Race, Empire, and the Idea of Human Development

In an exciting new study of ideas accompanying the rise of the West, Thomas McCarthy analyzes the ideologies of race and empire that were integral to European–American expansion. He highlights the central role that conceptions of human development (civilization, progress, modernization, and the like) played in answering challenges to legitimacy through a hierarchical ordering of difference. Focusing on Kant and natural history in the eighteenth century, Mill and social Darwinism in the nineteenth, and theories of development and modernization in the twentieth, he proposes a critical theory of development which can counter contemporary neoracism and neoimperialism, and can accommodate the multiple modernities now taking shape. Offering an unusual perspective on the past and present of our globalizing world, this book will appeal to scholars and advanced students of philosophy, political theory, the history of ideas, racial and ethnic studies, social theory, and cultural studies.

THOMAS McCARTHY is William H. Orrick Visiting Professor at Yale University and Professor Emeritus of Philosophy at Northwestern University.

Race, Empire, and the Idea of Human Development

THOMAS McCARTHY

CAMBRIDGE
UNIVERSITY PRESS

CAMBRIDGE UNIVERSITY PRESS
Cambridge, New York, Melbourne, Madrid, Cape Town, Singapore, São Paulo, Delhi

Cambridge University Press
The Edinburgh Building, Cambridge CB2 8RU, UK

Published in the United States of America by Cambridge University Press, New York

www.cambridge.org
Information on this title: www.cambridge.org/9780521740432

First published 2009

Printed in the United Kingdom at the University Press, Cambridge

A catalogue record for this publication is available from the British Library

Library of Congress Cataloguing in Publication data
McCarthy, Thomas, 1940–
Race, empire, and the idea of human development / Thomas McCarthy.
p. cm.
ISBN 978-0-521-51971-7 (hardback) – ISBN 978-0-521-74043-2 (pbk.)
1. Social evolution – Philosophy. 2. Race. 3. Imperialism. I. Title.
HM626.M43 2009
305.8009′04–dc22
2009006834

ISBN 978-0-521-51971-7 hardback
ISBN 978-0-521-74043-2 paperback

To the memory of my friend
Karl Ballestrem
1939–2007

Contents

Acknowledgments   *page* viii

Introduction   1

Part One   21

1   Political philosophy and racial injustice: a preliminary note on methodology   23

2   Kant on race and development   42

3   Social Darwinism and white supremacy   69

4   Coming to terms with the past: on the politics of the memory of slavery   96

Part Two   129

5   What may we hope? Reflections on the idea of universal history in the wake of Kant   131

6   Liberal imperialism and the dilemma of development   166

7   From modernism to messianism: reflections on the state of "development"   192

Conclusion: the presence of the past   230

Index   244

Acknowledgments

The names of those who contributed to this book by way of discussion, comment, and criticism are far too numerous to record. They include many of my colleagues and students at Northwestern and Yale Universities, and many participants in conferences and colloquia in which parts of it were presented. I do want to acknowledge my special debts to Robert Gooding-Williams and Jürgen Habermas who, in addition to being irreplaceable friends and interlocutors, commented on drafts of all the chapters. I want also to thank a number of friends and colleagues who provided helpful comments on large parts of the manuscript: Bill Barnes, Seyla Benhabib, Derrick Darby, Dilip Gaonkar, Maria Herrera, and Charles Taylor; or on particular chapters: Ken Baynes, Martha Biondi, Jim Bohman, Simone Chambers, Pablo De Greiff, Nils Gilman, Axel Honneth, Cristina Lafont, Karuna Mantena, Moishe Postone, Bill Rehg, Jim Sleeper, Carlos Thiebaut, Georgia Warnke, and Chris Zurn, who also doubled as a technical advisor. I have indicated some further debts in footnotes.

Earlier versions of parts of this book have appeared in print as follows: chapter 1 in S. Benhabib and N. Fraser (eds.), *Pragmatism, Critique, Judgment* (MIT Press, 2004); chapter 3 in *Contemporary Pragmatism* 4 (2007); chapter 4 in *Political Theory* 30 (2002); and chapter 7 in *Constellations* 14 (2007). They have all been revised and expanded.

I am greatly indebted to the Alexander von Humboldt Foundation for a Prize, to the National Endowment for the Humanities for a Fellowship, and to Northwestern University for a sabbatical, which afforded me the time free of teaching needed to complete the bulk of the work on this book.

Most of all, I am grateful to my wife, Pat, who, in addition to so much else, was always willing to discuss with me the topics on which I was writing.

Introduction

Racism and imperialism have been basic features of the modern world order from the start.[1] They have often appeared together: colonial regimes were usually racially organized, and racist beliefs and practices usually flourished in colonial contexts. And they have also been conceptually linked in various ways: in particular, both racial and imperial thought have drawn heavily upon developmental schemes, in which designated groups have been represented not only as racially distinct but also as occupying different stages of development, with their degree of advancement often being understood to depend on their race and to warrant various forms of hierarchical relations. Toward the end of the nineteenth century, for instance, social Darwinists understood the major groupings of human beings to embody different stages in the biological evolution of the species, which were manifested in their different stages (more or less advanced) of social evolution, and which warranted relations of domination ranging from peonage at home to imperialism abroad.

In its various renderings – as enlightenment, civilization, progress, social evolution, economic growth, modernization, and so forth – the conception of universal history as the ever-advancing development of human capacities has been fundamental to both the self-understanding of the modern West and its view of its relations to the rest of the world.[2] During the nineteenth century, this took the form of a hierarchical ordering of races and cultures along developmental gradients ranging from savagery to civilization, from barbarity to modernity. And in the twentieth century, developmental theory and practice became a basic means for interpreting and organizing difference in a global setting.

---

[1] The East India, West Indies, Virginia, and Royal Africa Companies were all founded in the seventeenth century.

[2] A number of the most important conceptions of "development" are discussed in some detail in chapters 2, 3, 5, 6, and 7, and I will not review them here.

Sharpening our understanding of such uses of developmental thinking in the past will put us in a better position to recognize and resist its continuing operation in racist and imperialist ideologies today, not only in popular culture and the mass media but in social science and social policy as well. Ideologies of race and empire may seem now to belong irretrievably to the past – driven there by, among other things, the scholarly opposition to race thinking that took shape in the 1920s and 1930s and was consolidated in the wake of the Holocaust, the decolonization struggles and civil rights movements of the post-World War II period, and the UN Charter and General Declaration of Human Rights. If that were so, this work would be an exercise in intellectual history and not, as it is meant to be, a contribution to the critical history of the present. So I shall begin by trying to make plausible, at least in a preliminary way, that various forms of "neoimperialism" and "neoracism" are of continuing significance in the contemporary world.

I

With *neoimperialism* or neocolonialism I can be very brief, as the idea has been current since the 1960s, soon after various struggles for national independence had achieved their goal.[3] The main line of thought was straightforward: although the newly emancipated ex-colonies were now formally independent, sovereign nations, they were in fact unfree to control their own fates. Ways were being found to maintain their subservience to former colonial powers without resorting to such classical mechanisms of subjugation as conquest and direct rule. This was, then, a "neocolonial" continuation of the systems of colonial domination and exploitation from which they had just formally emancipated themselves.

In what follows, I shall be using the terms "empire" and "imperialism" broadly to include all such systems and thus will not make use of the distinction that some authors draw between the "colonialism" of the settler and commercial colonies prior to the last quarter of the nineteenth century and the "imperialism" of the decades immediately preceding World War I – the "age of empire" in the narrower sense, which witnessed an intense struggle among competing national powers to secure overseas colonies, including the infamous "scramble for

---

[3] Robert J. C. Young, *Postcolonialism* (Oxford: Blackwell, 2001).

Africa," and at the end of which more than three-fourths of the globe was governed by colonial relations.[4] What is most important for my purposes is common to both the colonial and imperial formations in these more restricted senses, namely the domination and exploitation of the "periphery" by the "center," whether driven by settlers, private trading companies, or national governments. From the start, the expansion abroad of European economic interests in investment opportunities, natural resources, trading blocks, and the like went hand in hand with an extension of political and military power to protect and administer those interests;[5] and this money-power dynamic was common to the different forms. Across the many variations in its ideological representation, the "development" it propelled centered in fact on integration into economic relations with the colonizing country on terms and conditions that were favorable to the latter. This typically meant a transformation of the local economy that left it dependent on a new and unfair system of trade. For that purpose, forms of direct and indirect rule had to be put into place to regulate, administer, and enforce these unfair exchange relations, which meant more or less extensive restrictions on the scope and power of local government.

While this general pattern fits the classical modern empires of Britain, France, Holland, Spain, and Portugal, as well as the late nineteenth-century burst of imperialism by them and other more recent entrants into the "great game," the United States is something of an exception. For much of its history its imperial ambitions were focused on continental expansion by conquest and acquisition of contiguous territories. Only at the end of the nineteenth century did it too scramble for overseas colonies. Its more usual attitude toward European colonialism was critical: the trading blocks formed were barriers to its own ambition to expand abroad economically. At the same time, after the promulgation of the Monroe Doctrine in 1823, the United States practiced a form of hegemonic imperialism, without direct rule, in the Western Hemisphere, particularly in Central and South America, which was a precursor of the type of imperialism without formal

---

[4] E. J. Hobsbawm, *The Age of Empire, 1875–1914* (London: Weidenfeld & Nicolson, 1987).

[5] Hannah Arendt, *The Origins of Totalitarianism* (New York: Harcourt Brace Jovanovich, 1973), chap. 5.

colonies discussed today under the rubrics of "neocolonialism" and "neoimperialism."

Although military power has been repeatedly used from time to time to extend or defend such relations – as presently in Iraq – the preferred means of advancing geoeconomic and geopolitical interests today are less *overtly* violent, often indirect exercises of power and influence by strong states and transnational corporations over weaker states, whose sovereignty is nominally respected. The means in question include everything from establishing and/or supporting client states to controlling the international agencies that set the terms of global trade and finance. The striking imbalances of representation in such bodies as the IMF and World Bank – not to mention the G-7 – is an obvious illustration. And since the most developed countries are disproportionately former colonial powers, and the least developed are former colonies, the neoimperial system of domination and exploitation appears to be, in some considerable measure, a legacy of the five preceding centuries of colonialism and imperialism in their classical modern forms. If this is so, the present requirements of global justice include not only establishing relations of non-domination and fair terms of exchange but also, and interdependently, repairing the harmful effects of past injustice. This may well involve some forms of preferential treatment for the least developed societies – for instance, those artificial nations with arbitrary boundaries that resulted from the mad scramble for Africa – before they get to the point where they could develop themselves in a more equitable global system.

II

The relation of what, following Etienne Balibar and others, I am calling *neoracism* to earlier modalities of racism is less familiar and more controversial, and hence will require a lengthier introduction.[6] To begin with, whereas neoimperialism is a way of maintaining key aspects of colonial domination and exploitation after the disappearance of colonies in the legal-political sense, neoracism is a way of doing the same for racial

[6] Etienne Balibar, "Is There a 'Neoracism'?" in E. Balibar and I. Wallerstein, *Race, Nation, and Class* (London: Verso, 1991), pp. 17–28. See also Martin Barker, *The New Racism* (London: Junction Books, 1981), and Robert Miles, *Racism after "Race Relations"* (London: Routledge, 1993).

domination and exploitation after the displacement of "race" in the scientific-biological sense. Dividing the human species into natural kinds has a long and variegated history.[7] It is important to remember that the genetic conception of race that came to prominence in the twentieth century was the dominant conception for only a comparatively short period. "Race" could not be "in the genes" before the Mendelian revolution early in the twentieth century; and within a few decades, further developments in genetics itself helped to undermine it. Prior to that, racial essentialists tried to explain what it meant for "race" to be "in the blood" through a shifting variety of theoretical accounts, from Kant's idea of an original stock of racial germs to Darwin's idea of naturally selected and transmitted racial traits. But though arriving at a generally accepted theoretical account of the deepest biological roots of perceived racial differences required more than a century, investigations at levels closer to the surface proceeded apace. Thus comparative anatomists and physical anthropologists repeatedly studied such putative morphological characteristics of race as skull size and shape, facial angle, cranial capacity, and the like. And even closer to the surface, the usual classifications according to skin pigmentation, eye shape and color, hair texture, body type, and other "stigmata of otherness" (Balibar) continued without interruption. In short, though biological essentialism was characteristic of the modern idea of race, just how that was to be spelled out was a matter for ongoing conjecture until the "modern synthesis" in evolutionary biology finally ended the debate by calling into question the very idea that "race" was a useful scientific concept.[8]

It is also important to recall that these repeated attempts to spell out the idea that races are natural kinds in biological terms could make sense only after the scientific revolution of the seventeenth century. When Aristotle and his medieval followers talked of things being such-and-such "by nature," the idea of nature in question was articulated primarily in terms of "formal" and "final" causes rather than in terms of the "material" and "efficient" causes that came to dominate in modern science. Their conceptual and teleological approach to natural

---

[7] See, for instance, Ivan Hannaford, *Race: The History of an Idea in the West* (Baltimore: Johns Hopkins University Press, 1996).

[8] The current conception in population genetics of genotypically differentiated breeding populations does not support the amalgamation of phenotypic differences with mental and moral group differences that is characteristic of the modern idea of race under discussion here. See the remarks on this in chapter 3.

kinds was displaced only with the development of natural history in the eighteenth century, when the idea of natural kinds could be articulated largely in taxonomic terms. Racial description and classification could then proceed at this natural-historical level more or less continuously, despite the instability of depth-biological race theory before the modern synthesis in evolutionary biology. That is to say, although biological essentialism was characteristic of the mainstream of modern race theory, there was no general agreement concerning the biological "deep structure" of race prior to the twentieth century; and so *in practice*, the racialization of difference was carried out upon surface structures treated as generally available to the senses.

Moreover, "race" was never a *purely* biological construction. It always comprised a congeries of elements, including not only other "material" factors such as geographical origin and genealogical descent, but also a shifting array of "mental" characteristics such as cognitive ability and moral character, as well as a mobile host of cultural and behavioral traits. While such non-biological elements had previously been regarded as belonging to racial natural kinds, in the nineteenth century they came increasingly to be viewed as manifestations or expressions of deeper biological essences or causes – so that all of them could be said to be "in the blood" or, later, in the genes.

Finally, it is important to note that the ever-shifting theoretical attempts to get at the deep biological structure of race had little *immediate* effect on the social practices that reproduced racial formations. Because racial classification was a social construction out of such publicly available markers as somatic features, ancestry, geographical origins, cultural patterns, social relations, and the like, it remained relatively undisturbed in practice by short-term perturbations in theory.[9] And this is relevant to the conception of neoracism: since the structures of domination and exploitation embodied in differences of economic role, social standing, political power, and the like could be maintained across changes in scientific theories of race – in a self-reinforcing feedback loop with "common-sense" racist beliefs and practices – the disappearance of scientifically certified races did not bring an end to racial stratification. Just as postcolonial neoimperialism

---

[9] *Specific modalities* of racist thinking were, however, sometimes susceptible to critiques emanating from the cultural domains upon which they drew, from religion and philosophy to natural and social science.

could outlive the demise of formal colonies, post-biological neoracism could survive the demise of scientific racism. And just as the shift to neoimperialism required modes of domination and exploitation that were compatible with the nominal independence and equality of all nations, the shift to neoracism required modes that were compatible with the formal freedom and equality of all individuals.[10]

Whatever their specific form, content, and function, racial representations and classifications were generally mediated by power relations: they served to inform, interpret, and justify unfree and unequal social, economic, and political relations.[11] Although the studies in Part One focus on racist *ideologies*, their *functional contexts* are often visible in the background; in particular, the need for systems of coerced labor generated by colonial settlements in the Americas, which led both to the growth of the slave trade and to the rise of ideologies of blackness legitimating it; and the need after Reconstruction to keep recently emancipated slaves "down on the farm" (i.e. cotton plantations) and out of Northern industries, which furthered both the institutionalization of segregation and discrimination and the spread of a "scientific racism" that sought to rationalize them. And, as noted above, in other colonial contexts, the transformation of local modes of production and trade, so as to integrate them into economic systems that served the colonizers' purposes, required political and administrative regimes to enforce exploitative relations as well as ideologies to reconcile all this with the increasingly liberal cast of political thought in the European centers.

Another major context for modern racism appears only occasionally in these studies, and then principally in connection with the United States, and so I shall say a bit more about it here. It has become a commonplace of recent writing on racism to note its many affinities with nationalism.[12] The national imaginaries that served to unite disparate populations around putative commonalities of origin and descent, language and tradition, custom and culture increasingly overlapped with racial

---

[10] Thus the specific functions of neoracism differ from those of classical racism.

[11] For historical overviews of diverse power-knowledge interconnections that entered social constructions of "race," see Howard Winant, *The World is a Ghetto* (New York: Basic Books, 2001); and Bruce Baum, *The Rise and Fall of the Caucasian Race* (New York University Press, 2006).

[12] See, for instance, Arendt, *The Origins of Totalitarianism*, chap. 6; Etienne Balibar, "Racism and Nationalism," in Balibar and Wallerstein, *Race, Nation, and Class*, pp. 37–67; and Miles, *Racism after "Race Relations."*

imaginaries in the course of the nineteenth century. The Romantic emphasis on the unique spirit, mentality, and character of each people earlier in the century later tended to get displaced by, or combined with, a naturalistic emphasis on common ancestry and shared "blood." By the end of the century, with the near-total triumph of scientific racism in its post-Darwinian forms, race theory was applied not only to broader subdivisions of the species but to narrower national groupings, which were increasingly understood as races or distinct mixtures of races – the Anglo-Saxon race, the German race, the Irish race, the Jewish race, and so on.[13] This union of nationalism and racism was made easier by the many elective affinities between them: both invoked imagined collectivities with imagined similarities and differences; both operated with we/they dialectics of inclusion and exclusion; both encouraged identification across class and other divisions; and both identified certain "others" as special threats to racial and national purity. This was particularly true of alien bodies internal to the national body, such as European Jews. Racialized versions of nationalism thus gave traditional anti-Semitism an especially virulent new form, particularly in connection with such "pan" movements as Pan-German and pan-Slavic nationalism.[14] And it is also this sort of racialized nationalism that dominated debates about US immigration a century ago – and that, with cultural racism substituting for biological racism, still influences debates about immigration today.[15]

---

[13] This expanded application of the race paradigm meant, of course, that the putative somatic markers of racial difference were not so evident to the senses. But, as a look at the common caricatures of the period makes clear, the demands of the paradigm were nevertheless met, at least in regard to such negative stereotyping as the Irishman's simian appearance, the Jew's hooked nose, and so on.

[14] Arendt, *The Origins of Totalitarianism*, chap. 8.

[15] In this respect, some variants of contemporary neoracism construct "race" in ways similar to some constructions of "ethnicity." Although "ethnicity" usually centers on culturally transmitted customs, traditions, language, religion, and the like, some variants also stress ancestry and appearance – i.e. "blood." And just this type of culturally, genealogically, and somatically constructed identity/difference has tended to become salient in situations of domination, resistance, and conflict. So long as race thinking understood salient cultural differences to be biologically caused, there was at least a clear analytical distinction from thinking in terms of ethnicity. But now that the link between origins, ancestry, and appearance, on the one hand, and values, attitudes, and behavior, on the other, is usually taken to be cultural rather than biological even in race thinking, the differences narrow considerably. So contemporary neoracism is often (e.g. in the context of immigration debates) a form of "ethnoracism." My reasons for accentuating the "racism" component will become evident below.

The recent surge of racism in connection with immigration to the former colonial centers of Europe has been widely remarked – violent attacks on Third World immigrants, the rise of right-wing anti-immigration movements and parties, the continuing preoccupation of mainstream politics with "the immigration problem," and so on. Like other important contexts of contemporary neoracism – the continuing plight of African Americans in the US, for instance, or the gross inequities in life chances across the globe – this one evinces unmistakable continuities with the previous history of race relations. Following World War II, the acute shortage of labor power in reconstructing Europe was met in part by recruiting temporary migrant workers from other parts of the world, quite often from former colonies. When the need for migrant labor receded in the 1970s, many of these "guest workers" remained in their host countries, with an ever-increasing number of dependents but usually without full citizenship rights. And they were joined by growing numbers of political refugees and illegal immigrants. The presence of millions of "others" from third-world regions such as the Caribbean, the Indian subcontinent, Africa, Turkey, and so forth, in countries with high unemployment rates and expanding welfare rolls, and with heavily segregated housing patterns that gave rise to ethnoracial urban ghettos, intensified private and public racism across Europe. Familiar patterns of race thinking, particularly the construction of negatively charged stereotypes combining both physical and cultural elements, proliferated. Nonwhite immigrants from underdeveloped cultures were increasingly represented as foreign bodies that threatened the health of the nation.[16] This was particularly true when the raced bodies were the bearers of what was increasingly perceived to be a backward and violent Islamic culture.[17] Similar variations on racist themes familiar from the histories of colonialism and nationalism have been played, in different keys, outside of Europe as

---

[16] To mention only one example: campaign posters of the Swiss People's Party (SVP), currently (2008) the most powerful party in Switzerland's federal parliament, have displayed an image of dark-skinned hands snatching at Swiss passports, and another of three white sheep standing on the Swiss flag while driving a fourth, black sheep away.

[17] Of course, the growth of anti-Muslim sentiment across the West is not simply a matter of neoracism. It is everywhere a confusing mélange, in which the grammar of religious difference is one important ingredient and the fear of terrorism another. But there is usually also an element of neoracism in the mix, whereby Muslims are represented as non-white peoples from backward cultures.

well – for instance, in the increasingly heated debates about Latino immigration to the United States.

The point of applying the term "neoracist" to these and other recent discourses is to emphasize their logical and functional similarities to the classical paradigm. Real or ascribed somatic markers are taken as signs of deeper differences. Stereotypical representations combining phenotypic features with cultural and behavioral traits are used to include and exclude. And the negative stereotyping of "others" functions to explain and legitimate ongoing racial stratification. Raced bodies signifying differences in culture and psychology; racially inflected structures of inequality; and racialized grammars of difference serving as ideological justifications thereof seem grounds enough to continue to speak of racism after the demise of its relatively short-lived scientific version. To be more precise, what has been largely eliminated from academic and official discourse is the *natural*-scientific version of race theory anchored in biology. But what is referred to as "neoracism" or "cultural racism" does, in fact, come in *social*-scientific versions.[18] The discourses in the US about "the culture of poverty" in the 1960s and 1970s, and about the "socially dysfunctional behavior" of the "underclass" since the 1980s, as well as the ongoing discourse concerning the "dysfunctional cultural values" of "underdeveloped" societies are instances of a general pattern of ethnoracial thinking in social science and social policy.[19] In such discourses, depth biology no longer supplies the hidden links between phenotype and character: rather, the links were forged historically in various systems of racial oppression, adaptation to which by those oppressed gave rise to "cultural pathologies" of various sorts. According to the views I am characterizing as neoracist ideologies, such oppressive systems have long since been dismantled; but the pathologies have proved to be self-perpetuating and now function as a kind of independent variable in the etiology of poverty and

---

[18] Social-scientific versions of "cultural racism" are critically analyzed by Stephen Steinberg, *The Ethnic Myth* (Boston: Beacon Press, 2001); and Michael K. Brown *et al.*, *Whitewashing Race: The Myth of a Color-Blind Society* (Berkeley: University of California Press, 2003), among others. Richard H. King offers a useful overview in *Race, Culture, and the Intellectuals, 1940–1970* (Baltimore: Johns Hopkins University Press, 2004).

[19] See the works cited in the previous footnote and *Culture Matters: How Values Shape Human Progress*, ed. L. Harrison and S. Huntington (New York: Basic Books, 2000).

underdevelopment. Thus psychological and cultural patterns are used to explain social structures and processes rather than inversely or, better yet, reciprocally.[20]

It is, of course, a much debated question whether this shift from biology to culture amounts to the end of racism or to the rise of a new modality. There is no legislating in semantic matters, but from the perspective of critical theory, to regard it as the end of racism is not only to ignore the historical continuity of these discourses with classical racist ideologies, and their powerful synergies with the old-fashioned racism that is still rampant in everyday life; it is also to occlude the basic structural similarities cultural racism bears to biological racism. Both take stereotypical somatic differences to signify stereotypical differences of culture and character.[21] While these latter differences are no longer regarded as innate, they are regarded as deeply ingrained; and though they are not inherited biologically, they are passed on from generation to generation. They are, in Marxian terms, regarded as a kind of "second nature." Accordingly, the biological fixity of such traits gets replaced with their self-perpetuating character, and their absolute immutability with the difficulty of changing them. Perhaps the most striking continuity, however, is that this variant logic is generally applied to *the same basic subdivisions of humanity that were socially constructed in and through classical racism*. In the United States, for example, we are still talking about Native Americans, African Americans, European Americans, Asian Americans, and Hispanic Americans, notwithstanding the myriad cultural *and* genetic variations within each "racial" grouping. Phenotype and ancestry still rule here, it seems. And in the European debates, the great divide between white Europeans and colored non-Europeans still structures the experience and discourse of immigration. If one recalls the interpenetration of racism and nationalism at the end of the nineteenth century, when

---

[20] The social-scientific inadequacy of abstracting cultural and psychological patterns from their historical contexts of origin and societal contexts of reproduction, and treating them as an *explanans* but not as an *explanandum*, have been spelled out again and again. Nevertheless, methodological individualism has never lost its fatal attraction for Anglo-American social and political theory. See the remarks on institutionalized racism and the "behavior versus structure" debate in chapter 3.

[21] Which is no doubt one reason why so many Americans find Barack Obama "exotic."

nations or peoples were regarded as ethnoracial groupings, the continuities are even more evident: once again, ethnoracially "homoge-
neous" national communities are perceived to be threatened with
contamination by ethnoracially foreign bodies.

Some still insist that the shift from biology to history and culture
outweighs all these historical continuities and structural-functional
similarities, and so reject the terminology of "neo-" or "ethno-" or
"cultural racism." But it becomes difficult to keep the continuities and
similarities in mind when the terminology is dropped. And it also
becomes difficult to move back and forth between critical theory and
a social reality in which the racialization of "common-sense" discourse
in many spheres of life – from private conversation to mass media, from
political discourse to government policy – is omnipresent and deeply
entrenched.[22] For these and other reasons, emphasizing the continuities
and similarities of cultural with biological racism better serves the
purpose of ideology critique. Like racist discourses in the past, neoracist
discourses today attempt to explain away entrenched injustices by
reference to their victims' own shortcomings, which are now taken to
be cultural rather than biological in origin. In an influential neoconservative version, for instance, differences in social mobility or societal
modernization are said to be due to behavioral deficiencies in the disadvantaged underclass or underdeveloped society. While the historical
origins of these deficiencies in slavery, colonialism, or the like may be
acknowledged, this is not understood as a causal account of the inequalities in question, but at most as a confession of the sins of our fathers.
For in this version, such historical forces of oppression are no longer
active. The world today – at least in developed societies and the global
economy – is increasingly structured by free markets and equal opportunity. Under such conditions, the causes of failure in individuals and
societies are to be found not in forces outside them but in deficiencies
within them – in their own values, attitudes, habits, and the like. They
are biologically equal but culturally and psychologically inferior. And
so the proper remedy for the severely reduced life chances of members of
such (usually racially marked) groups is not a change in the system but a
change in their values, attitudes, and behavior. In the end, they can only
heal themselves. The ideological character of this prescription becomes
evident as soon as one tries to apply it, for instance, to the inner-city

[22] Robert Gooding-Williams, *Look, A Negro!* (New York: Routledge, 2006).

ghettos, dysfunctional public schools, chronic unemployment, and inequitable administration of criminal justice that afflict the US underclass, or to the massive asymmetries of money and power that face underdeveloped societies in the global economy. It becomes clear then that this culturalist form of ideology serves the important purpose of deflecting dissatisfaction and demands for change from established practices and institutions, policies and programs. It substitutes self-help for reconstruction and delegitimizes governmental efforts to combat racial inequalities.

My point here is certainly not to deny the role of sociocultural and social-psychological factors in the reproduction of poverty, underdevelopment, or other persistent inequalities; nor is it to deny the agency of oppressed groups and the importance of their engagement in processes of self-emancipation.[23] It is rather that by ignoring economic and political, structural and institutional causes of human misery, neoconservative diagnoses serve as ideological covers for the relations of domination and exploitation that perpetuate it. Not only are the historical roots of existing inequalities largely ignored, but present causes not pertaining to cultural or psychological stereotypes, particularly structural and institutional causes, also disappear from sight. Practically and politically, this means that types of collective action aimed at institutional reform, which could attack the roots of long-standing inequalities, are usually off the agenda. So it is not merely a theoretical nicety but an urgent practical necessity to insist on the neoimperialist and neoracist aspects of existing relations of domination and exploitation.

III

I shall conclude this introduction with a few preliminary remarks about the general approach adopted in the studies that follow. Coming here, they may well strike the reader as somewhat abstruse, but I trust they will become increasingly comprehensible in the course of the discussion.

1. The genre to which these studies belong is less "genealogy" in the Nietzschean or Foucauldian sense than "critical history with a practical

---

[23] This is already evident in the history of African-American emancipation from chattel slavery and Jim Crow, where black political agency was integral to the success of the abolitionist and civil rights movements. More generally, critical social theory is in its very design a theoretical undertaking with the practical aim of self-emancipation.

intent" in the Habermasian sense.[24] In specific, the interpretive framework I deploy has a normative dimension derived from Habermas's recasting of Kant's moral theory in the form of a "discourse ethics" and his reworking of Kant's legal and political theory into a "discourse theory of law and democracy."[25] For my purposes, what is most important in this is the translation of the Kantian categorical imperative into the discourse-ethical principle of equal participation by those affected in establishing the normative structures that govern their life together. As I hope will become evident, this can be used to decenter modes of theorizing that have underwritten Eurocentrism and white supremacy in the modern period. My guiding assumption is that the resources required to reconstruct our traditions of social and political thought can be wrested from those very traditions, provided that they are critically appropriated and opened to contestation by their historical "others."[26]

2. Borrowing from Kant by way of Habermas renders my relation to his work manifestly two-sided, for Kant is a topic as well as a resource: he produced early (i.e. late eighteenth century) but already well-articulated versions of hierarchical race theory and Eurocentric universal history. Chapter 2 focuses on those aspects of his work, not because

---

[24] However, critical theory in this latter sense also incorporates a genealogical moment, in that past and present forms of "existing reason" have to be ongoingly interrogated with regard to the elements of power invested in them. Such a "Nietzschean," metacritical moment was already built into the basically left-Hegelian approach of the early Frankfurt School by Horkheimer and Adorno in *Dialectic of Enlightenment*. On this point see Axel Honneth, "Rekonstruktive Gesellschaftskritik unter genealogischem Vorbehalt," in *Pathologien der Vernunft* (Frankfurt: Sukrkamp Verlag, 2007), pp. 57–69.

[25] Jürgen Habermas, *Moral Consciousness and Communicative Action*, tr. C. Lenhardt and S. Weber Nicholsen (Cambridge, MA: MIT Press, 1990); idem, *Between Facts and Norms*, tr. W. Rehg (Cambridge, MA: MIT Press, 1996). I do not, however, aspire to orthodoxy in my appropriations either of Kant or of Habermas.

[26] Thus critical history, as I understand it, contains elements of immanent, transcendent, and genealogical critique: "immanent" in that it starts from values, ideals, and principles embedded in the cultures and societies it analyzes; (context-) "transcendent" in that it reconstructs these values, ideals, and principles in terms of a general, discourse-ethical account of practical reasoning; and "genealogical" in that it is self-reflectively metacritical of the historical and contemporary forms of existing reason that it seeks to reconstruct as critical resources. See Thomas McCarthy, *Ideals and Illusions* (Cambridge, MA: MIT Press, 1991); McCarthy, "Philosophy and Critical Theory: A Reprise," in D. Hoy and T. McCarthy, *Critical Theory* (Oxford: Blackwell, 1994), pp. 8–100.

he was the worst offender of his age but because he was its best thinker. His valiant but vain efforts to reconcile moral-political normativism with anthropological-historical functionalism are highly instructive, as they render apparent and sharp the tensions between liberal universalism and liberal developmentalism, which lesser theorists have attempted to downplay or disguise. For this reason, Kant's views of development and difference function in this work as a kind of refrain, which regularly recurs, especially in Part Two, when I attempt to frame key issues in broadly philosophical terms. At the same time, adapting elements of Kant's practical philosophy to my purposes precludes any simple rejection of his ideas. Drawing upon a discourse-ethical version of his categorical imperative to respect all human beings equally as "ends in themselves," I can hardly claim neutrality regarding modes of ethical life. Accordingly, my approach to development theory is not merely deconstructive but also reconstructive: it includes an attempt to correct for the objectionable features of the ideologies of development that figured so centrally in modern racism and imperialism.

3. In this respect, my approach differs from those informed by wholehearted modernism, anti-modernism, or postmodernism. It starts from inescapable "facts" of global modernity and ideas of development used to conceptualize them, and undertakes to critically rethink them. The interpretation and evaluation of those facts and ideas are essentially contestable, and in the now global discourse of modernity contestation comes from the "margins" as well as from the "center." It is already evident that this increasingly polycentric and multivocal discussion has rendered untenable the monological, monocultural Eurocentrism of the received discourse of modernity.[27] In this altered context, global development may be reconceived, for example, in terms of collective action to improve the life chances of all inhabitants of this planet.[28] Undertaking such reconstructive efforts is all the more important today to counter the aggressive redeployment of traditional notions of development by neoliberal globalizers and neoconservative interventionists. And reconstruction involves much more than merely deflating the theological and metaphysical connotations of classical conceptions of development and relieving them of their teleological and normative excesses.

---

[27] Dipesh Chakrabarty, *Provincializing Europe: Postcolonial Thought and Historical Difference* (Princeton University Press, 2000).

[28] Amartya Sen, *Development as Freedom* (New York: Alfred A. Knopf, 1999).

4. To begin with, a critical theory of global development must get beyond the we/they structure of classical conceptions, in which "they" get developed by becoming more like "us" – through a kind of "colonial mimesis," as Homi Bhabha has put it, in which the imitation can never be quite like the original – not quite white.[29] Global development, in a sense that requires establishing a just and sustainable global order, is a challenge facing all of us together and not something that some of us do for (or to) others. In addition to being deflated and decentered, a critical conception of development must also be de-totalized. The overarching, all-inclusive conceptions of progress, modernization, and the like, which have informed the theory and practice of development from the eighteenth century into the twenty-first century, have to be disaggregated, for it has become only too evident that development in one domain (e.g. the technology of warfare) might be accompanied by regression in others (e.g. political morality).[30] There are different "logics" to developments in different areas, such that they may clash as well as harmonize. And the various "goods" that different lines of development promote are rarely all achievable at once and frequently at odds, such that more of one means less of the other.[31] In particular, the presently very influential, neoliberal conception of globalization, in which the development of "free-market" economies everywhere brings all good things, has to be seen for the delusion that it is. Deflated, decentered, and disaggregated in these ways, the idea of development no doubt loses much of its mobilizing power, for good and for ill. It can no longer serve as the sole or principal standard for evaluating social and political change; rather, it is demoted to the status of one important consideration among others in the assessment of "alternative modernities."[32]

[29] Homi Bhabha, "Of Mimicry and Man: The Ambivalence of Colonial Discourse," in F. Cooper and A. Stoler (eds.), *Tensions of Empire* (Berkeley: University of California Press, 1997), pp. 152–160.

[30] See, for instance, Reinhold Niebuhr, *Faith and History* (New York: Charles Scribner's Sons, 1951), and Christopher Lasch, *The True and Only Heaven: Progress and Its Critics* (New York: W. W. Norton, 1991).

[31] The general point about irreducible value pluralism was forcefully made by Isaiah Berlin. Charles Taylor has applied it to development theory in "Two Theories of Modernity," in D. Gaonkar (ed.), *Alternative Modernities* (Durham, NC: Duke University Press, 2001), pp. 172–196.

[32] See Gaonkar (ed.), *Alternative Modernities*; and the special issue of *Daedalus* 129:1 on *Multiple Modernities*, ed. S. N. Eisenstadt (Winter 2000).

5. As already noted, a major historical source of tensions in developmental theory and of depredations in its practice is the fact that it has had the concrete shape of the development of global capitalism. In consequence, liberal social and political theory has had repeatedly to reconcile universalist principles with the realities of domination and exploitation. As the dynamics of capital accumulation propelled an expansion of markets across the globe, the need to protect investments, secure raw materials, defend trading monopolies, and the like called for a corresponding expansion of political power. The multiple and shifting racial classifications and hierarchies that accompanied that expansion have to be understood in connection with the economic systems they served to organize and the political regimes that enforced them.[33] From Marx's early critique of capitalist globalization, which he saw hovering over the earth like some ancient fate, to contemporary critiques of neoliberal globalization, which has left much of the world in abject poverty, concerns about the possibility and limits of exerting political control over market economies have remained critical to development discourse, and those concerns are reflected in these studies.

6. Five centuries of imperialism and racism did not disappear without a trace in the fifty years since the postwar successes of decolonization and civil rights struggles. Whether or not they still play an important role in the contemporary world – and I shall be arguing that they do – the massive inequalities that are their historical legacy are scarcely deniable. Coming to terms with this past of racial and imperial injustice, and seeking to remedy the continuing harms that resulted from it are demands of reparative justice. Those demands figure, if sometimes only tacitly, in the way I approach the various topics that are the foci of the individual studies. In chapter 4, they are themselves a topic of discussion, specifically in connection with the history of racial slavery and segregation in the United States.

7. The exceptional (by comparison to other highly developed societies) importance of race as an internal organizing principle of domestic social and political order in the United States is one moment of what is commonly taken to be a more general American exceptionalism, which also finds expression in its external affairs. In chapter 3 I discuss this

---

[33] Winant, *The World is a Ghetto.*

claimed exceptionalism in connection with the theory and practice of social Darwinism, and in chapter 7 in connection with post-World War II development theory and practice. Both Part One, which is centered around race, and Part Two, which is centered around empire, begin with more general discussions of these themes – primarily with reference to thinkers and currents of thought in the Anglo-American and German traditions – and move to more specific treatments of them in the US context. This sharpening of focus is not only an indication of my own interests but also a reflection of the facts that the United States was the paradigmatic racial state of the nineteenth century and a hegemonic global power in the twentieth.

8. The chapters that follow are focused on ideas – selected thinkers and currents of thought from the late eighteenth through the twentieth centuries, not always in chronological order – rather than on the interests driving them or the historical contexts in which they arose. Interests and contexts are, to be sure, brought in at a number of points, but rather as backgrounds to ideologies than as focal points of analysis. It goes without saying that in dealing with topics so vast and issues so complex, these studies can aspire to be no more than provisional reflections on selected themes, with a rather severe reduction of the immense variety of views on them. They are thematically interlinked, however, and my hope is that their cumulative effect may be less an oversimplification in key respects than is any one of them taken alone. In any case, taken together they analyze a number of nodal points where developmental thinking has intersected with racism and imperialism from the late eighteenth century to the present, and thus make evident its centrality to the Eurocentric versions of universal history that have underwritten global white supremacy in the modern period.

9. It might bear repeating that I do not view the meaning of "development" to be exhausted by its (mis)uses in those connections. Like enlightenment ideas more generally, it is inherently ambivalent in character, both indispensable and dangerous. Thus, as suggested above, there is no alternative to its ongoing deconstruction and reconstruction. With that in mind, the heavily critical analyses that comprise the bulk of the individual chapters are typically accompanied or followed by normative and metanormative reflections on what global justice requires today. The perspective from which they are offered is expressly that of a multicultural universalism, in which multiple forms of sociocultural modernity are united by an overlapping consensus concerning

transnational norms and by institutionalized forms of democratic discourse about their interpretation, elaboration, and implementation. This is, I suggest, what becomes of the hope for perpetual peace that Kant once held out to universal-historical reflection from a cosmopolitan point of view. But without his teleology of nature and theodicy of history, and in view of the "glittering misery" of previous history and present circumstances, it is a hope pervaded by melancholy.

1 | *Political philosophy and racial injustice: a preliminary note on methodology*

In mainstream political philosophy, the history of European racism, with its vast implications for the theory and practice of modern liberalism, has long remained on the margins. This is nearly as astonishing as the theoretical marginality of gender until rather recently. I say "nearly," because while gender relations have deeply structured every human society, race relations, in the sense at issue here, have had major structural significance "only" for some five centuries. That is to say, they are contemporaneous with, and deeply implicated with, Western modernity from the first voyages of "discovery" to present-day neocolonialism. If one asked, in Rawlsian terms, which morally arbitrary facts about individuals and groups have had the greatest consequences for their legal and political standing in the modern world, gender and ascribed race would certainly be near the top of the list, along with class, though their comparative significance would vary from context to context. If the context were the global one of European expansionism since the fifteenth century, then racial classification would have a strong claim to being the most significant; for a central ingredient in the process by which more than three-fourths of the globe came to be under European and/or American rule before the start of World War I was the practice and theory of white supremacy.

Linking Western modernity to the conquest and exploitation of the non-Western world is a familiar form of critique. Marx already noted in the first volume of *Capital* that "The discovery of gold and silver in America, the extirpation, enslavement and entombment in mines of the aboriginal population, the beginning of the conquest and looting of the East Indies, the turning of Africa into a warren for the commercial hunting of black-skins, signalized the rosy dawn of the era of capitalist production."[1] But Marxism centered on class relations and generally treated race relations as derivative from them. An alternative tradition

---

[1] Karl Marx, *Capital* (New York: Random House, 1906), p. 823.

of critique, running through W. E. B. Du Bois to the critical race theory of the present, has, by contrast, regarded racism not merely as a dependent variable but as an irreducible dimension of social, cultural, and political relations in the modern world. On this view, the rise of overseas colonialism, the conquest and settlement of the Americas, the subjugation and extermination of indigenous peoples, and the massive expansion of the Atlantic slave trade in the early modern period were integrally bound up with the social construction of racial classifications and hierarchies. In the course of this global transformation, imperial ideologies of "Christians versus heathens" gradually gave way to those of "civilized Europeans versus uncivilized savages," which were understood in racial terms already in the eighteenth century. In the nineteenth century, the "age of empire," the rapid expansion of colonialism in Asia, the Pacific, and Africa, fueled a further development of racial ideologies, particularly in conjunction with the rise of physical anthropology and evolutionary biology. In short, there was a continuous interplay between colonialism and racism, between the establishment of imperial domination and the spread of racial ideologies.

From the perspective of this alternative tradition, these were not "mere" ideologies in the sense of epiphenomena of underlying social processes. Though they were social constructions, they were real social facts with real implications for the ordering of social relations. This is a view adopted, for instance, by Omi and Winant, as they explain how modernity came to be marked by the rise of "racial formations" at both national and global levels.[2] Systems of racial categorization centered around visible body types acquired not only expressive but also constitutive significance in modern society; they not only justified practices of racial domination but also entered into and informed them; and their rankings of racial capacity and incapacity did not merely reflect institutional reality but were essential to its very intelligibility and normativity. Such systems of "natural" racial differences were integral to arrangements as otherwise disparate as colonial labor regimes, US immigration policy, "Jim Crow" segregation, eugenics programs and extermination camps. In a word, "race" has functioned as a marker of inclusion and exclusion, equality and inequality, freedom and unfreedom throughout the modern period, both locally and globally. And despite the postwar successes of the civil

[2] M. Omi and H. Winant, *Racial Formation in the United States* (New York: Routledge, 1994).

rights movement here and decolonization struggles abroad, there is widespread agreement in this alternative tradition that the legacy of institutionalized racism is still with us, that is, that local and global relations of wealth and power are still structured along racial lines. On this view, the persistence of "race" as a significant ordering principle of social life, even after its theoretical deconstruction and legal dismantling, continues to be one of the major problems of our age – "the problem of the color-line."[3]

Since the 1960s, the centrality of race to the modern world in general and to the American experience in particular has permeated scholarship in most areas of the social sciences and the humanities. In mainstream political philosophy, however, the process has only recently begun – despite the evident facts that political discourses, practices, and institutions have been suffused with racism throughout the modern period and that racial politics persist into the present as the legacy of centuries of oppression.[4] As a result of this continuing marginalization, the development of political-theoretical tools for analyzing the racial dimension of political thought and practice has persistently lagged. But theoretical marginalization is only part of the story, and not the central part: most of the classical modern theorists were aware of and complicit in the emerging system of white supremacy. John Locke, for instance, famously declared America to be a "vacant land" occupied only by nomadic savages still in the state of nature, and hence a land ripe for European expropriation, as no ownership-conferring labor had yet been mixed with it. Less famously, he was an original shareholder in the Royal African Company, which was chartered in 1672 to monopolize the English slave trade. Thus, the same Locke who declared in the opening line of his *First Treatise* that "Slavery is so vile and miserable an estate of man, and so directly opposite to the generous temper and courage of our nation, that 'tis hardly to be conceived that an Englishman, much less a gentleman, should plead for it,"[5] did in fact

---

[3] As famously anticipated by W. E. B. Du Bois in 1903, *The Souls of Black Folk*, edited with an introduction by D. W. Blight and R. Gooding-Williams (Boston: Bedford Books, 1997), p. 45.

[4] And despite the best efforts of philosophers in the alternative tradition to bring this to the attention of mainstream political philosophy. Already in 1977–1978, for instance, there was a double issue of *The Philosophical Forum* devoted to "Philosophy and the Black Experience."

[5] John Locke, *Two Treatises of Government*, ed. Peter Laslett (Cambridge University Press, 1988), p. 141.

support it for the Africans being forcibly shipped to America to serve Englishmen.

Our first inclination might be to see this paradoxical combination as peculiar to him, or in any case untypical. But that is the problem: it is all too typical of Western political thought for the next two and a half centuries. Even Immanuel Kant, who developed what is arguably the philosophically purest version of European humanism, also developed what is arguably the most systematic theory of race and racial hierarchy prior to the nineteenth century.[6] In the course of his lectures on physical geography and anthropology, which he delivered annually from 1755 to 1796, he drew heavily upon the travel reports of explorers, settlers, missionaries, traders, and the like, which constituted a significant part of the "empirical" basis of comparative cultural studies in his day. As a result, the popular racism attendant upon European expansionism, "New World" conquest, the African slave trade, and the like found in his thought a highly resolved theoretical reflection, one that already displayed the chief characteristics of nineteenth-century racial "science": racial differences were represented as biologically inherited determinants of differences in talent and temperament. In consequence of such differences, Kant conjectured, non-European peoples could be incapable of autochthonously realizing their full humanity, and in particular, of attaining that perfectly just civil constitution which is the highest task that nature sets to mankind. Hence Europe would "probably legislate eventually for all other continents."[7] So already before the close of the eighteenth century, we had the makings of a theoretical rationale for global white supremacy, rooted in biology and featuring hereditary differences in ability and character, and replete with the civilizing mission of the white race – a rationale that had only to be further developed and adapted to meet the needs of the "floodtide of imperialism" in the nineteenth century.[8]

There were, to be sure, important variations on these themes from context to context and author to author. But there was also a general

---

[6] See chapter 2.

[7] I. Kant, "Idea for a Universal History with a Cosmopolitan Purpose," in *Kant: Political Writings*, ed. H. Reiss, tr. H. B. Nisbet (Cambridge University Press, 1991), p. 52.

[8] However, as I elaborate in chapter 2, Kant himself denied that there could be any right to chattel slavery and roundly condemned the European colonialism of his day.

pattern: non-European peoples were characterized as barbarous or uncivilized, as not possessed of fully developed rational capacities and incapable of fully rational agency, and hence were declared to be in need of tutelage, not only for the good of those who commanded them but also for their own good, for the full development of their capacities. In the course of the nineteenth century, that pattern was filled out with historical accounts of human development placing European civilization at the apex of social and cultural progress, and with allegedly scientific theories of racial difference and racial hierarchy. More recently, however, the widespread dismantling of colonial empires and of *de jure* discrimination has been accompanied by a change in the theoretical treatment of race. In liberal political theory, in particular, there is no longer any attempt to justify or accommodate racial subordination within a putatively universalistic framework. Instead, the treatment of this persistent feature of the messy political reality we inhabit tends to be consigned to the province of "nonideal theory."

Part of the background to this approach is the ambivalent attitude toward normative theory characteristic of the positivist views of social and political inquiry that had gained ascendancy by the mid-twentieth century, an attitude that Richard Bernstein described as follows: "On the one hand, there is an insistence on the categorial distinction between empirical and normative theory, but on the other hand, there is a widespread skepticism about the very possibility of normative theory."[9] That skepticism was based on a strict dichotomy between facts and values, the assignment of empirical science to the former domain and of normative theory to the latter, and the view that there could be no rational determination of anything so subjective as "values."[10] But just before he offered this diagnosis in the mid-1970s, a new venture in normative political theory had taken shape, one which by and large accepted the fact/value split, rejected the skepticism concerning rational

---

[9] R. Bernstein, *The Restructuring of Social and Political Theory* (Philadelphia: University of Pennsylvania Press, 1978), p. 45.

[10] Thus Richard Tuck notes "the absence of major works in political philosophy" in the English-speaking world "between Sidgwick and Rawls" and attributes it in part to the "fracture between ethics and the human sciences" and the view that "value judgments are not the product of systematic rational thought." "The Contribution of History," in R. Goodin and P. Pettit (eds.), *A Companion to Contemporary Political Thought* (Oxford: Blackwell, 1993), pp. 72–89, at pp. 72, 73, 78.

discourse about values, and proposed another, more cooperative division of labor between empirical science and normative theory: the theory of justice of John Rawls, which has remained the most influential paradigm of normative political theorizing to this day.

In this opening chapter, I want briefly to set the methodological stage for the studies that follow by (I) examining the division of labor between ideal and nonideal theory as it appears in Rawls's thought, (II) identifying some of the obstacles this dominant paradigm presents to an adequate treatment of racial injustice, and (III) suggesting how we might get beyond them by moving in the direction of a critical theory of race.[11]

I

As Susan Moller Okin and others have argued, Rawls effectively screened out gender and the gendered structure of the family from the purview of *A Theory of Justice* by designating the participants in the original position as "heads" or "representatives" of families.[12] Behind the veil of ignorance, not only was one's sex unknown to one, but participants also seemed to be unaware of the sex-gender systems that have deeply structured every society on record. Accordingly, the massively differential effect of the "morally arbitrary" fact of sexual difference did not become a central theoretical issue for justice as fairness. And although Rawls mentioned gender as a basic problem of our society in the introduction to *Political Liberalism* some twenty years later (*PL*, xxviii), it still remained untheorized therein. After a second round of criticism by Okin and other feminist theorists,[13] Rawls briefly

---

[11] A strong case for the inadequacy of mainstream political theory in regard to race and for the consequent need to develop a more historically and socioculturally informed critical approach was already made by, among others, Charles Mills in *The Racial Contract* (Ithaca: Cornell University Press, 1997) and *Blackness Invisible* (Ithaca: Cornell University Press, 1998). My approach here is indebted to that earlier work. For an opposing view, see Tommie Shelby, "Race and Social Justice: Rawlsian Considerations," *Fordham Law Review* 72 (2004): 1697–1715.

[12] S. Moller Okin, *Justice, Gender, and the Family* (New York: Basic Books, 1989). Rawls's works will be cited in the text with the following abbreviations: *TJ, A Theory of Justice* (Cambridge, MA: Harvard University Press, 1971); *PL, Political Liberalism* (New York: Columbia University Press, 1993); *CP, Collected Papers*, ed. Samuel Freeman (Cambridge, MA: Harvard University Press, 1999); and *LP, The Law of Peoples* (Cambridge, MA: Harvard University Press, 1999).

[13] S. Moller Okin, "Political Liberalism, Justice, and Gender," *Ethics* 105 (1994): 23–43.

addressed the matter in his 1997 piece on "The Idea of Public Reason Revisited" (*CP*, 575–615). There he endorses a principle of equal justice for women which requires that "wives have all the same basic rights, liberties, and opportunities as their husbands" (*CP*, 597). He notes that the gendered division of labor in the family has been implicated historically in the denial of such equality, and holds that such a division might persist in a just society only if and when it were "fully voluntary" and arrangements were made to ensure that it did not undermine the equal liberties and opportunities of women (*CP*, 600). It would seem to follow that such arrangements would have to be considered in the original position, and thus that the parties would have to be given access to the knowledge of "social theory and human psychology" (*CP*, 601) needed to agree rationally about them: sex-gender would have to be dealt with at the same level and in the same detail as other major axes of justice/injustice.

A similar issue might be raised concerning cultural and institutional patterns of racial domination. Charles Mills has remarked on the surprising insignificance of racial discrimination as an explicit theme (rather than a tacit subtext) of *A Theory of Justice*, which appeared in a highly charged political atmosphere a few short years after African Americans had finally won their centuries-long struggle for equal civil and political rights.[14] One might add to this the absence of any sustained discussion of colonialism in a world convulsed with the death throes of European–American global rule in its classical modern form. These, it seems, were features of the modern world about which parties in the original position were ignorant, and thus which they were not obliged to address explicitly in designing the basic structures of justice.

---

[14] Mills, *Blackness Invisible*, pp. 5, 152. This is not to deny that a deep concern with racial justice may well have been part of the motivation behind the argument of *TJ*, but only to point out that it is not systematically discussed therein – though there are scattered remarks on race and slavery; see, e.g., pp. 99, 158, 248, and 325, and the footnote to Martin Luther King (p. 364n.) in the extended discussion of civil disobedience in chapter VI. A number of theorists interested in questions of racial injustice have remarked on, and in various ways tried to make good on, this lack in *A Theory of Justice*, among them Bernard Boxill, *Blacks and Social Justice* (Totowa, NJ: Rowman & Allanheld, 1984); David Theo Goldberg, *Racist Culture* (Oxford: Blackwell, 1993); Howard McGary, *Race and Social Justice* (Oxford: Blackwell, 1999); Seana Shiffrin, "Race, Labor, and the Fair Equality of Opportunity Principle," *Fordham Law Review* 72 (2004): 1643–1675; and Tommie Shelby, "Justice, Deviance, and the Dark Ghetto," *Philosophy and Public Affairs* 35 (2007): 126–160.

At that time, however, though civil rights movements and decolonization struggles had eliminated some forms of *de jure* inequality, many
forms of *de facto* inequality remained in place – deeply entrenched in the
beliefs and values, symbols and images, practices and institutions,
structures and functions of national and global society. Hence, while
certain legalized forms of subordination like slavery and serfdom could
be, as Rawls later put it in *Political Liberalism*, "off the agenda" (*PL*,
151, n. 16), the same could not be said for racial injustice generally, as
he acknowledged in the introduction to that later work and as the
persistent debates about affirmative action and other proposals for
addressing the enduring legacy of legalized racism attested. Why,
then, if "race" was admittedly still among "our most basic problems"
(*PL*, xxviii), was it not theorized by Rawls?

An important part of the answer, I want to suggest, has to do with the
nature of "ideal theory," as he conceives it. Kantian in conception, ideal
theory starts with "rationally autonomous agents" and allows them only
so much information as is needed to achieve agreement on basic principles.[15] This point is reached, according to Rawls, when the parties in the
original position, represented now as symmetrically situated trustees of
free and equal, rational and reasonable citizens, know all and only those
"general," not particular or personal, "facts" about society – that is, laws,
theories, and tendencies pertaining to politics, economics, psychology, and
social organization – required to design a just *and* feasible basic structure.
Or, as Rawls also puts it in *The Law of Peoples*, ideal theory seeks to
construct a "realistic utopia" (*LP*, 6). In this respect, it follows Rousseau in
taking (a) "men as they are" and (b) "laws as they might be" (*LP*, 7, 13).

(a) Rawls understands the former phrase to mean "persons' moral and
     psychological natures and how that nature works within a frame-
     work of political and social institutions" (*LP*, 7). To take men as they

---

[15] Rawls described it this way in "Kantian Constructivism in Moral Theory,"
CP, 336. And despite his shift to a conception of political theory as
"freestanding," he continued to acknowledge the Kantian provenance of certain
key ideas. Thus the earlier characterization in *TJ* of the veil of ignorance as
"implicit, I think, in Kant's ethics" (*TJ*, 140–1) recurs in *PL*, where he
characterizes his preference for a "thick" veil of ignorance – in which "the parties
are to be understood so far as possible solely as moral persons and in abstraction
from contingencies" – as "a Kantian view" (*PL*, 273). For discussion of a
precursor to this approach, Kant's distinction between "pure" and "impure"
theory, see chapter 2.

are in this sense means to "rely on the actual laws of nature and achieve the kind of stability these laws allow" (*LP*, 12). Hence parties in the original position must have access to the relevant general knowledge about such laws. This has consistently been Rawls's position. In *TJ*, while the veil of ignorance rules out knowledge of particular personal or social circumstances, the parties do know "the general facts about human society" pertaining to politics, economics, psychology, and social organization. Indeed, "there are no limitations on general information, that is, on general laws and theories, since conceptions of justice must be adapted to the characteristics of the systems of social cooperation which they are to regulate" (*TJ*, 137–138). Some thirty years later, in *The Law of Peoples*, the same idea is expressed in similar terms: ideal theory is "realistic" when it depicts a social world that is "possible," that is, one that is "achievable" in light of what we know about "the laws and tendencies of society" (*LP*, 11). This way of delimiting what is known behind the veil of ignorance entails that certain kinds of "particular" knowledge required to understand and deal with racial injustice will not be available to parties in the original position – knowledge, for instance, about "the particular circumstances of their own society," or "to which generation they belong" (*TJ*, 137), or "the relative good or ill fortune of their generation" (*PL*, 273).

(b) Rawls understands the phrase "laws as they might be" to mean "laws as they should or ought to be" (*LP*, 7), and this too seems to entail that constructions of race have no place in ideal theory – for "race" *should not* be a structuring principle of political and social relations. It is, in short, *morally* irrelevant. But this threatens to render normative theory both unrealistic and unfair. To quote Mills: "Failure to pay theoretical attention to this history [of racial subordination] will then just reproduce past domination, since the repercussions of white supremacy for the functioning of the state, the dominant interpretations of the Constitution, the racial distribution of wealth and opportunities, as well as white moral psychology ... are not examined."[16] It is at this point, however, that Rawls's notion of *nonideal theory* comes into play. Taking the principles established by ideal theory as a guide, nonideal theory approaches the "noncompliance," "partial compliance," and "unfavorable conditions" of the real world

[16] Mills, *Blackness Invisible*, p. 108.

in a spirit of reform: it asks how political ideals "might be achieved, or worked toward, usually in gradual steps. It looks for policies and courses of action that are morally permissible and politically possible as well as likely to be effective" (*LP*, 89). Thus, though "the specific conditions of our world at any time ... do not determine the ideal conception," they "do affect the specific answers to questions of nonideal theory" (*LP*, 90). Does this division of labor work?

We can understand this as a question about the relative strengths and weaknesses of alternative theoretical strategies, for political theory may be practiced in a variety of ways, each with its peculiar advantages and disadvantages. One advantage of Rawls's neo-Kantian strategy is precisely the "purity" of the conception of social justice it constructs: social arrangements are based on equal respect for free and equal moral persons. Morally irrelevant particularities are systematically excluded or, when unavoidable, compensated for, inasmuch as even at this high level of abstraction there are certain "impurities" that cannot be simply excluded from ideal theory if the envisioned "utopia" is to be at all "realistic." Rawls already built some of these into *A Theory of Justice* – for instance, inequalities of birth and natural endowment – and in *Political Liberalism* he in effect added the persistence of deep cultural and ideological differences to the list: ideal theory has to accommodate, within its theory-construction, the "fact of reasonable disagreement" about the meaning and value of human life. And Rawls seems now to concede that feminist arguments for adding sex and gender to the list are irresistible: the "general fact" of the biological division of labor in the reproduction of the species should, it appears, be acknowledged by the parties in the original position and accommodated in their design of a basic structure so as to ensure women's substantive freedom and equality. Our question now is whether the same may be said of race? For Rawls, I think, the answer has to be "no." If "race," in the sense at issue here, is at bottom a social, cultural, and political formation established for purposes of subordinating certain groups to others, then it should simply be eliminated as a structuring element in a "well-ordered society."[17] In the ideal society, there would be a total absence of race in this sense. So ideal theory cannot be where it is theorized.

---

[17] At the same time, the evidence seems plain that ethnocentric modes of thought and action have been "general facts" or "general tendencies" of Western – but of course not only Western – society throughout recorded history. See, for instance,

In itself, this need not be a problem. Political theorizing has always been carried on at various levels of abstraction. There is no point in rejecting a priori even the most abstract – "Kantian" – levels, providing that they are not taken to be exclusively valid for, or inclusively adequate to, their objects. Given that Rawls's political theory is configured as a *multilevel* undertaking, with the intent of addressing relevant problems *at one level or another*, the question for us to consider is how his *overall strategy*, particularly the ideal/nonideal dichotomy, measures up against alternative strategies as a way of theorizing race.[18]

II

To begin with, general "facts" about the social world are, as anyone who has followed the discussions in postpositivist philosophy of social science will be aware, hardly the uncontroversial matter that Rawls represents them to be. Facts are stated in languages, and so long as there is no single general theory on which a consensus has formed within and among the relevant communities of investigators in any of the major domains of social life, the languages, and hence the facts – not to mention the "general laws" – of the social sciences are up for debate. Unless Rawls wants to take a firm position on, say, the century-old understanding/explanation debates – and build that position into his "freestanding" political liberalism – he will have to leave open the possibility that social and political inquiry have an ineliminable interpretive dimension and thus that what the general facts about social life are cannot be settled from the standpoint of a neutral observer or a reflective equilibrator.[19] If "realistic" political theory cannot be pursued

---

Ivan Hannaford, *Race: The History of an Idea in the West* (Baltimore: Johns Hopkins University Press, 1996). Whether there are any "general laws" at work here is hard to say, particularly as no stable meaning can be given to that concept in political theory, as I shall argue in section II.

[18] Rawls does not use the terminology of "levels" of theory, but of "parts" (ideal and nonideal) and of "stages" (the four-stage sequence). I shall be focusing on the former, but a full treatment of the issues I raise would require examining the latter as well. Thus Shelby, "Race and Social Justice," pp. 1706–1709, assigns antidiscrimination principles to the second, "constitutional" stage. My conjecture is that similar considerations would apply to this theoretical strategy as well, for the basic structure of justice is already set at the first stage; but I do not argue that here.

[19] See F. Dallmayr and T. McCarthy (eds.), *Understanding and Social Inquiry* (South Bend, IN: University of Notre Dame Press, 1977).

without incorporating into it knowledge of the general characteristics of the social systems to which it is meant to apply, then political philosophy will have to get involved in just the sorts of interpretive-historical and social-theoretical disagreements which, in its self-understanding as normative theory, it hopes to avoid. Moreover, interpretive approaches to the human world typically place more and different weight on historical modes of inquiry than do positivist or rational choice approaches. Hermeneutic understanding is inherently historical: it aims to comprehend social phenomena in their contexts and often in narrative terms. Hence, Rawls's strict separation of "general" from "particular" knowledge of society is problematic, if even the former always comes with an historical index, as hermeneutically inclined social theorists maintain. In any case, it is certainly not uncontroversial.

If political theorists do not dispose of interpretation-free general "facts" in the way that Rawls intends, neither do they have conflict-free political "values" at their disposal. Rawls himself explicitly characterizes the political values that his conception of justice seeks to articulate as belonging to the public political culture of a particular historical society and not to some ideal realm beyond the world. But then it follows that, as such, they do not come with fixed, clear, uncontested meanings; rather, they have to be interpretively worked up from the variable, particular, often conflictual political contexts in which they figure. As a result, the basic terms of his political conception cannot but reflect and project the particular forms of life and situations of conflict from which they are prepared; and they must be understood and assessed in relation to them. Specifically, his guiding conceptions of "persons" with two "moral powers" as both "free and equal" and "rational and reasonable," of "primary goods" as "specifying citizens' needs" in a way that provides a "practicable basis of interpersonal comparison," and of the "stability" of a "well-ordered society" are laden with particular – and contestable – interpretations and evaluations. It makes no sense to suppose that we could insulate their construction from the conflicts of interpretation and evaluation endemic to our public political culture, our constitutional tradition, our legal and political practices and institutions – including the conflicts surrounding "race" from the founding to the present. Working them up theoretically via reflective equilibrium or rational reconstruction cannot remove all traces of their conflictual origins, as Rawls himself appears to acknowledge.

In *A Theory of Justice*, Rawls was clear that the method of reflective equilibrium could not simply articulate an already existing consensus on basic political values, for the reason, among others, that such values had always been and continued to be debated in the public political culture. In view of the admittedly deep divisions on many of the matters to which he addressed himself – for example, the meanings and relative weights of liberty and equality – he did not understand his method of reflective equilibrium to be the hermeneutically conservative operation interpreters and critics sometimes mistook it to be. He remarked, for instance, that the kind of wide reflective equilibrium proper to moral philosophy might bring about a "radical shift" in our sense of justice (*TJ*, 49). It involved, as he put it a few years later, asking "what principles people would acknowledge and accept the consequences of when they had the opportunity to consider other plausible conceptions and to assess their supporting grounds ... [It] seeks the conception, or plurality of conceptions, that would survive the rational consideration of all feasible conceptions and reasonable arguments for them" ("The Independence of Moral Theory", *CP*, 289). But such "rational consideration" might well put the political theorist in the position of defending a comprehensive moral theory *within* the conflict of interpretations and reconstructions. And that is something, which Rawls's later stress on "overlapping consensus" explicitly disallows.[20]

In *Political Liberalism* and *The Law of Peoples*, the idea of the "reasonable" undergoes considerable dilution. The overriding concern of both these works is with the "feasibility" of liberal ideals and the "stability" of liberal institutions in the face of cultural and ideological pluralism. The irreducible plurality of basic views on the meaning and

---

[20] The resultant strain between "rational consideration" and "overlapping consensus" can, I think, be glimpsed in his "Reply to Habermas," *Journal of Philosophy*, 92 (1995), 132–180, where it appears as the tension between his characterization of discourse in civil society as an "omnilogue" in which citizens directly debate the relative merits of competing conceptions of justice (p. 140) and his account a few pages later of public justification as a kind of indirect – non-dialogical, non-dialectical – "overlapping consensus": "Public justification happens when all the reasonable members of political society carry out a justification of the shared political conception by embedding it in their several reasonable comprehensive [doctrines] ... [C]itizens do not look into the content of others' doctrines ... Rather, they take into account and give some weight to only the fact – the existence – of the reasonable overlapping consensus itself" (pp. 143–144).

value of human life makes it necessary, Rawls maintains, to construct a purely "political" conception of justice that "stands free" of "comprehensive doctrines" of any sort, including general philosophical views. This "strategy of avoidance" relocates the "reasonable" at some remove from the Kantian notion of reason, with its close connection to the idea of a critique that submits all claims to authority to the free examination of reason. The reasonable pluralism that we might expect to result from "the exercise of human reason under free institutions" (*PL*, 55–58) is, in Rawls's construction of a "political" conception of justice, replaced in effect by the *de facto* pluralism of comprehensive doctrines that satisfy the much weaker requirements set by his revised notion of toleration.[21] As a result, enlightenment and critique can play only a severely restricted role in normative theory of this sort, and that too makes it an unsuitable vehicle for theorizing racial injustice. Let me conclude these methodological reflections by gesturing toward an alternative theoretical strategy that will guide the studies in this volume.

III

In interpreting the languages of political thought, normative theorists too often take abstract formulations at their word, as if what were left out of the saying were left out of the meaning; they tend to ignore how key concepts and principles actually function in the multiplicity of contexts in which authors and their audiences use them and what their conditions of satisfaction and acceptability are in practice. They tend also to disregard the fact that general norms are always understood and justified with an eye to some range of standard situations and typical cases assumed to be appropriate, and that if that range shifts, then so too do the understandings and justifications of those norms, the conceptual interconnections and warranting reasons considered relevant to them. At the same time, recognizing that ideals and principles of justice, however abstract their form, always come with contentful pre-understandings that derive from their locations not only in systems of thought but also in forms of social and political life, does not in itself

---

[21] For the details of this argument, see my "Kantian Constructivism and Reconstructivism: Rawls and Habermas in Dialogue," *Ethics* 105 (1994): 44–63, and "On the Idea of a Reasonable Law of Peoples," in J. Bohman and M. Lutz-Bachmann (eds.), *Perpetual Peace* (Cambridge, MA: MIT Press, 1997), pp. 201–217.

commit us to sheer contextualism. In the matter at hand, liberalism's complicity with racial slavery, many of the ideas implicated in the justifications of slavery were also given more inclusive interpretations in the same broad contexts as the dominant exclusionary versions remarked above. That is to say, those contexts also provided resources for arguments against slavery on religious or philosophical grounds, including arguments to the effect that the basic rights possessed by all human beings as such forbade it. One could say, then, that there were competing meanings – networks of inferential connections, ranges of standard situations and typical cases – which partly overlapped and partly diverged, but which were sufficiently interlinked to make disagreements real disagreements and not just incommensurable mutterings. And one might then understand the work of critics as an ongoing effort to reweave those connections and redefine those ranges so as to promote more genuinely inclusive versions. In doing so, they could adopt the internal perspective of reflective participants and invoke the context-transcending claims of putatively universal ideals to argue that they had been betrayed, that existing formulations, though expressed in formally universal terms, were actually exclusionary.

On this view, the search for a genuinely inclusive theory of justice is a never-ending, constantly renewed effort to rethink putatively universal basic norms and reshape their practical and institutional embodiments to include what, in their limited historical forms, they unjustly exclude. What generally drive this effort are struggles for recognition by those whom the norms in their established versions fail to recognize.[22] And the intellectual form that takes is the ongoing contestation of essentially contestable articulations of the universal demands of justice. Judith Butler puts the point this way: "the provisional and parochial versions of universality" encoded in law at any given time never exhaust "the possibilities of what might be meant by the universal."[23] Contestation by subjects excluded under existing definitions and conventions is crucial to "the continuing elaboration of the universal itself," for "they seize the language of [the universal] and set into motion a 'performative contradiction,' claiming to be covered by [it] and thereby exposing the contradictory character" of conventional

[22] Axel Honneth, *The Struggle for Recognition*, tr. J. Anderson (Cambridge, MA: MIT Press, 1996).

[23] J. Butler, *Excitable Speech* (New York: Routledge, 1997), p. 89.

formulations.[24] Butler here captures the important insight that the possibility of challenging putatively universal representations is inherent in those representations themselves, or more precisely, in their context-transcending semantic import, and that historically this possibility has been exploited to greatest effect by groups who, though not entitled as a matter of fact under existing formulations of the universal, nevertheless appeal to that import in formulating more inclusive conceptions of justice.

Viewed in this light, as an element – albeit a reflective element – in historical processes of emancipation, normative theory is clearly not "freestanding" in any fundamental sense. And, as the shock-effects of Foucault's genealogies have made clear, the familiar enlightenment metanarrative of universal principles discovered at the birth of modernity and gradually realized ever since fails to acknowledge the impurity of the demands that have historically been made in the name of pure reason. Accordingly, there is a need for critical "histories of the present," the aim of which is to alter our self-understandings by examining the actual genealogies of accepted ideas and principles of practical reason.[25] This distinguishes critical approaches to social and political theory from approaches like Rawls's that seek to construct fundamental norms of justice from the "settled convictions" of our "public political culture" by way of "reflective equilibrium." Critical histories make evident that the political values from which political liberalism seeks to construct a political conception of justice have always been and still are deeply intricated with matters of power, desire, and interest, and that they are essentially contestable. More generally, such histories make us aware that the quite distinct, often conflicting ideas, principles, values, and norms that have variously been taken to express the demands of justice cannot adequately be comprehended, assessed, or rethought without understanding how elements of the contexts and situations in which they have been propounded have invariably entered into them.

---

[24] *Ibid.*
[25] Martin Saar, "Genealogy and Subjectivity," *European Journal of Philosophy* 10 (2002): 231–245. On the relation between Foucault's conception of genealogy and the type of critical theory I am espousing here, see "The Critique of Impure Reason: Foucault and the Frankfurt School," in Thomas McCarthy, *Ideals and Illusions: On Reconstruction and Deconstruction in Contemporary Critical Theory* (Cambridge, MA: MIT Press, 1991), pp. 43–75.

It is not only such "contexts of origin" that contemporary normative theory leaves largely unexamined, but "contexts of application" as well.[26] The distinction that Rawls and others draw between ideal and nonideal theory insulates political theorizing, at least initially, from the messiness of political reality. Subsequent forays into nonideal theory typically have a rather loose, *post hoc* connection to empirical work. Partly because of this, discussions of race following such a strategy usually end up as discussions of affirmative action in the broadest sense: since equal citizenship rights are now formally in place, the "unfavorable conditions" at issue are the substantive inequalities that are the enduring legacy of centuries of legalized oppression and discrimination.[27] Of course, one has to judge any proposed remedial measures, policies, and programs from a pragmatic as well as a moral point of view, for they are put forward as practical means to the desired end of eliminating or reducing those inequities. Hence the case for any concrete compensatory measures has to be made not just "in principle" but "all things considered," that is, it has to take into account empirically likely consequences and side effects, costs and benefits, comparative advantages and disadvantages of possible alternatives, political viability, long-term efficacy, and so on. So nonideal theorizing of this sort turns normative political theory back in the direction of the empirical social reality it began by abstracting and idealizing away from. But – and this is my main point here – there are no theoretical means at hand for bridging the gap between a color-blind ideal theory and a color-coded political reality, for the approach of ideal theory provides *no theoretical mediation* between the ideal and the real – or rather, what mediation it does provide is usually only tacit and always restricted.[28]

[26] This is the terminology employed by Jürgen Habermas in *Between Facts and Norms*, tr. W. Rehg (Cambridge, MA: MIT Press, 1996), chap. 9.

[27] This is the general approach to racial injustice taken by liberal theorists such as Bernard Boxill, Ronald Dworkin, Thomas Nagel, and Judith Jarvis Thompson, among others. An elaboration and defense of it can be found in Amy Gutmann's "Responding to Racial Injustice," in K. Anthony Appiah and A. Gutmann, *Color Consciousness* (Princeton University Press, 1996), pp. 106–178.

[28] An apparent – and for my purposes very interesting – exception in this regard is Shelby's "Justice, Deviance, and the Dark Ghetto." Shelby expressly draws upon his considerable knowledge of social theory generally and of the historical and social-scientific literature on race and racism to develop a nonideal theory of urban ghetto life on Rawlsian premises. In doing so, he relies on more or less the same theoretical and empirical assumptions as I do concerning the historical legacy and basic structures of contemporary racism, and he adopts more or less

On this last score, what Jürgen Habermas argues in *Between Facts and Norms* to be true of legal theory holds *ceteris paribus* of normative political theory as well – namely, that it always relies upon implicit background assumptions drawn from some preunderstanding of contemporary society's structures, dynamics, potentials, and dangers.[29] These implicit "images" or "models" of society tacitly enter into normative-theoretical constructions and often play a covert role in what appear to be purely normative disagreements. Deep differences in normative theory – for instance, those separating classical from social-welfare liberals, or those dividing both from their socialist, radical feminist, or postcolonial critics – often turn on disagreements about the "facts" being assumed, implicitly as well as explicitly, in regard to markets, classes, gender roles, global relations, and so forth. And as we know from the history of social and political theory, significant shifts in thinking often come about as a result of challenges precisely to what have previously been taken for granted as the natural, unalterable facts of social life – class-structured distributions of the social product, gendered divisions of labor, race-based hierarchies of social privilege, ethnocultural definitions of citizenship, and the like. These considerations strongly suggest that such understandings, images, or models of society, which are always at work, though usually only tacitly, in normative theorizing, have to become an explicit theme if political theorists hope to avoid exalting intuitive preunderstandings of their social contexts into universal ideals. But theorizing about politics would then have somehow to combine intuitive knowledge from the perspective of the "insider" with counterintuitive knowledge from the perspective of the "outsider," in the senses both of the observer and the excluded.[30] It would have to join the constructive and reconstructive aims of normative theory to the interpretive, analytical, and explanatory aims of history and other empirically based human studies, and to the practical aims of social and cultural

the same sort of interdisciplinary approach in addressing them. In my view, he largely succeeds in his aim, but only because he effectively treats the Rawlsian framework as an interdependent, rather than foundational, element of a broader critical enterprise. For instance, his analysis of unjust social structures – the interlocking syndrome of racial inequalities in housing, education, employment, and criminal justice – that give rise to systematic inequities and are stabilized by dominant ideologies betokens his willingness to step outside the bounds of that more individualistic framework.

[29] Habermas, *Between Facts and Norms*, chap. 9, "Paradigms of Law."

[30] I do not mean to imply here that "counterintuitive" knowledge could not also come from critical "insiders," as is argued by Michael Walzer in *The Company of Critics* (New York: Basic Books, 1988).

criticism. Given the existing institutionalization of research and scholarship, it would have to become interdisciplinary to the core.[31] And this means that even normative theory would have to become an *interdependent* – not "freestanding" – moment of a larger critical enterprise; that is, it would have to be pursued in a self-consciously interdisciplinary manner and remain theoretically responsive not only to the political struggles of the age but also to contemporary developments in historical, social, and cultural studies.

Of course, not all of these questions, perspectives, and methodologies, can be taken up in every – or any – single study. Interdisciplinarity can be realized only interactively, through ongoing communication across a multiplicity of discursive positions. The studies in this volume have been written in that spirit. They don't attempt to do everything at once but one thing at a time, though hopefully with an ear to the wider discussion of the matter under consideration. In particular, though the issues I take up are often framed in broadly philosophical terms, the resources I use to address them are drawn from a variety of other areas. And while normative issues are frequently the focus of discussion, the relevance of historical and other empirical materials to the way they are defined and addressed is never in doubt. The most narrowly focused of the studies is the close reading of Kant's views on race and development in the next chapter. This serves several purposes. For one thing, it provides a critical analysis of the complex theoretical interconnections among the central themes of this work, which persist, albeit in shifting forms, to the present day. For another, it offers a perspective on the developments in philosophical, historical, political, anthropological, and biological thought of the late eighteenth century that set the stage for the dominance of racial and imperial thinking in the nineteenth century. Finally, I repeatedly refer back to Kant's systematic treatment of these themes to frame some of the specific issues I take up in subsequent chapters.

---

[31] To be sure, critical race theorists from Du Bois onwards have typically worked in interdisciplinary ways. But their work has largely been ignored by mainstream political theory. So this chapter could also be construed as an argument for changing the canon.

2 | Kant on race and development

Derogatory characterizations of out-groups by in-groups are as old as recorded history. And various forms of bond-servitude, particularly in connection with conquest and captivity, are at least as old as settled agricultural societies. Christianity, despite its doctrine of the universal "brotherhood of mankind" as all God's children, generally accommodated itself to established practices of servitude and bondage: it was not until the latter half of the eighteenth century that there was sustained opposition to slavery *as such* from that quarter.[1] And the rationalized universalism of philosophy was no better in this respect: from Aristotle's justification of enslaving those who are inferior by nature, through medieval disquisitions on why man's fallen nature and spiritual bondage called for corresponding forms of earthly subordination and bondage, to modern liberal accounts of the civilizing mission of Europe toward savage and barbaric non-European peoples not yet ready for equal liberty. In this quarter too, the emergence of sustained opposition to racial slavery had to await the latter half of the eighteenth century.[2] The dismal record of philosophical thought in this regard raises the obvious question of how putatively universalistic, inclusive, moral doctrines could so readily countenance particularistic, exclusionary practices – and, as it seems, with surprisingly little cognitive dissonance. This question is no less important than it is obvious, both for coming to a better understanding of our history and traditions and also for heightening sensitivity to the presence of similar hidden dissonances in our current thinking. But we should not expect to find a single answer fitting the wide variety of circumstances with regard to which it might be raised.

[1] There was, to be sure, earlier opposition to enslaving other *Christians*. See Anthony Pagden, *Lords of All the World* (New Haven: Yale University Press, 1995); and David Brion Davis, *The Problem of Slavery in Western Culture* (Oxford University Press, 1988).

[2] There were, of course, earlier exceptions to this general pattern among religious and philosophical thinkers, as both Davis and Pagden remark.

In what follows, I will confine myself to asking "how possibly?" about a single instance – though arguably an exemplary instance – of modern universalistic philosophy, that of Immanuel Kant.[3] Writing precisely at the time when significant religious and philosophical opposition to racial slavery was emerging in Europe and America, Kant not only failed explicitly to condemn that "peculiar institution" but constructed one of the most – some would argue, *the* most[4] – systematic accounts of "race" prior to the flood tide of racial thinking accompanying late nineteenth-century imperialism. In the English-speaking world, his writings and lectures on anthropology and physical geography have only recently begun to receive the attention they deserve;[5] and one focal point of that attention is his treatment of race.[6] I want to take up that discussion here and connect it with the decisive role that Kant's developmental thinking plays in his efforts to reconcile moral-political

[3] In this respect, Kant is representative of Enlightenment thought more generally, which was pervaded by the ambivalence of reconciling universal ideals with deeply entrenched inequalities through hierarchical schemes allegedly based on reason and nature.

[4] See Robert Bernasconi's discussions of this in "Who Invented the Concept of Race? Kant's Role in the Enlightenment Construction of Race," in Bernasconi (ed.), *Race* (Oxford: Blackwell, 2001), pp. 11–36; and "Kant as an Unfamiliar Source of Racism," in J. Ward and T. Lott (eds.), *Philosophers on Race* (Oxford: Blackwell, 2002), pp. 145–166.

[5] Stimulated by the relatively recent publication (1997), in vol. XXV of the Academy edition of Kant's collected works, of seven transcriptions of student and auditor notes on his lectures in anthropology. *Kants Gesammelte Schriften*, ed. Deutsche Akademie der Wissenschaften zu Berlin, 29 vols. (Berlin: Walter de Gruyter, 1902–). Vol. XXVI, with transcriptions of notes on his lectures in physical geography, is forthcoming. Other transcriptions of student notes can be found at the Marburg Kant-Archiv website: www.uni-marburg.de/kant/webseitn/gt_v_ant. htm. A number of the transcriptions from vol. XXV will appear in English translation in *The Cambridge Edition of the Works of Immanuel Kant* (Cambridge University Press), in a volume entitled *Lectures on Anthropology*. The Academy edition will henceforth be cited as AA and the Cambridge edition by name.

[6] For some recent English-language discussions of Kant's views on race, in addition to the essays by Bernasconi cited in n. 4, see Emmanuel Chuckwudi Eze, "The Color of Reason: The Idea of 'Race' in Kant's Anthropology," in Eze (ed.), *Postcolonial African Philosophy* (Oxford: Blackwell, 1997), pp. 103–140; and in the same volume, pp. 141–161, Tsenay Serequeberhan, "The Critique of Eurocentrism and the Practice of African Philosophy"; Thomas Hill and Bernard Boxill, "Kant and Race," in Boxill (ed.), *Race and Racism* (Oxford University Press, 2001), pp. 448–471; and the essays in part II of E. Eigen and M. Larrimore (eds.), *The German Invention of Race* (Albany: SUNY Press, 2006).

universalism with anthropological-historical particularism, for ideas of "development" and "underdevelopment" are still central to Eurocentric thinking.

I Impure ethics

For some time now, the once all but exclusive focus on Kant's pure ethics in the English-speaking world has been broadening to include aspects of his impure ethics, especially his philosophy of history. More recently, the focus has expanded still further to include his views on the empirical study of human nature and culture generally.[7] If one looks back now at the specifically ethical works, one can readily see that this expansion is entirely appropriate: Kant repeatedly characterizes moral philosophy as comprising both a pure – rational – part and an impure – empirical – part. In the *Groundwork*, the former and leading part, which establishes the fundamental principles of morals, is said to be wholly independent of experience.[8] Everything having to do with the application of these principles to human beings is said to belong to the impure, empirical part, which he calls practical anthropology. In *The Metaphysics of Morals*, this sharp division is complicated some-what, insofar as the doctrine of virtue presents a mixed metaphysics in which pure rational principles are applied to *human nature in general*, an undertaking that requires some empirical knowledge of human beings, though presumably of a universal and noncontroversial sort.[9] To be sure, this purported knowledge of human nature in general can be and has been contested. But that is not my concern here, which is rather with Kant's views *on human nature in particular* – in particular times and places, cultures and races. Thus in his essays on the philosophy of history, Kant treats of different epochs and civilizations, and in the published manual for his anthropology course, *Anthropology from a*

---

[7] Good examples of this genre are Susan Meld Shell, *The Embodiment of Reason* (University of Chicago Press, 1996), and Robert Louden, *Kant's Impure Ethics* (Oxford University Press, 2000). See also B. Jacobs and P. Kain (eds.), *Essays on Kant's Anthropology* (Cambridge University Press, 2003).

[8] *Groundwork of the Metaphysics of Morals* [1785: AA IV, 385–463], in Cambridge edition, *Practical Philosophy*, tr. and ed. M. Gregor, with an intro. by Allen Wood (Cambridge University Press, 1996), pp. 43–108, at pp. 43–45.

[9] *The Metaphysics of Morals* [1797: AA VI, 203–493], tr. and ed. M. Gregor (Cambridge University Press, 1996). Allen Wood, *Kant's Ethical Thought* (Cambridge University Press, 1999), pp. 193–196, is helpful on this point.

Pragmatic Point of View, he offers an account not only of individual character and of the character of the species, but also of the characters of sexes, peoples, and races.[10]

The "pragmatic" anthropology sketched in that work is not meant to be a "value-free" or purely theoretical enterprise: it is undertaken from a "practical" perspective in the broadest sense, that is, one related to free human action of various sorts – "technical" (i.e. instrumental) and "prudential" (i.e. oriented to happiness), as well as "practical" in the narrower sense of "moral." But it is this narrower sense of "practical anthropology" as "moral anthropology" that Kant has in view when he uses the term to designate the impure or empirical part of ethics, the part that is concerned with the application of pure rational principles to concrete human beings in all their historical and cultural similarities and differences. The general aim of this moral-practical anthropology is to identify cultural and historical factors that help or hinder the establishment and efficacy of morality in human life. It deals with stages of cultural, institutional, and moral progress, and with cultural, political, and religious conditions for the realization of the highest good of the *species as a whole*, a global kingdom of ends.

But there is also a part of practical anthropology that deals with morally relevant differences among *subgroups within the species*, that is, differences that make a difference in regard to the duties owed them. As Kant puts it in a brief remark "On Ethical Duties of Human Beings toward One Another with Regard to Their Condition" in *The Metaphysics of Morals*: "[S]ince they do not involve principles of obligation for human beings as such toward one another, they cannot properly constitute a part of the metaphysical first principles of a doctrine of virtue.

---

[10] *Anthropology from a Pragmatic Point of View* [1798: AA VII, 117–333], tr. M. Gregor (The Hague: Martinus Nijhoff, 1794), part II, "Anthropological Characteristics." Louden, *Kant's Impure Ethics*, pp. 10–16, offers a differentiated account of the "degrees and kinds of impurity" in Kant's ethical thought. He distinguishes (a) the necessary moral laws of a free will in general, (b) morality for finite rational beings who can oppose the moral law (the level of the *Groundwork*), (c) the determination of moral duties for human beings as such (the level of *The Metaphysics of Morals*), (d) moral or practical anthropology, concerned with the development, spread, and strengthening, of morality in human culture and history, (e) practical anthropology, concerned with the morally relevant conditions and relations of various subgroups of human beings, and (f) moral judgment in specific situations (catechism, casuistry). It is primarily with levels "d" and "e" that I am concerned here.

They are only rules modified in accordance with the differences of the subjects to whom the principle of virtue (in terms of what is formal) is applied in cases that come up in experience (the material) ... a transition which, by applying the pure principles of duty to cases of experience would schematize these principles, as it were, and present them ready for morally practical use."[11] As examples of such "schematized" moral principles, Kant mentions rules that apply to the treatment of people "in accordance with their differences in rank, age, sex, health, property, or poverty, and so forth," or according to whether they belong to "the cultivated or the crude."[12] I shall be concerned here with Kant's practical anthropology in both general and particular aspects, more precisely with both his developmental philosophy of universal history and his anthropological "characteristics" of particular racial subgroups.

Kant's popular lecture course on anthropology and his published notes thereto dealt not with practical anthropology in the narrower sense of moral anthropology but with practical anthropology in the broader sense that pertains to all forms of free action: that is to say, they dealt with pragmatic anthropology.[13] He distinguishes "anthropology from a pragmatic point of view" from "physiological anthropology" by noting that the latter studies only what nature makes of man, whereas the former considers "what man as a free agent makes, or can and should make, of himself."[14] Pragmatic anthropology thus includes moral-practical anthropology but is not restricted to it: it studies humankind in respect to, and for the sake of, human agency in all its dimensions, not only the moral. Partly for textual reasons, then, our concern with Kant's "impure ethics" will be pursued in this broader context. But this is also the context required by the logic of Kant's reflections on human destiny, which renders highly problematic any attempt sharply to separate the workings of nature – particularly as culturally formed – from those of freedom: mixed creatures such as we, with one foot firmly planted in each realm, have to realize the ends proposed by the laws of freedom in the realm of nature. The construction of a moral world, of a kingdom of ends, which practical reason enjoins as the highest good, cannot but use the materials that nature,

---

[11] *The Metaphysics of Morals*, p. 214.   [12] *Ibid.*

[13] Kant lectured on anthropology every winter semester from 1772–1773 until his retirement in 1796. His lectures on physical geography began in 1755 and also continued until retirement, alternating semesters with the anthropology lectures after 1773.

[14] *Anthropology*, preface, p. 3.

including human culture and civilization, provides. And this means, in the terminology of the passage from *The Metaphysics of Morals* cited above, that the laws of freedom can be put into effect only if they are "schematized" in some sense, so that purely "formal" principles can be applied to the "material" of experience. Impure ethics is not, then, merely a convenient but unnecessary addition to pure ethics; it is, as Derrida might say, a necessary supplement, if morality is to have any purchase at all on human life. And this means that however "purely rational" the derivation of first principles may be, their application will require ongoing "schematization" to deal with the impurities of experience.

It is as if the pure rays emanating from ideas of practical reason could illuminate human life only once they are refracted through the denser medium of human nature, culture, and history. This is, at least, the division of labor that Kant proposes. Moreover, because particularity and contingency are ineliminable from the human condition in his view, there can be no complete, systematic knowledge of it. Thus pragmatic anthropology will, he maintains, never achieve the status of a strict science; it is not only practically interested but also unavoidably incomplete. This lower epistemic status gives cause for concern about the sources and uses of such knowledge, and Kant does advise his readers and auditors to exercise great caution in using the travel reports, histories, biographies, literature, and the like, which were the standard sources in his day for knowledge of other cultures. But he frequently failed to follow his own advice. And as the "denser media" in which his pure rational ethics was refracted were shot through with the prejudices of the age, his operative views on differences of gender, race, ethnicity, class, culture, religion, and the like were "impure" in more than one sense. My concern here, however, is primarily with his theory of racial differences.[15]

---

[15] The most important published works for this purpose are "Observations on the Feeling of the Beautiful and the Sublime" [1764: AA II, 205–256], "Of the Different Races of Human Beings" [1775/1777: AA II, 427–443], "Determination of the Concept of a Race of Human Beings" [1785: AA VIII, 89–106], "Of the Use of Teleological Principles in Philosophy" [1788: AA VIII, 159–184], and *Anthropology from a Pragmatic Point of View* [1798: AA VII, 117–333]. The most important unpublished materials from Kant's own hand are lecture notes for his courses in physical geography and anthropology, and various *Reflexionen* (notes, fragments, course announcements) collected in vol. XV of AA. In addition there are the aforementioned student and auditor transcriptions of his lectures. I shall be citing the published works, which, on the points that concern me here, are not different in substance from the unpublished materials.

II Race

One thing that should be noted straightway regarding Kant's theorizing of "race" is that he was not only at the forefront in Germany of the emerging discipline of anthropology, he was also fully abreast of contemporary discussions of the natural history of the human species. Thus his interchanges with Johann Friedrich Blumenbach, who is often deemed to have invented the modern, scientific notion of race, were not unidirectional.[16] In particular, it seems to have been Kant who introduced the idea of explaining racial differentiation by postulating in our original ancestors a fund of four germs or seeds [*Keime*], each of which contained *in potentia* one set of racial characteristics; which germ developed in a given genetic line and which remained inactive, and thus which set of racial characteristics was actualized, was determined by geographical – especially climatic – conditions; and once developed, racial characteristics were invariably inherited in a genetic line, for no reversion to the original stem was possible.[17] One of Kant's chief aims in developing this theory of race was to defend monogenesis and the biological unity of the human species against the polygenetic views of authors like Voltaire and Lord Kames, views that had developed in response to the intensified European encounter with alien peoples in Africa and the Americas over the preceding century.[18] That is to say, Kant intended his account of racial diversity also to preserve the unity in difference of the human species, in line with the Biblical narrative of creation and the traditional doctrine of the "brotherhood of mankind" under God.[19] The costs of doing so via a theory of biologically based racial differentiation were, as we now know, much too high.

[16] On Kant's relation to Blumenbach, see J. H. Zammito, "Policing Polygeneticism In Germany, 1775," and R. Bernasconi, "Kant on Blumenbach's Polyps," both in Eigen and Larrimore (eds.), *The German Invention of Race*, pp. 35–54 and 73–90. As noted below in chapter 3, it was Blumenbach's version of race theory that had much the more significant influence on the development of race thinking in the nineteenth century.

[17] Attributing racial differences to climatic and other environmental factors was not unusual in this period. It is the notion of *Keime* as the biological basis of racial characteristics that is new.

[18] In "Of the Different Races of Human Beings," tr. J. M. Mikkelsen, in R. Bernasconi and T. Lott (eds.), *The Idea of Race* (Indianapolis: Hackett, 2000), pp. 8–22, Kant explicitly addresses himself to Voltaire's polygenetic hypothesis, at p. 19.

[19] For Kant, this biological unity of the species underpins its ultimate cultural and political unity, and thus is a condition of its final moral unity, as I shall elaborate below.

In addition to being familiar with earlier developments in natural history and contemporary developments in anthropology and ethnology, Kant was an avid reader of travel reports of all kinds, written by explorers, traders, missionaries, settlers, and others involved in direct contacts with distant peoples; and at that time such reports were still a principal source of knowledge in Europe about many of them. He warned repeatedly of the unreliability of such sources, but rely on them he did. As a result, his characterizations of the different races – which he distinguished primarily by skin-color: red, black, yellow, and white – largely repeated the racist commonplaces of the period.[20] And in his account these commonplaces were naturalized through being biologized. Thus his ranking of the innate capacities of the major subdivisions of the species is fleshed out in terms of their different *Naturanlagen* or natural predispositions.[21] Part II of the published manual on anthropology, which deals with the "characteristics" of persons, sexes, peoples, races, and the species, is subtitled "On How to Discern Man's Inner Self from His Exterior."[22] There we read that "physical character" belongs to the world of nature, "moral character" to that of freedom.[23] The former, what nature makes of us – which would seem to be properly a concern of "physiological" rather than "pragmatic" anthropology – includes our individual natures [*das Naturell*] and our temperaments. In the lectures on anthropology, individual nature is said to be the basis of natural abilities or talents, and temperament to be the basis of inclinations, insofar as they are related to bodily constitution.[24]

---

[20] Most of Kant's detailed remarks about the various races of human beings are to be found in unpublished materials, especially in his *Reflexionen zur Anthropologie*, the *Menschenkunde* transcription of his anthropology lectures, and the notes to his lectures on physical geography (edited by Theodor Rink); but his published remarks, while fewer in number, are not substantively different.

[21] See the definition of *Naturanlage* in "Of the Different Races," p. 13, and Wood's explication of it in *Kant's Ethical Thought*, p. 211.

[22] *Anthropology*, p. 149. This is, of course, an instance of the theoretical linking of physical and mental stereotypes that is characteristic of race thinking.

[23] *Ibid.*, p. 151.

[24] Wood, *Kant's Ethical Thought*, p. 205, emphasizes that character, in the full sense, involves the "taking over" and "transforming" of these "physiological endowments" by free agents, so that in his view Kant's anthropology is not a naturalistic determinism. But it remains that, for Kant, the natural medium in and through which human freedom must express itself is differentiated by sex and race in ways that result in significantly different "propensities" and abilities of the

Such differences in talent and temperament are what Kant has in mind when he speaks of the "innate" [*angeboren*] differences between the races.[25] Because racial differences are adapted in large part to geographical differences, abilities and inclinations suited to one environment may be dysfunctional in another. In particular, the weaker impulse to activity suited to tropical climes, according to Kant, renders their native inhabitants – for example blacks – less energetic and industrious than the native inhabitants of temperate zones – for example whites – and thus less capable of self-improvement.[26] Because the growth of culture and civilization depend on such things, we can understand why, in Kant's view, the advancement of the species is, and will continue to be, centered in Europe.[27] Reflecting – often in distressing detail – the character of European contacts with non-Europeans, he represents Native Americans as too weak for hard

corresponding human subgroups. On the whole, I agree with Louden's assessment of the strict dichotomy between physical and moral character in Kant's anthropology as "hard to swallow" (*Kant's Impure Ethics*, p. 81). On this issue in the context of the anthropology lectures, see Brian Jacobs, "Kantian Character and the Problem of a Science of Humanity," in Jacobs and Kain (eds.), *Essays on Kant's Anthropology*, pp. 105–134.

[25] He also regards some of the differences between "peoples" or "nations" as "innate" or "in the blood," owing to the "mixture of races" that produces them. See, for instance, *Anthropology*, pp. 315, 319. I shall be only marginally concerned with that in this essay, though it is relevant to his conception of nation-states and thus of cosmopolitan order. I discuss it briefly in "On Reconciling National Diversity and Cosmopolitan Unity," in C. Cronin and P. DeGreiff (eds.), *Global Justice and Transitional Politics* (MIT Press, 2002), pp. 235–274.

[26] Like other Enlightenment thinkers, Kant regarded adaptation to extreme climates as generally bad for a people's character. Thus he explains the "diminished life power" of American Indians in part through their having adapted to extremely cold climes as they migrated over many generations from Northeast Asia to Northwest America. ("Of the Different Races," p. 16) It should be noted that Kant variably classified as "white" peoples other than European. In "Of the Different Races," for example, that classification includes – in addition to Europeans – Moors, Arabs, Turkish-Tatars, and Persians. But, his philosophy of history makes clear that in his view, however dispersed earlier advances in culture may have been, European whites alone drive cultural and political progress from the modern period onward.

[27] European whites were consistently given top ranking by Kant from early on – see *Observations on the Feeling of the Beautiful and Sublime* (1764), tr. J. T. Goldthwait (Berkeley: University of California Press, 1960), pp. 109–112 – but his relative ranking of Africans and American Indians shifted in favor of the former.

labor and resistant to culture; Africans as accepting the culture of slaves but not of free people; and both as incapable of creating for themselves an orderly civil society. Asians (China and Hindustan) are depicted as civilized but static and lacking in spirit. Whites, by contrast, are said to possess all the drives, talents, and predispositions to culture and civilization that make for progress toward perfection.[28] The specifics of these comparative assessments are not of interest here; but their general result is a naturalistic rationale for existing power relations between Europeans and the nonwhite world. As we shall see, in the context of Kant's philosophy of history, his natural-historical account of racial hierarchy merges into a philosophical and even theological justification: it becomes part of a theodicy justifying God's ways to humankind. And it is in this larger setting that Kant's strictures against race mixing should be understood: it is against nature and thus against the plan of divine providence.[29] How, then, is this natural, God-willed hierarchy of human types, possessing markedly different capacities for culture and civilization, to be reconciled with the all-inclusive demands of morality as figured in a global kingdom of ends?

The path of attempted reconciliation is a teleological one, and it proceeds in several stages. At every stage, the guiding principle of teleological judgment is understood to be "reflective," not "constitutive." That is, it properly functions as a heuristic principle needed by us humans to make sense of nature and history; but it is not appropriate for "determinant" judgments concerning the actual grounds of the appearance of natural purposiveness, which may in fact be causal mechanisms. Viewing nature as if some end were the ground for the existence of this or that regular feature of it, does not, then, exclude our

---

[28] See, for instance, "Of the Different Races," pp. 16–18, and "On the Use of Teleological Principles in Philosophy," tr. J. M. Mikkelsen, in Bernasconi (ed.), *Race*, pp. 37–56, at pp. 47–49. For additional remarks and sources, see Louden, *Kant's Impure Ethics*, pp. 98–100, and Wood, *Kant's Ethical Thought*, pp. 338–339, n. 3.

[29] See, for instance, "Of the Different Races," p. 10, and *Anthropology*, p. 320. At the same time, Kant appears to be aware that most nations were the result of interbreeding of one sort or another. Kant's complex and – at least on first appearance – inconsistent views on this matter are sorted out in different ways by Susan Shell, "Kant's Concept of a Human Race," and Mark Larrimore, "Race, Freedom, and the Fall in Steffens and Kant," both in Eigen and Larrimore (eds.), *The German Invention of Race*, pp. 55–72 and 91–120.

eventually being able to explain that feature in causal terms. But it does enable us to give systematic unity to what would otherwise be an indeterminate collection of contingent facts and laws. This is particularly important in the move from mere "natural description" to "natural history," for the systematic ambitions of the latter can be fulfilled only by assuming a purposiveness underlying its classificatory divisions.[30] In the case of organic beings, this underlying purposiveness means that functionally significant similarities and differences are to be traced back to natural predispositions: they are "originally implanted" as part of "the plan of nature," so to speak.[31] Thus, for example, in the human species the differences between the sexes are understood teleologically in terms of the different natural predispositions of males and females, which suit them to their different functions in the natural and cultural reproduction of the species.[32] The differences among the races are to be understood in terms of different natural predispositions suiting them to different geographical conditions. The principle of natural teleological judgment – that nature does nothing in vain – prompts us to inquire after the natural purposiveness of such differentiation; and that is said to lie in nature's plan that human beings populate the entire globe. The biological differences attendant upon this functional adaptation prominently include heritable skin-color: as the principal means for ridding the body of harmful elements, perspiration, and thus skin composition, are central to survival in a given environment. But those differences – rooted, as we saw, in which germ is activated and which others "stifled" or "extinguished" by climatic and other geographical conditions experienced over long periods – also importantly include differences in temperament and ability. So, as with the subdivision of the sexes, the subdivision of the races for biological purposes is linked with fateful differences at the level of "mental powers" and "culture." The resultant hierarchical scheme thus provides a natural-historical underpinning to the deep social and cultural inequalities that Kant takes to be characteristic of the human condition. To make moral sense of those sociocultural differences requires now that we extend

[30] "Of the Different Races," p. 13, n. 1.

[31] See "On the Use of Teleological Principles in Philosophy," pp. 42–44.

[32] See *Anthropology*, pp. 166–173. Not surprisingly, these functionally rooted biological differences entail, for Kant, that women are less suited by temperament and ability to engage in public life.

the principle of (reflective) teleological judgment from natural history in the narrower sense to human history proper.

III Development

To understand nature in the broadest sense, including human history, as a systematic unity, we must have recourse to an "ultimate end of nature" [*letzter Zweck der Natur*] beyond the natural ends that explain specific features of specific kinds of organic beings; and according to Kant that ultimate end is the full development of the natural capacities of the human being. Even beyond this, to understand why nature as a whole, with its systematic purposiveness oriented to that ultimate end, is itself not simply an unintelligible fact, we have to have recourse to a "final end" [*Endzweck*] that stands outside of nature and possesses its own intrinsic worth; and that Kant takes to be "the highest good" in the form of a "kingdom of ends." Racial differentiation and hierarchy will have to make sense, then, both in the context of human sociocultural development naturalistically conceived, and, at the same time, in the context of the species achieving its highest good morally conceived. For our purposes, it is important to examine Kant's views on race in this expanded context, for though teleological thinking has largely been displaced from biology by Darwinian thinking, it still plays a role in conceptualizing the history of the species.

In Kant's view, over the course of human history the biological unity of the species is destined to become, first, a legal-political unity – a cosmopolitan federation of nation-states – and then, finally, a moral unity – a "Kingdom of God on earth." The teleological philosophy of history in which he sketches this development does not attribute it directly to the conscious intentions of historical actors but rather to "a purpose of nature behind this senseless course of human events," a "plan of nature" informing the "history of creatures who act without a plan of their own."[33] In thus anticipating the better-known Hegelian version of the cunning of reason in history, Kant lays down the basic (teleological) principles of (reflective) judgment in this domain: "all the natural capacities [or predispositions: *Naturanlagen*] of a creature are

---

[33] "Idea for a Universal History with a Cosmopolitan Purpose," [1784: AA VIII, 15–31], tr. H. B. Nisbet, in H. Reiss (ed.), *Kant: Political Writings* (Cambridge University Press, 1991), pp. 41–53, at p. 42.

destined sooner or later to be developed completely," and "in man (as the only rational creature on earth), those natural capacities which are directed toward the use of reason are such that they could be developed only in the species, but not in the individual."[34] Using this as his guiding thread, Kant produces a reading of history that is progressivist and cosmopolitan while remaining decidedly Eurocentric – that is to say, a reading in the Enlightenment mold.

Unlike instinct, reason "requires trial, practice, and instruction to enable it to progress," and thus it will "require a long, perhaps incalculable series of generations, each passing on its enlightenment to the next, before the germs implanted by nature in our species can be developed to the degree which corresponds to nature's original intention."[35] As our rational capacities turn on the ability to set ourselves ends and select means to them, our development is essentially a matter of progressive cultivation; for culture is precisely the aptitude in a rational being for setting and pursuing ends generally, that is, not just moral ends but any ends whatever.[36] There are different aspects of this progressive cultivation of the species. At a general level, Kant distinguishes the negative aspect of discipline – liberation from the despotism of desire – and the positive aspect of skill [*Geschicklichkeit*] – the ability to attain chosen ends. And under the latter aspect he distinguishes the development of the arts and sciences, of taste and refinement, and of the rule of law, particularly in nation-states organized as constitutional republics and in a cosmopolitan federation of such states. In his historical essays, Kant emphasizes this last, legal-political, dimension of historical development, so much so that some commentators have taken this to be "the ultimate end of nature" in his eyes, rather than sociocultural development more broadly. But the broader view can accommodate that emphasis as well, for Kant holds that "the highest purpose of nature – i.e. the development of all natural capacities – can be fulfilled only in society," and indeed only in a "civil society [*bürgerliche Gesellschaft*] which can administer justice [or law: *Recht*] universally."[37] And that will require, in the end, "a law-governed external relationship with other states," in the form of a "civil union [*bürgerliche Vereinigung*]

---

[34] *Ibid.*, First and Second Propositions, p. 42.   [35] *Ibid.*, pp. 42–43.
[36] *Critique of the Power of Judgment* [1790: AA V, 165–485], Cambridge edition, tr. P. Guyer and E. Matthews (Cambridge University Press, 2000), p. 299.
[37] "Universal History," p. 45.

of mankind," a "universal cosmopolitan condition [*weltbürgerlicher Zustand*]" as the "matrix [or womb: *Schoß*] within which all the original predispositions of the human species will develop."[38] Securing external freedom through the rule of coercive law [*Zwangsrecht*] is a basic condition of, and thus a central ingredient in, the full development of species capacities. Cultural advances and advances in legal-political organization go hand in hand.

Kant distinguishes these natural developments from *moral development* – which, as commentators have repeatedly pointed out, is a difficult notion to make sense of in a system that rigidly separates the noumenal realm of timeless freedom from the phenomenal realms of nature and history. Be that as it may, there is little doubt that Kant's philosophy of history treats cultural progress, conceived in naturalistic terms, as a necessary condition for the realization of nature's *final end*, the global moral community, which must itself be the work of freedom. That is, the "final end of nature" – which makes sense of there being any nature at all, rather than nothing – unlike the "ultimate end of nature" – which unifies nature, including human nature and history, into a systematic whole – lies beyond nature. What redeems nature, so to speak, is human freedom in its complete or perfect form of a kingdom of ends. Human destiny [*Bestimmung*], as the destiny of the mixed beings that we are, requires the cooperation of nature with freedom; it comprises both the development of our natural predispositions and the gradual realization of our moral end, the highest good – which is itself dual, combining the well-being that is the object of our natural desires with the moral disposition [*Gesinnung*] that can only result from free choice. The bridge between nature and freedom is, then, human history, in which raw human nature is gradually cultivated to the point at which the realization of a moral world in nature/history becomes not a certainty but a rational hope.[39]

If the republican constitutional state, and ultimately a global federation of all such states, is the matrix within which our natural predispositions may fully develop, organized religion is the institutional means through which moral community develops and – this is the hope – may lead eventually to a global kingdom of ends, figured in religious terms as the Kingdom of God on earth. That is, only when a

---

[38] *Ibid.*, pp. 47, 51.
[39] I shall have more to say about this Kantian idea of hope in chapter 5.

world civil society under the rule of coercive law is combined with a *world moral community* under laws of freedom or virtue do we have the final goal of history, which it is our duty consciously to promote. Overcoming the war of all against all that has been the rule in international relations requires that republican nation-states relativize their particularistic claims to absolute sovereignty in a global *Völkerstaat*, a world republic of all republics, under the rule of cosmopolitan law [*Völkerstaatsrecht*].[40] And overcoming the mutual suspicion, contempt, and hostility that have characterized relations among organized religions requires that historical faiths transcend their sectarian claims to offer the one true path to salvation and gradually come to understand themselves as purely rational, moral faiths. To be sure, for mixed beings such as ourselves, pure moral-rational faith cannot of itself effectively ground moral community; for us the invisible moral union of hearts requires visible symbols and supports, in the form of historical ecclesiastical faiths with sacred scriptures, and the like, if it is to take root in people's lives and spread across the whole species. In a variation on a familiar Enlightenment theme, however, Kant regards the particular "vehicles" or "shells" of pure rational faith as inessential to its core content, which is purely moral. Sometimes he writes as if they will gradually disappear; but most often he envisions their gradual transformation through a growing consciousness that they are inessential outward forms of pure moral religion, forms which may be retained, if needed, but only after having been freed from the illusions and superstitions that plagued their historical manifestations. When Kant writes that there are many historical faiths but only one true religion, when he envisions historical faiths gradually coming to realize this and thereupon making themselves more suitable vehicles for a universal ethical community encompassing all peoples, he is unclear as to what specific roles the various world religions might play in such a, so to speak, second-order convergence of religious self-understanding. On the whole, however, and in keeping with his generally Eurocentric perspective, Kant decidedly privileges Christianity. Not only was it originally taught by its founder as a moral (rather than statutory) religion, it was presently (i.e. at the close of the eighteenth century) much further along the road to a pure moral religion. So here too, it seems, as with progress

---

[40] For an elaboration of this interpretation of Kant's cosmopolitan ideal, see my article cited in n. 25.

in law and politics, art and science, European developments will set the pace and provide the models for the rest of the world. Ethico-religious community, like legal-political union, will arrive not through some form of dialectical or dialogical mediation of differences, but through the global diffusion of Western ways.

On the other hand, though eighteenth-century Europe had, in Kant's view, already advanced significantly in culture and civilization, its moralization lagged seriously behind. The radical transformation of moral disposition which would put the general advances in the development of human capacities to good use, that is, to the creation of a world in which justice, virtue, and happiness were united, was still outstanding. This transformation of men's and women's hearts, which must come in significant part from the purification of religion (as well as from the reform of education), is, according to Kant, the most difficult step along the path to realizing our final end. But without the passage from civilization to moralization, humanity's growing aptitude for attaining ends of all sorts will increasingly be made to serve the worst sorts of purposes. If civilization is to be more than the "glittering misery" that it has so far been, a profound moral change is required, so that the ends we pursue with increasing skill will be good ends, ends that can be approved and shared by all.[41] For this, however, we cannot rely on the cunning of nature: it is something that we have to do for ourselves as free, moral beings. Philosophy of history with a practical interest can provide no guarantees in this regard, it can only show that there is a rational basis for hope and thus no need to despair.

It is critical to Kant's conception of the highest good as a kingdom of ends that the legal-political side of global unification be complemented and completed by the ethico-religious side. For without a corresponding, reinforcing transformation of moral character, attitudes, and motivations, any legally established cosmopolitan order would be in constant danger of being undone by the depravity of human nature.[42] Beyond this pragmatic worry, the need for a specifically moral conception of the final end of nature is built into Kant's system, since a moral world is the unconditional collective end that practical reason as such

---

[41] As enjoined by the categorical imperative, particularly in the formulation of humanity as an end in itself.

[42] "Perpetual Peace" [1795: AA VIII, 341–386], tr. Nisbet, in Reiss (ed.), *Kant: Political Writings*, pp. 93–130, at pp. 103–105.

commands. Considered apart from our moral destiny, even with highly developed skills we are but "a mere trifle in relation to the omnipotence of nature."[43] Again: "In the system of nature, a human being (*homo phaenomenon, animal rationale*) is a being of slight importance ... Although a human being has, in his understanding, something more than [the rest of the animals] and can set himself ends, even this gives him only an extrinsic value for his usefulness ... But a human being regarded as a person, that is, as the subject of morally practical reason, is exalted above any price; for as a person (*homo noumenon*) he is not to be valued as a means to the ends of others or even to his own ends, but as an end in himself, that is, he possesses a dignity (an absolute intrinsic value) by which he exacts respect for himself from all other rational beings in the world. He can measure himself with every other rational being of this kind and value himself on a footing of equality with them ... [H]is insignificance as a human animal may not infringe upon his consciousness of his dignity as a rational human being."[44] But if equal dignity and respect define the kind of world which, to borrow a formulation from the *Religion*, a moral being "would create, under the guidance of practical reason, were such a thing in his power, a world into which, moreover, he would place himself as a member,"[45] how does Kant make moral-rational sense of the racial inequality that he takes to be part of our natural history? To grasp the essentials of Kant's version of Christian–Stoic theodicy, we shall have to take a closer look at how he conceives the "radical evil" inherent in human nature and its essential role in human development.

IV Theodicy naturalized

A concise indication of Kant's conception of the role of evil in human history can be found in the "Fourth Proposition" of his "Idea for a

---

[43] "A Renewed Attempt to Answer the Question: 'Is the Human Race Continually Improving?,'" Second Part of *The Conflict of the Faculties* [1798: AA VII, 1–116], tr. Nisbet, in Reiss (ed.), *Kant: Political Writings*, pp. 177–200, at p. 185.

[44] *The Metaphysics of Morals*, pp. 186–187. These considerations, which are set forth in a section entitled "On Servility," directly give rise there to such injunctions as the following: "Be no man's lackey [*Knecht*]. Do not let others tread with impunity on your rights."

[45] *Religion within the Limits of Reason Alone* [1793/1794: AA VI, 1–203], tr. T. M. Greene and H. H. Hudson (New York: Harper & Row, 1960), p. 5.

Universal History with a Cosmopolitan Purpose": "The means which nature employs to bring about the development of innate capacities is that of antagonism within society, in so far as this antagonism becomes in the long run the cause of a law-governed social order. By antagonism, I mean in this context the *unsocial sociability* of men, that is, their propensity to enter into society, coupled however, with a continual resistance [thereto] that threatens to break it up."[46] This structure of motivation, Kant notes, is "obviously rooted in human nature"; and in various places he spells out his version of what is in essence a familiar story about the continual war between good and evil in the human breast. The evil side is fleshed out in terms – again, not unfamiliar – of basic desires, affects, and passions that lead us away from the path of reason – self-love, ambition, greed, desire for honor and power, and the like – which Kant sums up as "the unsocial characteristic of wanting to direct everything in accordance with [one's] own ideas."[47] We want to have things our own way, as do others; we resist one another and expect resistance from one another. And "it is this very resistance which awakens all men's powers ... and drives [them] to seek status among [their] fellows," through gaining honor, power, property, and so forth.[48] Without these "self-seeking pretensions" and other "asocial qualities," human talents would have remained "forever in a dormant state ... [T]he end for which [men] were created, their rational nature, would be an unfilled void."[49] In short, "nature" uses evil to achieve good. This might seem an odd combination until we recall that many eighteenth-century authors – from Mandeville and Smith to Rousseau and Turgot – were wrestling with the problem of what might be called "the dialectic of progress," that is, the inextricable entanglement of good and evil in human development, which some of them understood also to include the unintended good consequences of actions undertaken for selfish reasons (the invisible hand, the cunning of reason, and the like).[50] Kant's version of this invokes "the hidden plan of nature" or "Providence," which systematically turns evil to good: "Nature should thus be thanked for fostering social incompatibility, enviously competitive vanity, and insatiable desires for possession or even power. Without these desires, all man's excellent natural capacities would

---

[46] "Universal History," p. 51.   [47] *Ibid.*   [48] *Ibid.*   [49] *Ibid.*, p. 45.
[50] I elaborate further on the dialectic of progress in chapter 5.

never be roused to develop ... They would thus seem to indicate the design of a wise creator."[51]

The basic structure of the human condition – mutual interdependence pervaded by mutual antagonism – and the "propensity to evil" that it subtends, mark both the state of nature, which Kant depicts as a "condition of savagery" [*Zustand der Wilden*], and the civilized state, which he repeatedly characterizes as a "glittering misery" [*schimmerndes Elend*]. The source of the problem in the state of nature is the "crudeness and vehemence of those inclinations which belongs more to our animality"[52] – for the developmental plan of nature or providence entails that this part of us would predominate in the earlier stages of our history.[53] And it continues to predominate during the long passage through cultivation and civilization on the way to moralization: "[E]ven under a civil condition, animality manifests itself earlier and, at bottom, more powerfully than humanity ... Man's self-will is always ready to break forth in hostility toward his neighbors, and always presses him to claim unconditional freedom, not merely independence of others, but even mastery of other beings that are his equal by nature – something we can see in even the smallest child. This is because nature within man tries to lead him from culture to morality and not (as reason prescribes) from morality and law, as the starting point, to a culture designed to conform with morality ... This education from [Providence] is salutary but harsh and stern; nature works it out by way of great hardships, to the extent of nearly destroying the whole race."[54]

Among these great hardships is, of course, war, which at times threatens the "barbarian devastation" of the achievements of culture and civilization; however, in the larger scheme of things, it serves as a valuable spur not only to the constructions of peace meant to contain it but also to other cultural advances driven by the competitive mobilization of forces it occasions.[55] Another great hardship that proves to be

---

[51] "Universal History," p. 45.   [52] *Critique of the Power of Judgment*, p. 300.
[53] Which means, of course, that human reason has continually to do battle against the very conditions that give rise to it. In his "Conjectures on the Beginning of Human History" [1786: AA VIII, 107–123], tr. Nisbet, in Reiss (ed.), *Kant: Political Writings*, pp. 221–234, Kant figures the initial break with instinctual life and the start on the long road to morality as a "fall": "When reason began to function and, in all its weakness, came into conflict with animality in all its strength, evils necessarily ensued ... From the moral point of view, therefore, the first stage beyond this state was a fall" (pp. 227–228).
[54] *Anthropology*, pp. 188–189.
[55] See "Universal History," pp. 47–49; "Conjectures," pp. 230–232.

functional for the perfection of the species is the gross inequality and oppression that accompany the advance of culture and civilization. The progress of the arts and sciences, of taste and refinement has largely been the work of leisure classes who could count on the labor of others, the dominated and exploited, to attend to the necessities of life.[56] In sum, then, for Kant the history of human progress has been anything but a pretty story; rather, his view of it anticipates in some respects Walter Benjamin's later judgment that all civilization is a monument to barbarity. And yet, in his view "this glittering misery is bound up with the development of the natural predispositions in the human race, and the end of nature itself, even if it is not our end, is hereby attained ... to make us receptive to higher ends than nature itself can afford."[57] So it is an ugly story with a happy ending, in which human morality finally overcomes the empirical (animal) conditions of its own possibility. The chief cause of the ugliness, according to Kant, is that in the premoral stages of cultivation and civilization, nature has no other means to combat our unsociability but that unsociability itself, "for it is compelled by its own nature to discipline itself."[58] Antagonism is checked by antagonism, self-interest by self-interest, and the resultant teleological inversions thus also contain the seeds of their disintegration, until the moralization of culture is further along.

A crucial consideration here – and one which Kant never tires of emphasizing – is that nature's purpose in history is not human happiness but human development. "Without these asocial qualities (far from admirable in themselves) ... men would live an Arcadian, pastoral existence of perfect concord, self-sufficiency, and mutual love. But all human talents would remain hidden forever in a dormant state, and men, as good-natured as the sheep they tended, would scarcely render their existence more valuable than that of their animals. The end for which they were created, their rational nature, would be an unfilled void ... Man wishes concord, but nature, knowing better what is good for his species, wishes discord."[59] And it is this same consideration that is behind his infamous remarks on the Tahitians: "Does [Herder] really

[56] See *Critique of the Power of Judgment*, pp. 299–300.

[57] *Ibid.* Again, I leave aside the question of how, in Kant's system, there can be empirical conditions for a non-empirical moral disposition.

[58] "Universal History," p. 46.

[59] *Ibid.*, p. 45. On this point in the larger context of the anthropology lectures, see S. M. Shell, "Kant's 'True Economy of Human Nature': Rousseau, Count Verri,

mean that, if the happy inhabitants of Tahiti never visited by more civilized nations, were destined to live in their peaceful indolence for thousands of centuries, it would be possible to give a satisfactory answer to the question of why they should exist at all, and of whether it would not have been just as good if this island had been occupied by happy sheep and cattle as by happy human beings who merely enjoy themselves?"[60]

In the context of this reading of history, it would not be surprising if Kant viewed the oppression and exploitation specific to racially structured forms of injustice as another dimension of the same dialectic of progress, that is, as just another form of developmentally functional evil. It is, then, noteworthy that he sharply condemns the contemporary forms of European settlement and colonization on grounds of morality and right.[61] And yet, it seems that he cannot but rely on them for teleological purposes, that is, precisely as the vehicles at that time for the spread of European culture and civilization, law and religion throughout the world. His position here is thus similar in important respects to the one he took on the French Revolution: he condemned its violence on moral grounds while welcoming the legal and political advances it brought with it.[62] In both cases – and, indeed, more generally – there is a lack of fit between how things look from the normative point of view of morality or right and how they look from the functional point of view of human progress: what appears to teleological judgment as a crucial evolutionary vehicle, may well stand condemned by morality and justice. The two standpoints are in tension.[63]

With respect to chattel slavery, Kant's position is similarly ambivalent. He denies that there is any right to bondage that can be acquired through conquest: "Still less can bondage [*Leibeigenschaft*] and its legitimacy be derived from a people's being overcome in war ... [L]east of all can hereditary bondage be derived from it; hereditary bondage as such is absurd."[64] Or through contract: "[A] contract by

and the Problem of Happiness," in Jacobs and Kain (eds.), *Essays on Kant's Anthropology*, pp. 194–229.

[60] Review of Herder's *Ideas on the Philosophy of History of Mankind* [1785: AA VIII, 43–66] tr. Nisbet, in Reiss (ed.), *Kant: Political Writings*, pp. 201–220, at pp. 219–220.

[61] *The Metaphysics of Morals*, pp. 53, 121–122; "Perpetual Peace," pp. 106–107.

[62] See "Is the Human Race Continually Improving?"

[63] I discuss this "dilemma of development" further in chapter 6.

[64] *The Metaphysics of Morals*, p. 118.

which one party would completely renounce its freedom for the other's advantage would be self-contradictory, that is, null and void, since by it one party would cease to be a person and so would have no duty to keep the contract but would recognize only force ... The contract of the head of a household with servants can therefore not be such that his use of them would amount to using them up; and it is not for him alone to judge about this, but also for the servants (who, accordingly, can never be in bondage [*Leibeigenschaft*])."[65] The only basis in right for bondage is as punishment for certain crimes, and then only as legally institutionalized: "The exception is someone who has lost [the dignity of a citizen] by his own crime, because of which, though he is kept alive, he is made a mere tool of another's choice (either of the state or of another citizen). Whoever is another's tool (which he can become only by a verdict and right) is a bondsman [*Leibeigener*] ... [H]e still wants to live, and this now is possible only if others provide for him. But since the state will not provide for him free of charge, he must let it have his powers for any kind of work it pleases (in convict or prison labor) and is reduced to the status of a slave [*Sklavenstand*] for a certain time, or permanently if the state sees fit."[66] But in no case is bondage heritable: "children (even those of someone who has become a slave [*Sklaven*] through his crime) are at all times free. For everyone is born free."[67] So it is clear that, on Kant's view, there is no basis in right for enslaving people or otherwise placing them in bondage which would even begin to legitimate the African slave trade, of which he had an extensive knowledge. And then, too, Kant expresses sharp disapproval of existing practices and institutions of slavery, for instance when he refers to "the Sugar Islands, that stronghold of the cruelest and most calculated slavery ... And all this is the work of powers who make endless ado about their piety, and who wish to be considered as chosen believers while they live on the fruits of iniquity."[68] Or when he writes: "For if the master is authorized to use the powers of his subjects as he pleases, he can also exhaust them until his subject dies or is driven into despair (as with the Negroes on the sugar islands); his subject will in fact have given himself away, as property, to his master, which is impossible."[69] And

---

[65] *Ibid.*, p. 66.
[66] *Ibid.*, pp. 104–106. On p. 33, Kant classes *Leibeigene* and *Sklaven* together.
[67] *Ibid.*, p. 66.   [68] "Perpetual Peace," p. 107.
[69] *The Metaphysics of Morals*, p. 104. Bernasconi gives this passage an opposed reading in "Kant as an Unfamiliar Source of Racism."

yet it remains that Kant did not explicitly intervene in the debates about the slave trade that were raging at the time and often commented on the chattel slavery of Africans in the tone of a disinterested observer.[70] This, together with his frequent disquisitions on the inherent inferiority of Africans, their ready adaptation to slave routines, and their innate inability to raise themselves from the state of nature, make it not unreasonable to conclude that, *from a historical-developmental perspective*, Kant understood slavery to be one of those evils that contributed to the advance of the human race through the diffusion of European culture, a part of its "civilizing mission." Be that as it may, in trying to make moral sense of history, he ironically constructed an early version of the very rationale – biological and cultural – that would serve as the dominant proslavery ideology later in the following century.

V Coda: problems with the Kantian idea of progress

For more than two centuries now, critics have remarked on the fault lines running through Kant's developmental schema. Some of them are peculiar to Kant's own construction and those modeled closely upon it; others, however, signal problems that have to be faced by liberal developmentalism more generally. To the former belong the various tensions caused by his strict *bifurcation between freedom and nature*. It never becomes clear how, on this account, there could be natural – biological, social, cultural, legal, political – conditions for the progress of morality, which is supposed to be the work of freedom alone, or how there could be phenomenal, temporal supports for and impediments to a noumenal, timeless, condition of the *Gesinnung*. Nor is it clear how there could be anything like moral progress and what that might mean for the moral equality of all human beings.[71] Then there is a host of problems attendant upon Kant's *theodicy of history* – and, more generally, upon ontotheological schemes of development similar to his in requiring that out of evil come good. That requirement comes from the need to justify the ways of God to humankind – or, in Kant's less expressly

---

[70] Infamously, in commenting on the most effective way to discipline blacks in his lectures on Physical Geography. The passage in question appears in English translation by E. C. Eze and K. M. Faull, in Eze (ed.), *Race and the Enlightenment* (Oxford: Blackwell, 1997), p. 61.

[71] On this point, see Paul Stern, "The Problem of History and Temporality in Kantian Ethics," *Review of Metaphysics*, 39 (1986): 404–545.

theological language, to show that a world order replete with suffering and evil is the sort of world which a moral being "under the guidance of practical reason" would nevertheless create. That the world as a whole makes moral sense in this way is a burden of proof that more consistently naturalized developmental accounts need not assume. Finally, Kant's reliance on a strong *teleology of nature* – summed up in the maxim that "nature does nothing in vain" – with his frequent references to the purposes and plans of nature, generate yet another array of problems. The skepticism regarding causal explanation of biological phenomena, which underlay his teleological approach, was largely dispelled by the Darwinian revolution. Few evolutionary biologists would today be tempted to argue that, say, the full development of the natural capacities of human beings is the "aim" or "plan" of nature as a whole.

Even if we bracket Kant's two-world doctrine, his theodicy, and his teleology of nature, his account of historical development is inherently unstable. For one thing, tensions between the developmental and the moral standpoints are built into any such construction of the "cunning of reason"; but for Kant they are more of a problem than they are for, say, Hegel or Marx, since he requires that history make *moral* sense. And morally speaking, the end does not justify the means: the war, oppression, injustice, and other evils that appear from the former standpoint as functional – even functionally necessary – for the progressive improvement of the species are, from the latter standpoint, no less violations of the fundamental moral injunction to treat human beings as ends-in-themselves, and never only as means.[72] So even if we granted, for the sake of argument, his account of the progressive development of *species* capacities, we could not morally justify the sacrifice, on what Hegel famously called "the slaughter bench of history," of countless *individuals*, each of whom, Kant tells us, possesses infinite moral worth, nor the dire circumstances of the numerous earlier generations who serve merely as stepping stones on the way to the kingdom of ends. That is to say, the reflective judge who discerns the invisible hand of progress at work in history and the moral agent who is appalled by its depredations are not easily harmonized within a single breast.

---

[72] See Tsenay Serequeberhan's critical analysis of "Kant's double game" in "The Critique of Eurocentrism."

As noted above, Kant explicitly eschews looking for purpose in the dimension of human happiness: "It seems that nature has worked more with a view to man's rational self-esteem than to his mere well-being ... [It] does not seem to have been concerned with seeing that man should live agreeably, but with seeing that he should work his way onwards to make himself by his own conduct worthy of life and well-being."[73] But this "perfectionist" component of his species perfectionism is no less troubling than its species component. The tension here is between treating concrete human beings as ends-in-themselves and treating the humanity in their persons as an end-in-itself.[74] *On the one hand*, both our "humanity" and our "personality" are inherently tied to our rational capacities.[75] "Humanity" refers to rational nature in general and "personality" to rational nature in its capacity to be morally self-legislative. The development of our predisposition to humanity is, correspondingly, understood to be the development of our capacity to set and pursue ends through reason generally, and not just moral-practically; thus it is coincident with the development of culture and civilization, as Kant understands them. So races that are incapable, or less capable, of progress in these dimensions would be incapable, or less capable, of developing the humanity that morality commands us to respect. And races that are capable of advancing in culture and civilization, but not through their own initiative, could not achieve "rational self-esteem" on their own. *On the other hand*, Kant repeatedly characterizes human beings as such as rational beings and as worthy of respect;[76] and his cosmopolitan society and kingdom of ends are repeatedly said to be the destiny of human beings generally, inclusive of all the peoples of the earth. But it is never made clear how the biologically inferior endowments of non-whites could be consistent with this destiny. What is clear is that the path Kant projects toward this end-state is marked, even prepared, by an unevenness of development among various races and peoples; and that from the start of the modern period, at the latest, progress

---

[73] "Universal History," pp. 43–44.

[74] See Kant's discussion of the humanity-as-an-end-in-itself formulation of the categorical imperative in the *Groundwork*, pp. 79–81.

[75] *Religion*, pp. 74–76. Accordingly, the derivation of the humanity-as-an-end-in-itself formulation turns on the idea of our "rational nature." On this point, see Wood, intro., pp. 124–132 (see n. 8 above), and his contribution to Jacobs and Kain (eds.), *Essays on Kant's Anthropology*, "Kant and the Problem of Human Nature," pp. 38–59.

[76] For instance, in the same discussion of the humanity formulation, *Groundwork*, p. 79.

in cultivation, civilization, and moralization is and will continue to be a process of diffusion from the West to the rest of the world. Not only will Europe eventually bring republican government to all other peoples; progress in the arts and sciences, as in technology and society, will also spread from there over the entire earth. And even in the sphere of religion, the rationalized, demythologized version of Protestant Christianity serves as an exemplar of moral religion for the rest of the world. In short, progress in non-European societies seems to mean gradual assimilation in central respects to European culture and civilization.[77] With regard to Kant's systematic intentions in practical philosophy, this projection raises an obvious problem: Is the convergence model of progress, with its attendant – even if not explicitly advocated – civilizing mission of the West, compatible with a future in which the passive recipients of development are on a cultural, political, and moral par with its active originators? The problem becomes all the more pressing as the factors behind developmental unevenness are said to include biologically rooted, and thus unalterable, inequalities of natural endowment.[78] Here too, it seems, Kant's pure ethics is not

---

[77] But not in all respects: Kant warns against the "amalgamation" [*Zusammenschmelzung*] of diverse peoples in a world state ("Perpetual Peace," pp. 102, 113) and against interethnic or interracial "mixture" [*Vermischung*] (*Anthropology*, p. 182).

[78] It seems that Kant himself was not as troubled by such inequalities as we might be. Thus, in *The Metaphysics of Morals*, he explains that civil equality, as he understands it, is not incompatible with a distinction between active and passive citizens, where "all women" and "underlings" (roughly, those who live from the sale of their labor) belong to the latter class and thus have no right to vote or other wise participate actively in government. Nor does he regard this difference in status as incompatible with their "freedom and equality as human beings" (pp. 91–92). Furthermore, whereas underlings may work their way up to active status, women are, by virtue of their natural endowments, permanently passive citizens. (On this point, see Susan Mendus, "Kant: 'An Honest but Narrow-minded Bourgeois'?," in H. Williams (ed.), *Essays on Kant's Political Philosophy* [University of Chicago Press, 1992], pp. 166–190.) Likewise, in "On the Common Saying: 'This may be true in theory, but it does not apply in practice'" [1793: VIII, 273–313], tr. Nisbet, in Reiss (ed.), *Kant: Political Writings*, pp. 61–92, Kant explains that the equality of subjects before the law is "perfectly consistent with the utmost inequality in the amount and grade of their possessions, whether in the form of material or mental superiority over others" (p. 75). Equality under the law does not mean equal right to make the law: "Anyone who has the right to vote on this legislation is a citizen ... The only qualification required by a citizen (apart, of course, from being an adult male) is that he must be his own master (*sui iuris*) and must have some property (which can include any skill, trade, or fine art or science) to support himself" (pp. 77–78). In the case of women, then, it is clear that Kant's understanding of republican

only complemented but also confounded by his impure ethics: the internal relation between the two made it possible for his universalistic humanism to be placed at the service of European expansionism, whatever his own intentions.

The tendencies toward monoculturalism that surface in Kant's account of progress, the insignificant role he envisions for *reciprocal* intercultural learning, is prefigured in his fundamentally monological conceptions of reason and rationality. Though the empirical materials that "practical anthropology" deals with are pervaded by contingency and particularity in his view, the normative standpoint from which they are reflectively judged is not. It is fixed once and for all by the pure rational principles, ideas, and ideals disclosed by the critique of reason. There is scant recognition of the inherent contestability of the latter enterprise, of the essentially social nature of reason and rationality, or of the inescapable interdependence of the universal and the particular. Factoring those into the self-understanding of practical anthropology would reveal its ineluctably interpretive and evaluative character. It would call into question the extramundane standpoint of transcendental philosophy, undermine the pure/impure structuring of moral and political theory, and make evident the intrinsically dialogical nature of the discourse of modernity. It would, in short, require a reconstruction of Kant's moral vision to make room for multicultural universalism and multiple modernities.

> government was compatible with permanent inequalities rooted in biological differences. Thus there may be no theoretical bar, in his mind, to the "world republic" of federated national republics (the ideal form of cosmopolitan union) containing those and other such biologically based – and hence unalterable – inequalities. Perhaps we are being anachronistic when we see that as an inconsistency in his thought.

3 | Social Darwinism and white supremacy

In a recent analysis of contemporary American imperialism, Cornel West traces its roots to the arrested development of democracy in America.[1] The latter, he argues, can only be understood historically; and a – if not the – principal lens under which it must be examined is the pervasiveness of white supremacy in our history. The failure to come fully to terms with the deeply racist and imperialist strains in our national past remains a fundamental weakness of our political culture. Until critical historical consciousness of that past informs political discourse in the present, the "self-deceptive innocence" and avoidance of "painful truths about ourselves" so characteristic of debate in our public sphere will persist.[2] West stresses the profound interconnections between race and empire in our nation's history. He highlights the constitutive tensions between freedom and domination, inclusion and exclusion, national independence and imperial expansion in that history, and the racist worldview that informed them. In this chapter I want to take up one strand of the critical history of the present he calls for: the ascendancy of social Darwinist thinking about race and empire in the period from the end of Reconstruction to the start of World War I.

In the wake of Darwin's *Origin of the Species* (1859), and through the intermediation of Herbert Spencer and his American disciples, social Darwinism became the dominant ideology in a period that saw the establishment of a racial caste system in the South, the completion of Indian removal in the West, the shift from continental expansion to international imperialism in the war with Spain, and the rise of organized opposition to immigration from Southern and Eastern Europe in the Northeast, and from Asia, especially China, in the West. "Race" played a critical role in the public discourse about each of these

[1] Cornel West, *Democracy Matters: Winning the Fight against Imperialism* (New York: Penguin, 2004).
[2] *Ibid.*, p. 41.

formative processes; and in contrast to the racial ideologies of the antebellum period, it was conceptualized in explicitly evolutionary terms. As we shall see, this formulation provided a particularly potent and protean version of the hierarchical scaling of difference that had been characteristic of liberalism in the two preceding centuries.

Section I sketches some relevant background concerning the development of race theory in the US and connects it with the enduring sense of American exceptionalism, the shifting spirit of American nationalism, the fusion of the latter with an increasingly racialized nativism, and the transformation of manifest destiny into a racial destiny. Section II then focuses on the forms of social Darwinist thinking that came to pervade and dominate American intellectual life toward the end of the nineteenth century, as well as the chief ideological uses to which the new racial imaginary was put in domestic and foreign affairs. Finally, section III traces the decline of this dominant ideology and its replacement with a cultural theory of racial differences, which is functionally equivalent in important respects.[3]

I

Kant had no significant influence on the development of racial thinking in America, but his younger contemporary and correspondent, Johann Friedrich Blumenbach, did. Lines of research into racial differences that he had opened were pursued here, especially the comparative measurement of skull sizes, facial angles, brain capacity, and the like. In the newly constituted United States, however, racial thinking of this sort had not yet dislodged religious belief in the brotherhood and equality of men in the eyes of God or enlightenment faith in the unity and improvability of the human family in all its branches – the ongoing enslavement of Africans and dispossession of Indians to the contrary

---

[3] Douglas Lorimer sketches a similar general trajectory for the discourse of race in Britain during this period, in "From Natural to Social Science: Race and the Language of Race Relations in Late Victorian and Edwardian Discourse," in D. Kelly (ed.), *Lineages of Empire* (Oxford University Press, forthcoming 2009). The particular differences are also instructive, as the overwhelming British concern with colonial administration gave to the ethnography of non-European peoples a centrality that it did not have in the American context of post-Civil War race relations. On this point, see George W. Stocking, Jr. *Victorian Anthropology* (New York: Free Press, 1987).

notwithstanding.[4] More particularly, the exceptional status of the American nation was not yet represented in racial terms.[5] The self-understanding of the Puritan colony as a new Israel – whose exodus to this promised land sealed a new covenant with God, and which, in its ascetic Christian purity, would light the way to regenerate a corrupted humankind – was combined after the Revolution with a robust self-consciousness of being the first genuine republic, founded on the natural rights of man and guaranteeing the liberty of all its citizens. Thus America came widely to understand itself as a religious-political project of world-historical significance, providentially assigned to lead the way to a "new order for the ages," as the motto of the Great Seal put it. The religious and political streams of thought feeding into this sense of American exceptionalism were joined by literary and historical streams flowing from European Romanticism. German Romantic notions of ancient Teutonic virtue, particularly a primordial form of freedom, flowed together with the English view of the Anglo-Saxon line of Teutons as having rescued that freedom from historical disrepair and given it the modern form of political liberty. And the American branch of the Anglo-Saxon line was widely understood by Americans to be in the forefront of that advance.[6] The world-historical mission of the United States was to carry out a great experiment for the benefit of mankind and, as Jefferson put it, to expand the empire of liberty. And while it is true that many nations have at times come to regard themselves and their places in history as special in various ways, the multiple streams of thought flowing into America's sense of being a providential nation were powerfully reinforced by its extraordinary bounty and mounting successes, beginning with the defeat of the world's greatest military power and the doubling of its size through the Louisiana Purchase not long thereafter. Thus ascetic Protestants, liberal enlighteners,

---

[4] Thomas Jefferson's well-known ambivalence regarding both practices is indicative of a more general state of intellectual affairs.

[5] In what follows, I draw upon Reginald Horsman, *Race and Manifest Destiny: The Origins of American Racial Anglo-Saxonism* (Cambridge, MA: Harvard University Press, 1981), and Anders Stephenson, *Manifest Destiny: American Expansion and the Empire of Right* (New York: Hill and Wang, 1995).

[6] Dorothy Ross, *The Origins of American Social Science* (Cambridge University Press, 1991), elucidates the important role of this Teutonic/Anglo-Saxon genealogy of American exceptionalism in the formation of American "historico-political" science, in both the antebellum and the post-Civil War periods (pp. 37–42, 64–77).

Romantic nationalists, and ambitious entrepreneurs could all embrace the idea of America's special destiny, however variously they understood it.

By the time that John O'Sullivan coined the phrase "manifest destiny" in connection with the annexation of Texas in 1845, however, that idea had become markedly racialized. Given the centrality of African slavery and Indian removal to American life, and the pervasiveness and deep-rootedness of the racial beliefs and attitudes that went along with those practices – not only, but especially, in the South and on the ever-receding frontier – race could not but acquire much greater saliency in American thought than in European. And when deep wounds to its Christian and republican ethos were opened – as they were by the intensified debates over abolitionism in the 1830s and the relentless expulsion of Indians beyond the Mississippi during the Jacksonian era – the intellectual response often included some attempt to patch them up with elaborations of race theory. Thus, in the 1830s and 1840s, the superiority of Anglo-Saxon political institutions metamorphosed into a racial superiority, the providential nation into a providential race, and its historical destiny into a racial destiny. "In the middle of the nineteenth century a sense of racial destiny permeated discussions of American progress and of future American world destiny ... The contrast in expansionist rhetoric between 1800 and 1850 is striking ... By 1850 the emphasis was on the American Anglo-Saxons as a separate, innately superior people."[7]

In the period when "manifest destiny" entered explicitly into America's discourse about itself, there was another powerful spur to its racialization: the vast expansion of America – even vaster than the Louisiana Purchase – through the annexation of Texas, the Southwest, and California. The dominant ideology in the 1848 war with Mexico already comprised a central racist strand: Mexicans were racially inferior "half-breeds," a "mongrel race" incapable of establishing or maintaining free institutions on their own. Thus, if freedom was to be expanded on this continent, it would have to be through incorporating into the empire of liberty, by force if necessary, all territories between the Atlantic and the Pacific, north of the Rio Grande and the 32nd parallel, and south of the 49th parallel. America was, in this ideology, the last outpost of that westward expansion of civilization carried by

---

[7] Horsman, *Race and Manifest Destiny*, pp. 1–2.

Aryan peoples from the ancient Near East into Greece and Rome, further extended by Teutonic tribes into Britain, and borne by Anglo-Saxons from there to America. The manifest historical destiny of the American branch of this family was now to extend that civilization, in its fully developed form, to the utmost boundary of the Western world. There would then only remain the historical task of projecting it across the Pacific to complete the circle of civilization.

There were, of course, dissenting voices. It was repeatedly pointed out that the British were not a single consanguineous people, let alone the Americans, and more generally that commonalities of language, culture, and nationality did not map onto biological lines of consanguinity. But these voices were drowned out in the floodtide of racial thinking, which represented Americans as innately endowed to shape the destiny of the world and other, innately inferior, races as biologically destined to be subjugated or annihilated. One important development supporting the growing racialization of America's destinarian self-understanding in the 1830s and 1840s was the increasing influence of scientific race theory, particularly as propounded by the American school of ethnology. Samuel George Morton's *Crania Americana*, published in 1839 and based on his comparative study of the world's largest collection of skulls – some 800 of them, assembled in Philadelphia – conferred scientific respectability on the treatment of difference in terms of distinct, innately unequal races. In fact, Morton went so far as to espouse the controversial thesis of polygenesis, that is, of multiple creations of separate races in different parts of the world. Despite its religious heterodoxy, the polygenetic position itself became increasingly respectable in scientific circles, especially after its adoption by Louis Agassiz, the famous Swiss naturalist, subsequent to his immigration to the USA in 1846. But whether or not scientists endorsed polygenesis, "by 1850 there were very few [of them] prepared to defend the inherent equality of the different races of the world."[8]

Morton had studied the crania of American Indians, and concluded that their intellectual capacities were decidedly inferior to those of Caucasians. His follower, Dr. Josiah C. Nott, a defender of slavery,

---

[8] *Ibid.*, p. 60. At about the same time, in Europe, pre-Darwinian race theory reached a certain culmination with Comte Arthur de Gobineau's four-volume *Essay on the Inequality of the Human Races* (1853–1855); and Robert Knox's *The Races of Man* (1850).

made a cognate case for the separateness as species of blacks and whites, the innate superiority of the latter, and the consequent need for subordination of the former. In short, well before the rise and spread of Darwinism, race theory had already established itself in the US as an important framework within which to theorize human difference and an essential ingredient in comprehending the contours of human progress. In this regard, social Darwinism composed new variations on already familiar themes, and those variations dominated American intellectual life in the half-century following the Civil War.

II

The label "social Darwinism" has been applied to a considerable variety of views, bearing stronger or weaker family resemblances to one another.[9] Darwinian ideas were omnipresent in scholarly and popular discourse by the end of the nineteenth century, and they were being used in very different contexts and for very different purposes. Reformers invoked them as well as defenders of the status quo, anti-imperialists as well as imperialists, classical laissez-faire liberals as well as new social liberals. For the purpose at hand, I shall be examining only the uses of evolutionary schemes to rationalize the emerging racial caste system at home and the projection of American imperial power abroad: they belonged to "the natural order of things" and thus allowed of no reasonable disagreement. However important in their own right, the uses of analogical reasoning from biological to social evolution to underwrite the ongoing subordination of women, the massive economic inequalities of the Gilded Age, the restriction of immigration by non-Northern European peoples, the widespread employment of IQ testing, the eugenics movement, and even Nazi doctrines of Aryan superiority will be noted here only in passing. As this list suggests, however, social

[9] For a sample of the disputes this has engendered, see the pathbreaking work by Richard Hofstadter, *Social Darwinism in American Thought* (Philadelphia: University of Pennsylvania Press, 1944); the critical reconsideration by Robert C. Bannister, *Social Darwinism: Science and Myth in Anglo-American Thought* (Philadelphia: Temple University Press, 1979); and the wide-ranging adjudication by Mike Hawkins, *Social Darwinism in European and American Thought, 1860–1945* (Cambridge University Press, 1997). My approach owes most to Hawkins.

Darwinism was certainly one of the most multifunctional, all-purpose ideologies of the late nineteenth and early twentieth centuries.

It is important to note that the Darwinian ideas we are considering here stem from the original, pre-"modern synthesis" account of biological evolution laid out in such works of Darwin as *On the Origin of Species* (1859), *The Descent of Man* (1871), and *The Expression of the Emotions in Man and Animals* (1872). Though Mendel's work on heredity was published at about the same time, Darwin was unaware of it, and the development of Mendelian genetics had to await its rediscovery at the turn of the century. In fact, while Darwin emphasized the operation of natural selection in the origin and extinction of species, he did not completely break with the Lamarckian idea of the inheritance of acquired characteristics, though it occupied only a subordinate place in his evolutionary theory. Consequently, in the application of evolutionary schemes to society, Lamarckian ideas intermingled with more narrowly Darwinian ones until the rise of Mendelian genetics began to drive them out early in the twentieth century. As might be expected, reform-minded social Darwinists generally tended to give Lamarckian mechanisms more scope than did the thinkers I shall focus on. But various combinations of the two were typical of social evolutionary thinking in the late nineteenth and even early twentieth century. Another point worth noting is that Darwin was not only the progenitor of a theory of biological evolution in the restricted scientific sense, but also the propagator of a broader evolutionary worldview, which he repeatedly articulated, though never in a wholly systematic fashion. Thus, many of the ideas – on women and race, for instance – that Darwin's defenders often attribute to the *mis*use of his thought by ideologues unschooled in biology can already be found in Darwin.[10] That having been said, it is nevertheless true that the spread of evolutionary thinking into the broader culture was chiefly propagated by social Darwinist thinkers who were not trained biologists, such as the British thinker Herbert Spencer and his American disciple William Graham Sumner.[11] Spencer, in fact, came to his influential conception of social evolution as part of cosmic evolution prior to the publication of

[10] Carl N. Degler, *In Search of Human Nature: The Decline and Revival of Darwinism in American Social Thought* (Oxford University Press, 1991), pp. 10–16.

[11] Stephenson, *Manifest Destiny*, p. 81, deems Spencer "the single most influential Anglophone thinker of the latter part of the nineteenth century."

Darwin's *Origin*. He was subsequently able to incorporate Darwin's account of natural selection as the mechanism of evolution into his conception and to render its gist in the pithy phrase "survival of the fittest," which Darwin himself adopted in the fifth edition of *Origin* (1869).

Given the multifarious sources of social Darwinism, it could only be a shifting concatenation of interrelated and somewhat indeterminate ideas. Even so, it was the wellspring of a continual supply of metaphors used to represent certain social relations and processes either as "natural" – and thus beyond our power to change – or as "unnatural" – and thus to be avoided or eliminated. Spencer, for example, famously represented laissez-faire liberalism, in which individuals were free to compete for survival and only the fittest survived, as the natural order of things. Government intervention to protect the weak, aid the needy, or the like amounted to interfering with the laws of nature and was doomed to fail. At most it could have the unnatural result of helping the unfit to survive and thus contributing to the degeneration of the population. The metaphors that most concern us here, however, are those that configure race and empire in evolutionary terms. To begin with, the different races – or permanent varieties of the human species – are typically represented as embodying different stages in the evolution of the species, with "inferior races" embodying earlier stages. Thus, Africans and American Indians are figured as human beings at arrested stages of development, while Caucasians are portrayed as furthest along the scale of human evolution. And since ontogeny recapitulates phylogeny, race relations are further figured as similar to the relations between children and adults. Hence inferior races require, for their own good, subordination and tutelage by superior races – as do women by men and lower classes by upper classes – such as might be effected through a racial caste system or colonial administration. As long as Lamarckian elements were part of the scheme, such tutelage *could* be figured as leading *in the long run* to maturity and independence. When they were absent, as they increasingly were after the turn of the century, the hierarchy could only be represented as permanent.[12] To some extent, obviously, all this amounted only to grafting preexisting racial ideas and attitudes onto evolutionary theory. But that grafting significantly enhanced the

[12] Degler, *In Search of Human Nature*, pp. 20–22.

ideological repertoire and scientific standing of racist thinking for a generation and more.

Though Darwin himself officially repudiated teleological readings of evolution, he often joined the mainstream of social Darwinism in connecting evolution with progress. Spencer was less equivocal on this point: the struggle for existence and survival of the fittest led to cumulative, progressive developments in society. Human history is the story of the survival and improvement of some groups at the expense of others. It is a naturally directional process with evaluative significance: the mental and behavioral traits that make adaptation and survival possible – increasing rationality and morality, for instance – mark the ongoing development and perfection of successful individuals and groups. With few exceptions – one of whom was Spencer's chief American disciple, William Graham Sumner – social Darwinists accepted this developmental, progressive view of history. Of course, that view too predated Darwin. But its incorporation into the foundations of the emerging social sciences, particularly sociology, invested the latter with a social evolutionary strain and helps explain its failure to develop an adequate account of racial formations.[13]

In the surpassingly racist decade of the 1890s, then, it appeared that racism had science on its side. After the massacre at Wounded Knee in 1890, American Indians were no longer a threat and seemed in fact destined to disappear, as social Darwinist views led many to expect. And after the last federal troops were withdrawn from the South in 1877, the disenfranchisement of blacks and the establishment of Jim Crow segregation – upheld by *Plessy* v. *Ferguson* in 1896 – proceeded apace. Social Darwinist views served that cause too: the inherent inferiority of blacks made them unfit for full citizenship and incapable of competing successfully with whites; their only hope for survival was to submit themselves to the discipline and guidance of the inherently superior race. Joseph Le Conte, for example, the president of the American Association for the Advancement of Science and the author of *The Race Problem in the South* (1892), declared that Darwin's evolutionary theory had revolutionized sociology. In particular, it was now evident that "the struggle for life and the survival of the fittest ... is applicable to the races of man also." The inevitable result of contact

---

[13] See James B. McKee, *Sociology and the Race Problem* (Urbana: University of Illinois Press, 1993).

between races that differ widely in the "grade of race evolution ... will be, must be, ought to be, that the higher race will assume control and determine the policy of the community."[14] For "the Negro," slavery had initially been the optimal arrangement, while for "the Indian," extermination had been unavoidable. Though slavery was no longer appropriate for Negroes, who had evolved further under its harsh discipline, they were still unable "to walk alone in the paths of civilization" and so required continued control by those who were.[15] In particular, they should not expect to vote. On this point, Sumner and many other social Darwinists concurred. The South should be left to work out its racial problems alone: "The negro is unquestionably entitled to good government, but giving him political rights has made it harder to give him good government."[16] And nearly a decade later, Woodrow Wilson, soon to be elected president of Princeton, reaffirmed the view that during Reconstruction "a host of dusky children [were] untimely put out of school," which had almost led to the South's ruin until "at last the whites who were the real citizens got control again."[17] The widespread acceptance of evolutionary views on race at the turn of the century also helps to explain why the sweeping reforms of the Progressive Era left racial oppression largely untouched. To reject those views meant to reject science, and that is something that most progressive reformers did not choose to do.

Imperialism was a different matter, for despite the near universality of racial evolutionary assumptions, there was wide disagreement as to whether or not they justified imperial conquest. Spencer himself, for instance, was opposed to imperialism. Though he regarded competition between peoples as the very stuff of history, he held that violent conflict belonged to an earlier, militant stage of development, which had given way to the present industrial stage, in which nonviolent, economic competition was the order of the day. But a broad stream of social Darwinism held that violent conflict was not only unavoidable but desirable from an evolutionary point of view: it remained a central form of the struggle for existence and dynamic of progress.

---

[14] Quoted in Hawkins, *Social Darwinism*, p. 201.
[15] *Ibid.*, p. 202.   [16] *Ibid.*
[17] Quoted in Thomas F. Gossett, *Race: The History of an Idea in America* (Dallas: Southern Methodist University Press, 1975), p. 284.

In post-Reconstruction America, destinarian thought and action had shifted from a focus on continental expansion – which, as Frederick Jackson Turner noted in 1893, had largely been completed – to a concern with the extension of national power abroad. The staggering economic growth and recurrent economic crises of this period, which reached a high point in the depression of 1893, as well as the social unrest they engendered, made the acquisition of external markets and raw materials sources seem indispensable. The intensified European imperial rivalries in Africa and Asia reinforced this view; and the still powerful religious sense of America's redemptive mission in the world lent overseas expansion widespread legitimacy. The entwinement of nationalism with racism earlier in the century, and the racial rethinking of America's destiny that it fostered, reached new heights with the rise of social Darwinism. As in the 1840s, the objection by anti-imperialists that America's greatness stemmed from values and institutions of liberty that were incompatible with old-European forms of imperialism was overcome by the proponents' argument that America's greatness stemmed precisely from its world-historical role in expanding the empire of liberty. Thus when the US gained its first extra-continental colonies and dependencies after the declaration of war with Spain in 1898 – that is, when it seized Cuba, Puerto Rico, Guam, Wake Island, and the Philippines from Spain, annexed Hawaii, and partitioned Samoa with Germany – and announced its "Open Door" policy toward China, sent troops to put down the Boxer Rebellion there, and assisted Panama's separation from Colombia in exchange for rights to construct a canal, it could count on support from the many ideological sources that came together on this matter. In this spirit, President McKinley called upon Americans to uphold the great trust placed upon the nation "under the Providence of God and in the name of human progress and civilization," and he assured them that "our priceless principles ... go with the flag."[18] One of his congressional supporters, the ardent Albert Beveridge of Indiana, reminded Americans that they were "a people imperial by virtue of their power, by right of their institutions, by authority of their Heaven-directed purposes."[19] On the eve of the

[18] Quoted in Michael H. Hunt, *Ideology and U.S. Foreign Policy* (New Haven: Yale University Press, 1987), p. 38.

[19] Quoted in *ibid*. Stephenson, *Manifest Destiny*, notes that the "sacred-prophetic" impulse did not wane in late nineteenth- and early twentieth-century America, as it did in Europe. The American ideology of empire remained more providential

Spanish–American War, in referring to Ulysses Grant, he (misleadingly) declaimed: "He never forgot that we are a conquering race and that we must obey our blood and occupy new markets, and, if necessary, new lands. He ... beheld, as part of the Almighty's infinite plan, the disappearance of debased civilizations and decaying races before the higher civilization and the more nobler and virile types of man."[20] On this widespread view, the providential destiny of the Anglo-Saxon race bearing liberty to the world converged now with the pursuit of national and international greatness by its American branch, and with America's material interest in expanding and protecting its economic prerogatives abroad, particularly in Asia.

This imperialist variation on the familiar theme of manifest destiny received a powerful and influential articulation in social Darwinist terms, which provided not only a readily comprehended interpretation of international affairs but also a persuasive justification of America's role in them. In some respects, the situation was not so different from the debates surrounding Indian removal and the war with Mexico earlier in the century. Racial thinking had played a crucial ideological role then too. Many of the same arguments concerning Anglo-Saxon superiority and America's civilizing mission reappeared now in a new, evolutionary form, which lent them scientific legitimacy. As Thomas Gossett notes: "The war of 1898 was not the first American war in which an appeal had been made to the manifest destiny of the Anglo-Saxons ... [But] by the time of the Spanish–American War, the idea of race had deeply penetrated nearly every field ... [and] had immense philosophic and scientific backing ... Darwin himself had invested the westward movement of the American nation with all the force of a law of nature."[21]

To be sure, power politics and the pursuit of American interests in international affairs did not require social Darwinism. But Darwinian ideas proved particularly well suited to represent and justify them: it was nature's way that inferior races yield to superior races. This was not merely a question of power, but also of right; for inferior races were inherently incapable of establishing institutions of liberty. This had to be done for them by superior races, even if that sometimes required

and messianic than the European, which went further in translating such impulses into "liberal-secular" projects of a political nature.

[20] Quoted in Stephenson, *Manifest Destiny*, p. 98.

[21] Gossett, *Race: The History of an Idea in America*, pp. 310–311.

force and imposition. In the racial imaginary of late nineteenth-century America, the heavily Negroid Latins in Cuba, Puerto Rico, and elsewhere required such tutelage, as did our "little brown brother," as William Howard Taft put it, in the Philippines. "Orientals" were also naturally less gifted than whites; and so the threat of their growing numbers in America to Anglo-Saxon purity had to be met with the Chinese exclusion acts in the 1880s and 1890s. But they were naturally more gifted than Indians and Africans; and so it was in America's interest to be centrally involved in the economic development of Asia, especially China. In these and other ways, the widespread influence of social Darwinism reinforced long-standing prejudgments and made it possible to reformulate them in terms of a "competition of the races."[22] Anglo-Saxons would undoubtedly triumph in this competition, but for the benefit of the whole of mankind, whom they would lead in the progress of civilization. It was in the midst of these imperial undertakings, and to urge them on, that Rudyard Kipling published his proverbial poem, "The White Man's Burden," which was widely reprinted in American newspapers as a call to arms.

The confluence of God and Nature, History and Destiny in the most influential versions of social Darwinism is reminiscent in some ways of Kant's thoughts on race and development a century earlier. In the views I have been considering, however, though certainly not in all, that confluence was used to justify racial subordination and not just to explain it. Kant "justified" war and oppression only from the point of view of eternity, so to speak, that is, in a kind of theodicy of history. He did not justify, but roundly condemned them from the moral agent's point of view. This was also true of some social Darwinists, who condemned racial oppression and militant imperialism. But the mainstream of social Darwinist thought was prone to elide putative laws of nature with putative norms of natural law, and thus to close the "is/ought" gap before it opened. Darwinian biology was used to "naturalize" relations of power in both these senses at once. Racial thinking no doubt lent itself to such an elision, and social Darwinism especially so. But it is important to note that biological ideas of race were not

---

[22] This was the formulation of the Rev. Josiah Strong in his enormously influential book, *Our Country* (1885). He completed this thought with the words: "And can anyone doubt that the result of this competition will be the 'survival of the fittest'?" Quoted in Hofstadter, *Social Darwinism*, p. 179.

indispensable in this regard: a similar operation could be performed by employing ethnocultural ideas – as, for example, in John Stuart Mill's writings on imperialism, which were appearing at about the same time as Darwin's *Origin*. It is an operation typically called for when liberal political thinkers try to resolve the tension between ideals and reality, principles and practice, by justifying illiberal uses of power as "tutelage" and "benevolent despotism."[23]

III

Mill was certainly not the only social or political theorist to raise doubts about the explanatory power of race theory in the second half of the nineteenth century.[24] But dissidents became an increasingly marginal minority in the USA as social Darwinism reached its high point in the 1890s. Its deep and pervasive influence can be seen in the oft-noted fact that Darwinian racial assumptions were common to all sides of the major debates about racial and imperial domination, as well as in the relative inattention to race issues during the period of progressive social reform early in the next century.[25] At the turn of the century, belief in the scientific status of racial explanations of cultural differences ruled supreme. Physical anthropology since Blumenbach and evolutionary biology since Darwin seemed to place them beyond empirical question. However, storm clouds were developing on both fronts. Franz Boas, a German Jew who immigrated to the USA at the age of 29, and who was a recognized authority in physical anthropology as well as a founding father of cultural anthropology in America, began to question the foundations of race theory in the 1890s. In biology, the rediscovery of Mendel's work at the turn of the century, and the development of experimental genetics thereafter, put increasing pressure on the classifications and explanations of race theory. These countertendencies took a

---

[23] I shall discuss this aspect of Mill's liberalism in chapter 6.

[24] See Stocking, *Victorian Anthropology*.

[25] But see Ralph E. Luker, *The Social Gospel in Black and White* (Chapel Hill: University of North Carolina Press, 1991), who stresses the role of American social Christianity in establishing the National Council of Churches in 1909, the National Association for the Advancement of Colored People in 1910, the National Urban League in 1911, and other organizations and programs dealing with racial conflict. A bit later, in the teens and twenties, left progressives such as John Dewey, Horace Kallen, and Randolph Bourne rejected doctrines of racial inequality and the policies they were used to justify.

while to gather force in the scientific community at large, for social Darwinism had contributed significantly to shaping the emerging human sciences, particularly sociology and psychology. As a result, most American social scientists regarded the theory of race as belonging to the presuppositions rather than to the subject matter of their disciplines: the hierarchy of races was part of the natural order.[26] Thus, the *American Journal of Sociology* contained only one article on race – in Europe! – from 1895 to 1900 and only eleven more from 1900 to 1910. The exceptional work of W. E. B. Du Bois on this topic was largely ignored by white sociologists. It was not until the 1920s that the sociology of "race relations" became an established field of inquiry through the work of Robert Park and the Chicago School.

In the meantime, Boas had not only launched an empirical challenge to the basic assumptions of anthropometry – by demonstrating that key measurements of 17,000 immigrants and their children evinced significant differences between children and parents, owing to the changed environment of American life – but had published *The Mind of Primitive Man* (1911), undercutting the received correlation between cultural formations and racial types.[27] An architect of the fieldwork approach to cultural anthropology and an advocate of understanding alien cultures in their own terms rather than forcing them into a pre-established scale of civilization, he founded the most important tradition of cultural anthropology in America, counting among his disciples Alfred Kroeber, Robert Lowie, Melville Herskovits, Ruth Benedict, and Margaret Mead, among others. Boas and his disciples undercut the standard racial typologies by, for instance, evincing their basic confusion of "race" with shifting combinations of ethnicity, nationality, religion, geography, language, and culture, as well as the never-ending

---

[26] McKee, *Sociology and the Race Problem*. He mentions Lester Ward and W. I. Thomas as among the few American sociologists of the period who were skeptical of prevailing race theories (pp. 29–30). For a broad overview of the development of the social sciences in America during this period, which accentuates their ties to the changing vision of American exceptionalism, see Ross, *The Origins of American Social Science*.

[27] Elazar Barkan, *The Retreat of Scientific Racism* (Cambridge University Press, 1992), notes that Boas, educated in Germany before immigrating to the US, was influenced by German historicism, which provided a counterweight to the German physical anthropology that was so influential among American race theorists (pp. 76–90).

inconsistencies that marked their construction and deployment by different race theorists.[28]

These criticisms were reinforced and made decisive by developments in genetics after 1900, which led to the eventual elimination of Lamarckian ideas from biology and made the reconceptualization of social science as an independent mode of inquiry plausible. It is worth keeping in mind, however, that though scientific racism was increasingly discredited in scholarly circles, it did not completely lose its academic respectability until the atrocities of Nazism finally drove even the most recalcitrant scientists, scholars, and intellectuals away.[29] The growing power of the eugenics movement after 1900, with its increased emphasis on biological inheritance over social environment, was a factor in its continuance.[30] Another was the design of the Stanford-Binet intelligence test by American psychologists in 1916 and its deployment to measure differences between races, which were then grounded in a hereditarian theory of racial inequality. Moreover, it was only with the development of the "modern synthesis" in evolutionary theory during the 1920s and 1930s that the biological validity of race, in its received sense, was definitively undermined.[31]

Eventually, however, the anthropological and biological critiques of scientific racism eroded its scholarly respectability. By the end of the 1920s, studying race was increasingly a matter for the sociology of race relations rather than for evolutionary biology, and sociologists had come generally to accept the biological arguments against racial inequality. But they did not generally accept the anthropological assumption of the equality of cultures.[32] The sociological tradition had from the start been centrally concerned to comprehend the rise of "modern" society, and its founding fathers had developed conceptual

---

[28] Boas and most of his disciples retained the idea of biologically different races, but held that the most important differences between human groups were cultural. See Vernon J. Williams, Jr., "What is Race? Franz Boas Reconsidered," in J. Campbell, M. Guterl, and R. Lee (eds.), *Race, Nation, and Empire in American History* (Chapel Hill: University of North Carolina Press, 2007), pp. 17–39.

[29] Barkan, *The Retreat of Scientific Racism*.

[30] Hawkins, *Social Darwinism*, chap. 9.

[31] This did not, however, put an end to the biological study of human diversity, as the "postscript" to this chapter explains. But it did shift the primary locus of scientific racism from the natural to the social sciences, as is explained in what follows.

[32] McKee, *Sociology and the Race Problem*, p. 6.

schemes organized around a series of contrasts with "traditional" society: *Gemeinschaft* and *Gesellschaft*, status and contract, mechanical and organic solidarity, and the like. Social scientists trained in this tradition were generally disposed to treat racial differences in developmental terms. In particular, American sociologists depicted blacks living primarily in the rural South at the time as a premodern people, whose folkways rendered them unfit for modern life. The solution to "the Negro problem" would depend, then, on their gradual modernization and assimilation to white society. That would take time, and thus full equality had to be deferred, and the passage to it had to be managed by the socioculturally more advanced sections of the white population. However, as the "great migration" of Southern blacks to Northern cities picked up steam – from 1910 to 1940, 1.8 million Southern blacks migrated to the North – and the African-American population became increasingly urbanized, the frame of interpretation was altered, but without altering the assessment of sociocultural inferiority. In the new frame, African-American culture and institutions were generally interpreted as reaction-formations to the trauma of slavery and its aftermath, which had resulted in values, attitudes, and behavioral patterns that were now dysfunctional in a modernizing society, whatever survival value they may once have had. On this line of interpretation too, eventual assimilation to white society was the only remedy.

The most influential work in this genre was Gunnar Myrdal's two-volume study, *An American Dilemma*, which was published in 1944 and cited in the *Brown* v. *Board of Education* Supreme Court decision of 1954, and which continued to frame the social-scientific study of race for another decade.[33] Adopting a normative standpoint premised on integration, Myrdal judged that "American Negro culture is not something independent of general American culture. It is a distorted development, or a pathological condition of the general American culture … [I]t is to the advantage of American Negroes as individuals and as a group to become assimilated."[34] The main obstacles to this, in his view, were white racism ("prejudice") and the institutionalized discrimination it supported. Overcoming black cultural pathologies thus required both enlightening the white majority and changing social institutions. This general approach to the sociology of race predominated well into

[33] Gunnar Myrdal, *An American Dilemma* (New York: McGraw-Hill, 1944).
[34] *Ibid.*, vol. II, pp. 928–929.

the 1960s, among black as well as white scholars. To mention only one prominent example, E. Franklin Frazier, who had studied with Parks at Chicago, generally endorsed Myrdal's diagnosis of black culture and institutions.[35] And like him, he identified the main problem as white racism and the socioeconomic inequalities it reproduced, and the main antidote as institutional change guided by social-scientific knowledge.

Frazier focused early on the damage done to the black family by slavery, Jim Crow, and the migration of rural Southern blacks to the urban centers of the North.[36] That focus later became central to a rather different diagnosis and prescription. In his 1965 report to President Johnson, *The Negro Family: The Case for National Action*, Daniel Patrick Moynihan singled out the deterioration of the black family as the principal source of the "pathology" that marked Negro American life.[37] Though its historical origins in slavery and segregation were acknowledged, there was an important shift of etiological emphasis from the oppressive social, economic, and political conditions established and maintained by white racism, which Myrdal and Frazier had stressed, to "the present tangle of pathology [that] is capable of perpetuating itself without assistance from the white world."[38] Cause and effect were being transposed.

It was chiefly to this culturalist version of African-American inferiority that critics responded in the late 1960s by emphasizing the elements of creativity and resistance in black culture.[39] My interest here, however, is not in tracing the various twists and turns of the debate about the strengths and weaknesses of African-American culture.[40] My concern, rather, is with the culturalist turn in the scholarly discussion of race itself, and with the new modality of racial ideology it spawned: cultural

---

[35] See the discussions of Myrdal and Frazier by Richard H. King, *Race, Culture, and the Intellectuals, 1940–1970* (Baltimore: Johns Hopkins University Press, 2004), chaps. 5, 6.

[36] E. Franklin Frazier, *The Negro Family in the United States* (New York: Dryden Press, 1948).

[37] Printed in Lee Rainwater and William C. Yancy, *The Moynihan Report and the Politics of Controversy* (Cambridge, MA: MIT Press, 1967).

[38] *Ibid.*, p. 93.

[39] They were also responding to social-psychological versions, especially the "Sambo" personality structure posited by Stanley Elkins in *Slavery: A Problem in American Institutional and Cultural Life* (University of Chicago Press, 1959).

[40] For overviews, see King, *Race, Culture, and the Intellectuals*; and Daryl Scott, *Contempt and Pity* (University of Chicago Press, 1997).

racism.[41] As I explained in the introduction, the main feature of this new modality is the replacement of a biological inferiority putatively warranted by natural science with a cultural inferiority putatively warranted by social science, which still has the effect of reinforcing racial stereotypes and the diminished status and opportunity they foster. Thus, unlike the founding figures in the sociology of race, neoconservative theorists treat "underclass" values, attitudes, behavior, and the like as independent variables and make them the causes of the social, economic, and political inequities afflicting its members.[42] Extreme residential segregation, failed schools, dire poverty, chronic unemployment, and the breakdown of the black family are thereby regarded as effects of irresponsible behavior rather than as its causes or as both its causes and effects. Accordingly, the remedy proposed is self-improvement rather than institutional change or than some combination of both. Institutional racism, on this view, is a thing of the past. There is now sufficiently equal opportunity for all to achieve socioeconomic success, so that the failure (statistically) to do so by members of any group must be due to internal deficiencies and not to external factors.

This "blaming the victim" version of cultural racism is in many ways a mirror image of the blaming-the-racist version widespread in the sociology of race relations. There the chief explanatory factor is white racism, elaborated in terms of individual and group prejudices and the discriminatory practices they promote. From this perspective, the causes of racial inequality lie rather in the culture and psychology of white racism, of which the culture and psychology of black underprivilege are effects. Neoconservative critics typically counter that racism of this sort is on the wane and can no longer plausibly be regarded as the root cause of the African-American predicament. But while the data on anti-black attitudes among whites clearly indicate a sharp drop since the 1960s, they also indicate a considerable persistence. Orlando Patterson, for

---

[41] See Stephen Steinberg, *The Ethnic Myth* (Boston: Beacon Press, 2001); Martin Barker, *The New Racism* (London: Junction Books, 1981); and Robert Miles, *Racism after 'Race Relations'* (London: Routledge, 1993).

[42] See, for example, Thomas Sowell, *Ethnic America: A History* (New York: Basic Books, 1981); Shelby Steele, *The Content of Our Character: A New Vision of Race in America* (New York: St. Martin's Press, 1990); and Dinesh D'Souza, *The End of Racism: Principles for a Multiracial Society* (New York: Simon & Schuster, 1996). For a more scholarly, extensively documented argument to similar effect see Stephan and Abigail Thernstrom, *America in Black and White: One Nation, Indivisible* (New York: Simon & Schuster, 1997).

instance, estimates on this basis that one in five white Americans harbors strongly racist feelings toward black Americans – which, if it were true, would mean that there were significantly more hard-core racists in the country than there are African Americans.[43] In any case, this mode of explanation points to a different set of psychological and cultural factors that must be taken into account when thinking about race in America.

There is another approach to white racism that remains broadly at the cultural-psychological level but focuses less on conscious prejudices than on widespread stereotypes. While the proportion of whites harboring expressly racist feelings toward blacks may have declined to 20 percent or less, the proportion harboring racist stereotypes of blacks seems to be many times that.[44] As a number of studies have shown, action premised on such stereotypes – for example hiring or housing decisions, policing or sentencing decisions – may be discriminatory in effect without being so in intent. And even when such stereotypes reflect statistical realities – for example differential crime patterns – their widespread application to dealings with all or most individuals belonging to the group so stigmatized seriously impairs the equality of opportunities open to them and thus diminishes their life chances. This is, then, another factor that has to enter into the explanatory mix.

A type of explanatory factor that tends today to get too little attention is the institutional racism mentioned above. While the racist institutions of slavery and segregation were established and administered by individuals harboring racist attitudes within racist cultures, they eventually gave way to formally non-discriminatory institutions that are, however, systematically biased in their consequences – that is, whose normal operation consistently produces outcomes that disadvantage African Americans but that function across a wide variety of mindsets on the part of those who participate in them.[45] Thus, for example, the

---

[43] Orlando Patterson, *The Ordeal of Integration* (Washington, DC: Civitas/ Counterpoint, 1997), p. 61.

[44] David K. Shipler, *A Country of Strangers: Blacks and Whites in America* (New York: Knopf, 1997), reports a University of Chicago study in which over 50% of whites rated blacks as less intelligent than whites, over 60% thought they were lazier, and over 75% considered them more likely to prefer welfare to work.

[45] Eduardo Bonilla-Silva, *Racism without Racists* (Lanham, MD: Rowman & Littlefield, 2006); Douglas S. Massy, *Categorically Unequal: The American Stratification System* (New York: Russell Foundation, 2007).

operation of an educational system based on local funding of local schools may systematically disadvantage the children of urban black ghettos, without that being the aim of particular participants. To put the normative point in Rawlsian terms: if the institutions of the "basic structure" are unjust, then the distribution of rights, opportunities, and goods they structure will be unjust.[46] It is arguable that the basic institutions of our society – the institutions that structure housing, education, employment, family formation, criminal justice, and other domains – are unjust in this sense, that is, that they *routinely* function to the systematic disadvantage of African Americans in distributing basic opportunities and primary goods. And if the basic structure is unfair, justice requires that it be changed, which is what those calling for a "third reconstruction" have in mind.

Another factor at work in sustaining neoracist responses to racial stratification is the invisibility of the historical causes of existing racial imbalances. Relatively few Americans seem to be aware, for instance, of the central role that New Deal programs played in perpetuating inequality of opportunity in labor markets (the Wagner Act legalizing labor unions intentionally omitted anti-discrimination provisions), in housing (only a very small portion of Federal Housing Administration [FHA] and Veterans Administration [VA] insured home mortgages were made available to African Americans), and social security (the initial exclusion of agricultural and domestic workers left roughly three-fourths of black workers uncovered by the Social Security Act, as intended). But the patterns of social inequality in employment, housing, and wealth they helped weave into the fabric of American life are still quite visible. Thus it is all too "natural" – especially among the overwhelming majority of Americans who came of age or immigrated after the passage of the Civil Rights Act, the elimination of *de jure* discrimination, and the gradual reduction of overt bigotry – to point to a lack of personal responsibility in making decisions about marriage, school, education, work, crime, and the like to explain those patterns. Historical unconsciousness of institutional racism in the past feeds unconscious neoracism in the present.[47]

---

[46] See Tommie Shelby, "Justice, Deviance, and the Dark Ghetto," *Philosophy and Public Affairs* 35 (2007): 126–160.

[47] See Michael K. Brown, Martin Carnoy, Elliott Currie *et al.*, *Whitewashing Race: The Myth of a Color-Blind Society* (Berkeley: University of California Press, 2003), pp. 26–30, 223–228.

In my view, there is ample evidence for the significance of all these types of factors in explaining racial injustice: prejudice and discrimination, dysfunctional attitudes and behavior, pervasive negative stereotyping, the structure and functioning of basic institutions, as well as historical unconsciousness of the causes of intergenerational patterns of racial stratification. And, as I have noted, they operate in a vicious causal circle, as reciprocal causes and effects, to form a self-reinforcing nexus of feedback loops.[48] Hence efforts to achieve racial justice that aim to be adequate to the complexities of racial injustice will have to address all of them. Preaching tolerance and training for diversity are no more likely to succeed on their own than are self-improvement and racial uplift. And negative stereotyping is unlikely to disappear before the racial stratification that feeds it. At the same time, while desegregation processes demonstrated that institutional change can sometimes foster sociopsychological and sociocultural change, the failure of any number of bureaucratic initiatives to solve the problems they targeted strongly indicates that institutional changes unaccompanied by changes in individual attitudes and behavior on both sides of the racial divide are unlikely to be ineffective. As the first and second reconstructions have made clear, it is usually when both agency and structure are in play that institutionalized racial injustice can be effectively ameliorated. The civil rights revolution of the 1960s is unthinkable without the agency of black and white activists, the support of black and white churches, the solidarity within the black community, and with significant segments of white America; but it is also unthinkable without the intervention of the federal government, which was finally enlisted to reconstruct some of the discriminatory structures of legalized racism. Thus the all too familiar opposition between agency and accountability, on the one side, and structures and institutions, on the other, is a false dichotomy. On this point we can still learn from Karl Marx, who long ago noted that human beings make their own history, only not under conditions they

---

[48] One can find similarly vicious causal circles at work in the ethnoracial – Turkish, Algerian, Afro-Caribbean, South Asian, African, etc. – ghettos that have taken shape in a number of European countries. There too, such "structural" factors as residential segregation, chronic unemployment, and widespread poverty are enmeshed in feedback loops with such "cultural" factors as educational underachievement, alienation from the dominant culture, single parenthood, and high crime rates. And there too, today's problems are in part a legacy of past injustice.

choose but under those inherited from the past. That is to say, neither voluntarism nor determinism is adequate to the task of remedying the conditions of racial injustice we have inherited from three centuries of slavery and segregation.

Neoracist ideologies obscure not only the historical roots of racially distributed disadvantages, but also the continuing role of institutionalized structures in reproducing them. To extract character traits and cultural values from their historical and institutional contexts, treat them as individual and group failures, and make them responsible for the whole mess is, methodologically viewed, indefensible. But the main point of doing so is political rather than methodological: taking a sharp culturalist turn on the theoretical side obviates institutional reform on the practical side. Rather than attacking the massive structural inequalities of opportunity under which African Americans still suffer, the dysfunctional-culture approach stigmatizes the victims anew, blames them for their plight, and leaves it largely to them to correct the situation. Reconstruction is taken off the political agenda and moral exhortation put on. Thus, while social-scientific neoracism no longer serves the same legally institutionalized, structure-forming functions as classical racism, it does serve to sustain institutional racism through shaping public debate and public policy in a wide variety of areas from immigration and education to urban affairs and criminal justice.

In this respect, then, the demise of scientific racism in its evolutionary-biological form did not mean the end of racist thinking in scholarly discourse altogether. A new, post-biological modality of neoracism is now widespread in social science and public policy: historically disadvantaged, racially identified groups are ascribed stereotypically negative culture and character traits, which then are used to explain and legitimate the social, economic, and political inequities under which they live. And though "common sense" has lagged behind in shedding assumptions of biological inferiority, there too the substitution of cultural for biological inferiority is well along.[49] The way for this substitution had already been cleared by the correlation between biological and cultural inferiority in classical race theory. One had only to disengage

[49] Donald R. Kinder and Lynn M. Sanders, *Divided by Color* (University of Chicago Press, 1996), chap. 5, report a study in which about 75 percent of whites rejected the proposition that blacks come from a biologically inferior race, against about 10 percent who agreed with it (p. 326, n. 60).

the deficiencies of talent and temperament from their putative biological basis and reattach them to sociocultural, sociopsychological patterns. It was scarcely necessary to alter the phenotypical, psychological, and cultural stereotypes in the process.[50] These shifts in the scholarly and, with some delay, popular understanding of group differences within America were accompanied by similar shifts in the understanding of difference between Americans and other nations. Biological evolution was absent from the discourse of development that dominated the comparative study of society after World War II. Instead, the developmental schemes of classical sociological theory were combined with development economics to explain and justify the global dominance of the West in general and of the United States in particular.[51] In "the underdeveloped world" too, it was no longer racial inferiority but sociocultural retardation and pathology that had to be overcome.[52]

What is striking about the practice of racial difference in the US over the two centuries following the Revolution is how constant the assumptions of superiority and inferiority and the policies of domination and deferral have remained throughout the many vicissitudes of theory. Whether theorized in terms of the philosophy of history, physical anthropology, evolutionary biology, the sociology of modernization, or cultural theory, difference typically means deficiency. One important variation is whether that deficiency is figured as "natural," and thus unalterable, or sociocultural, and thus in principle improvable. In the one case, difference means permanent inferiority, in the other, deferred assimilation. In both cases, the theory of difference is closely linked with the practice of difference. Like other forms of social and political theorizing, thinking about race reflects the basic social structures, material interests, cultural patterns, and political forces of the context in which it is carried on. At the same time, the ideas through which that context is understood, serve to orient and guide perceptions, motivations, and actions within it. Given that the United States was formed around the core processes of Indian removal, African enslavement, and Mexican annexation, it is no surprise that throughout its history, racial thinking played a leading role in its self-understanding and self-

---

[50] See McKee, *Sociology and the Race Problem*, chap. 2 and pp. 230–236.

[51] I discuss this in chapter 7.

[52] This view is still widespread. See, for example, the collection edited by Lawrence E. Harrison and Samuel P. Huntington, *Culture Matters: How Values Shape Human Progress* (New York: Basic Books, 2001).

legitimation. From this perspective, social Darwinism was only one chapter in a long history of thinking white supremacy. But it was a very important one, as it "scientifically" represented racial domination as the natural order of things and thus as neither requiring nor permitting full emancipation and equality. Overcoming it was vital to renewing the hope for racial justice in post-World War II America, as is overcoming the various forms of neoracism for redressing the legacy of that long history today.

Postscript

Scientific racism combined biological differences with behavioral differences in such a way that the former were the basis of the latter. It was, in this regard, a species of biological determinism. Since World War II the natural-scientific study of human diversity has, roughly, recognized the sociopolitically constructed character of the racist meanings historically attached to biological differences between human populations, while pursuing an interest in biological variation itself.[53] After the development of molecular biology, population genetics could provide more precise information about the variation in gene (or allele) frequencies across the relatively isolated breeding populations that resulted from the early human migrations out of Africa and their evolutionary adaptations to various geographical conditions. The results of this work have tended to confirm in part the received notion of biologically distinct "races," insofar as five of the six genetic "clusters" that have been identified more or less match the historically identified racial groups associated with major geographical regions of the world: Africa, East Asia, Melanesia (or Oceana), the Americas, and Eurasia (Europe, the Middle East, and South Asia).[54] But they also diverge from the received notion of "race," insofar as the genetic variation found within such large populations is far greater (c. 95 percent) than that between them (c. 5 percent); and the variation in genetic frequencies between populations is continuous and graduated, so that some

---

[53] For brief historical overviews, see Bruce Baum, *The Rise and Fall of the Caucasian Race* (New York University Press, 2006), chap. 6; and John Arthur, *Race, Equality, and the Burdens of History* (Cambridge University Press, 2007), chap. 2.

[54] The 2002 issue of *Science* (298) contains useful summaries of work connected with the Human Genome Diversity Project.

subpopulations in each larger cluster are genetically closer to subpopulations in other large clusters than to some in their own. They diverge
too in assigning little biological significance to the genetic differences
underlying conventional surface markers of racial difference such as
skin color, eye shape, hair texture, facial features, and the like. Most
importantly, they do not treat the variations in genetic frequencies they
have identified as a biological explanation of cultural differences across
populations.

Many have judged these divergences from received notions to be
sufficient to warrant abolishing the terminology of races altogether.
Whatever the terminology, however, the biological diversity identified
by research in population genetics has posed anew a question inherited
from scientific racism: are these variations in gene frequencies across
regional breeding populations correlated with any significant differences at the behavioral level? That is, are these genetic variations
important for explaining differences in human behavior? For one
thing, medical and pharmacological research has established that
there are different patterns in the incidence of certain diseases and the
effectiveness of certain medications across genetic populations and
subpopulations; but that has nothing to do with the judgments of
inferiority/superiority characteristic of scientific racism. On the other
hand, there is an area of research that does seem to fit that model:
intelligence testing has repeatedly ascertained "gaps" in scores on stan-
dardized tests across racially identified populations. There are also data
correlating differences in the results of IQ testing (and other standar-
dized tests) with differences in educational performance and economic
success, among other things. So the question of how these test-score
differences are to be explained has become a politically sensitive issue,
particularly in connection with the test-score gap between white and
black Americans.[55] Some have argued that it is genetically based.[56]
Others have argued for the empirical significance of a host of other,
non-genetic factors: methodological bias in the design and administration of the tests; teachers' perceptions and expectations; social-
psychological factors such as "stereotype threat" and the burden of

[55] Christopher Jencks and Meredith Phillips (eds.), *The Black–White Test Score Gap* (Washington, DC: Brookings Institution Press, 1998).
[56] Richard J. Herrnstein and Charles Murray, *The Bell Curve: Intelligence and Class Structure in American Life* (New York: Free Press, 1994).

"acting white" (sometimes used in microeconomic analyses of the achievement gap); sociocultural factors such as the relative infrequency of middle-class parenting practices; and structural factors such as the poor quality of *de facto* segregated elementary and secondary schools.[57] This is, in short, an area of ongoing controversy. One thing is clear normatively: if there were genetically based statistical variations in the results of intelligence testing *between* populations demarcated by gene clusters, they would have no more relevance to our basic principles of moral, legal, and political equality than do such variations *within* them. But they could complicate the theory and practice of equal opportunity to which those principles commit us.

In any case, the forms of neoracism currently widespread appeal for scientific validation not to biological studies of human diversity but to social-scientific accounts of cultural difference, especially of the "cultural pathology" variety. Moreover, the persistence and strength of negative racial stereotypes, as well as the discriminatory practices and failed policies they inform, appear to be largely independent of the twists and turns of population genetics. As things stand, it is not the natural-scientific but the social-scientific study of race that serves to rationalize continuing racial injustice.

---

[57] For brief overviews see Arthur, *Race, Equality, and the Burdens of History*, pp. 165–197; and Roy L. Brooks, *Atonement and Forgiveness* (Berkeley: University of California Press, 2004), pp. 75–97.

4 | Coming to terms with the past: on the politics of the memory of slavery

We can no longer afford to take that which was good in the past and simply call it our heritage, to discard the bad and simply think of it as a dead load which by itself time will bury in oblivion ... This is the reality in which we live.

Hannah Arendt[1]

It seems that wherever one turns these days questions of how to deal with difficult pasts have risen to the top of national and international agendas.[2] The general premise of this chapter is that the United States has not yet adequately dealt with the many forms of racial injustice endemic to its national past; and its general approach is that our thinking about this failure, its consequences, and possible remedies can be sharpened by drawing upon the German case, particularly Germany's renewed efforts in the 1980s and 1990s to face the painful truth of the National Socialist past of the 1930s and 1940s. In that situation, the forum in which public memory was exercised and consciousness raised was a debate among historians – a *Historikerstreit* – that spilled over into public awareness. That peculiar circumstance allowed the links between changing public memory and changing political culture and collective identity to appear in sharp relief. One key issue in that debate concerned the role that anti-Semitism, as a racialized mode of perception

---

[1] Hannah Arendt, *The Origins of Totalitarianism* (New York: Harcourt Brace Jovanovich, 1973), "Preface to the First Edition" (1950), p. ix.
[2] See Ruti G. Teitel, *Transitional Justice* (Oxford University Press, 2000); Priscilla Hayner, *Unspeakable Truths* (London and New York: Routledge, 2000); Martha Minow, *Between Vengeance and Forgiveness* (Boston: Beacon Press, 1998); Elazar Barkan, *The Guilt of Nations* (Baltimore: Johns Hopkins University Press, 2000); John Torpey (ed.), *Politics and the Past* (Lanham, MD: Rowman & Littlefield, 2003); J. Torpey, *Making Whole What Has Been Smashed* (Cambridge, MA: Harvard University Press, 2006); and Margaret Urban Walker, *Moral Repair: Reconstructing Moral Relations after Wrongdoing* (Cambridge University Press, 2006). See also the website of the International Center for Transitional Justice: www.ictj.org/en/.

and interaction, played in the Holocaust. Others concerned the collective liability of present-day Germans for state-sanctioned and state-implemented atrocities in the past; the cultural, and political costs of suppressing painful memories and refusing to mourn; the relation of professional to popular history, and of both to public sites and rituals of commemoration; and the forms of patriotism and collective identity suitable to a democratic society with an oppressive past. In these and other respects, I suggest, the German historians' debate may throw some new light on our own tortured attempts to come to terms with a past of racial injustice.[3]

I shall focus here on only one of the major racial formations that disfigure our past and present, the one associated with racial slavery and its aftermath. The "logics" and "dynamics" of the constellations associated with the dispossession and near extermination of Native Americans, the forceful subjection of the inhabitants of territories conquered from Mexico, the involuntary incorporation of native Hawaiians, Puerto Ricans, and Alaskan Eskimos, and the exclusion or oppression of various groups of immigrants are sufficiently different to warrant separate treatments. Moreover, it is the black/white divide that has most deeply marked the topography of American racial politics from before the Civil War to the present day. The first, post-Civil War Reconstruction not only failed to repair the damages of two centuries of racial slavery, it soon gave way to another century of racial caste relations. The "second reconstruction," which culminated in the civil rights legislation of the 1960s, ended most *de jure* discrimination but did not repair the massive *de facto* inequalities it left behind. "Great Society" programs and policies, including affirmative action, contributed importantly to correcting these inherited disadvantages; but the "Reagan Revolution" and the conservative realignment of national

---

[3] Another feature of German efforts to come to terms with the past that is relevant to our situation is the reparations paid to Jews since the end of the war and, more recently, to forced and slave laborers of diverse ethnic backgrounds, for there has been a recent resurgence of interest here in the question of reparations for slavery and segregation. A Reparations Coordinating Committee, founded by Charles Ogletree of Harvard Law School and Randall Robinson of TransAfrica, has prepared class-action lawsuits for that purpose. I discuss some pros and cons of this approach in "Coming to Terms with the Past, Part II: On the Morality and Politics of Reparations for Slavery," *Political Theory* 32 (2004): 750–772, and "Repairing Past Injustice: Remarks on the Politics of Reparations," forthcoming in H. McGary (ed.), *Reparations for African Americans*.

politics have increasingly squeezed the life out of them. In addition to the massive shift of party allegiance in the South and the significant role of the radical right in Republican politics, there were also socio-structural factors involved in the post-1960s transformation of racial politics. For one thing, rapid economic globalization and the transition of advanced capitalist societies from "Fordist" regimes of mass production to postindustrial regimes of "flexible production" led to large losses in the types of unionized jobs that generations of workers had used to climb into the middle class and abetted the deterioration of government-sponsored social programs. For another, the enormous increase in US immigration since the mid-1960s, especially from non-European regions of the world such as Asia and Latin America, has refracted the black/white politics of race into a wider and more variegated spectrum. When one adds to this the many negative rulings of federal courts in matters of affirmative action – so that, notwithstanding the recent ruling by the Supreme Court in *Grutter* v. *Bollinger*, this avenue of repair has been considerably narrowed – the prospects of remedying the lingering effects of slavery and segregation seem bleak, despite Obama's election.

In this conjuncture, it might be of some use to examine the US failure to deal with its racist past under a lens shaped by a more or less successful attempt to do so elsewhere. Accordingly, the first section will focus on the recent debates in Germany concerning the role that publicly working through past injustice can play in reshaping national culture and identity. Section II will use insights gleaned from that discussion to review the US's failure to come to terms with a past in black and white. I will conclude, in the last section, with some thoughts on how a politics of public memory might figure in debates about policies that address the legacy of slavery and segregation.

I

From the close of World War II to the present, Germany has been engaged in an ongoing effort to come to terms with its Nazi past – in shifting circumstances and with varying aims, approaches, and results.[4]

---

[4] See Richard J. Evans, *In Hitler's Shadow* (New York: Pantheon Books, 1989) for a sketch of these shifts and a good account of the historians' debate of the 1980s. I shall be concerned here with the West German story; the East German story was quite distinct, until their separate trajectories began to merge after reunification.

Immediately after the war, a defeated and divided Germany had various measures relating to its recent past imposed upon it by the victorious Allies – war crimes trials, denazification procedures, reeducation processes, and the like. From 1949 through the early 1960s, however, dealing with the past was largely – though not completely – suspended, as energies were marshaled in the service of *Wiederaufbau*, or rebuilding. During that period, a general turning away from the Nazi period was supported by the dominant view, in public life and in the schools, that the twelve years of National Socialism were an aberration in German history foisted upon the people by Hitler and his henchmen. Reparations were made to Israel, the "economic miracle" proceeded apace under Adenauer and Erhard, and the Nazi affiliations of major public figures were concealed behind a wall of silence. A number of German intellectuals who grew to young adulthood under National Socialism and came to maturity after the war protested this curtailment of critical investigation into the past already in the late 1950s, but with limited effect until, in the second half of the 1960s, student radicalism and the accession of the Social Democrats to power tipped the balance in favor of a determined effort to come to terms with the past. As a result, and aided by new access to Nazi documents, in the 1970s there began a steady stream of scholarly studies that left little room for doubting or denying the character and extent of Nazi crimes, the complicity of various German elites, the widespread support among large segments of the population, or the roots of Nazism in German history and culture. But in the 1980s, after the Christian Democrats returned to power under Helmut Kohl, conservative intellectuals were encouraged to take advantage of the new political climate to reclaim political-cultural dominance from the left opposition. This was the setting for the well-known *Historikerstreit*, or historians' debate, of the mid-1980s, which I shall be considering here.[5]

Ernst Nolte, Michael Stürmer, Andreas Hillgruber, and other professional historians undertook to reinterpret the events of the Nazi period in ways that reduced their singularity and enormity – for instance, by comparing the Final Solution to other mass atrocities of the twentieth

---

[5] Many of the relevant documents, in English translation, are collected in James Knowlton (ed.), *Forever in the Shadow of Hitler*, tr. T. Cates (Atlantic Highlands, NJ: Humanities Press, 1993), and Peter Baldwin (ed.), *Reworking the Past* (Boston: Beacon Press, 1990).

century, from the massacre of the Armenians by the Turks to the Stalinist purges of the 1930s. Indeed, the Bolshevik Revolution and its aftermath also served as the major explanatory factor in their account of the recent German past: Hitler and Nazism were a response to the threat of Bolshevism from the East. In addition to "normalizing" and "historicizing" the Holocaust in these ways, historical work from this quarter also promoted a shift in perspective from solidarity with the victims of Nazism to solidarity with the valiant German troops fighting on the Eastern front and with ordinary Germans suffering through the war's grim end. There was, of course, a political-cultural point to all of this: it was time for Germany to leave behind its Nazi past, turn toward the future, and assume its rightful place among the leading nations of the world. It was worse than an intellectual error to view a proud German history solely through the distorting lens of a twelve-year aberration; it was a political failing as well, for it impeded formation of the strong national identity and confident national purpose needed for effective action in rapidly changing European and global settings. By that time, most of the country's inhabitants had been born after the war or had been too young during the Nazi period to bear any individual responsibility for it. Dwelling on a past that was not theirs served no better purpose than public self-flagellation and blocked the normal development of patriotic identification with the fortunes of the nation.

With such arguments, and in concert with their political allies, the conservative historians were putting revisionist history to public use in the interests of reshaping public memory – and thus German self-understanding – and of relieving public conscience so as to revitalize German patriotism. And it was precisely to this political-cultural challenge that Jürgen Habermas, Hans Mommson, and other German left-liberal intellectuals responded in the *Historikerstreit*.[6] I want now to consider briefly their responses concerning the public use of history, and to do so from the interested standpoint of the US's own difficulties in coming to terms with the past.

---

[6] In addition to the collections mentioned in the preceding note, see the helpful discussions by Evans, *In Hitler's Shadow*, and Charles S. Maier, *The Unmasterable Past* (Cambridge, MA: Harvard University Press, 1988). A number of Habermas's contributions to the debate have appeared in English translation in a collection of his essays, *The New Conservatism*, tr. S. Weber Nicholsen (Cambridge, MA: MIT Press, 1989).

The overriding political-cultural issue behind the historians' dispute might be put as follows: what should be the attitude of present-day Germans toward a Nazi past in which most of them were not directly implicated? Often enough the collective past is a burden on the present, and the stronger the memories of it the greater the burden. If the past in question involves terrible crimes for which amends can never really be made, the problems for collective identity and collective action can be immense. With worries of this sort in mind, many Germans felt in the mid-1980s that forty years of dealing with the Nazi past was enough and that it was time for Germany to move on – to reestablish continuities with the many glorious aspects of its history and traditions, to foster a more positive self-understanding, and to play a more self-confident and self-interested role in international affairs than its postwar pariah status had permitted. Those who argued against this – successfully in the end – noted that the process of publicly facing the past had gotten fully underway only in the late 1960s and was already throttled in the early 1980s by the *Tendenzwende*, or change of direction, set in motion when the Christian Democrats regained power under Kohl. And the character of that change – particularly the heavy-handed attempts to reverse the political-cultural accomplishments of the 1970s and to renew German patriotism, encapsulated by the infamous events at Bitburg in 1985 – made it clear that Germany had not yet effectively worked through its past but was rather in the process of trying to repress it.[7] The questionable work of the conservative historians enlisted in these efforts only proved the point: professional history was being misused to improve Germany's weak self-image by touching up the ugly picture of its recent past.

There were, of course, historiographic criticisms of that work by other historians; but the line of criticism I want to focus on stressed rather the political implications of this effort to leave the painful past behind. Jürgen Habermas, in particular, advanced the argument that German national identity was inseparable from its historical

---

[7] The Bitburg incident involved a Kohl-staged memorial ceremony at a German military cemetery, during which then-President Reagan laid a wreath to honor the dead, among whom were a number of Waffen-SS troops. See Geoffrey Hartmann (ed.), *Bitburg in Moral and Political Perspective* (Bloomington: Indiana University Press, 1986). Not long thereafter, Kohl appeared at a congress of German expellees from Silesia and voiced his support for the German state boundaries of 1937 – which include about one-third of present-day Poland.

consciousness, and that any major shifts in German public memory would leave their mark upon German self-understanding, with practical-political consequences. If those shifts were in the direction of denying and repressing the past instead of confronting and dealing with it, they would likely lead to forms of "acting out" rather than "working through," symptoms of which could already be discerned in German public life, most notably in various expressions of a mounting xeno-phobia. For what was at issue here was not a temporary aberration but a catastrophe with deep roots in German history and culture. Historians of the Holocaust had, for instance, pointed to a virulent strain of popular anti-Semitism as a contributing factor, a diagnosis later reinforced and sharpened in Daniel Goldhagen's *Hitler's Willing Executioners*.[8] Long-standing, widespread, and deeply rooted views of German racial super-iority and Jewish racial inferiority had shaped a popular mindset that was, Goldhagen maintained, a necessary, if not sufficient, condition for the attempted Judeocide. Even those born later, who bore no individual moral guilt in that connection, had a continuing responsibility to work up, on, and through such elements of German political culture in an effort to break with the past. Failure to do so, Habermas argued, would come back to haunt German public life, for allowing the motivational force of such beliefs and attitudes to persist would only heighten the risk of repeated outbreaks of racially imbued thinking and acting, as already evinced in the growing conflicts over asylum and immigration. It would also amount to a renunciation of Germany's collective obliga-tion to make amends for the past and a show of disrespect for its many victims.

On this point, referring to Walter Benjamin's idea of reversing the usual triumphal identification with history's winners for an anamnestic solidarity with its victims, Habermas writes: "There is the obligation incumbent upon us in Germany ... to keep alive, without distortion, and not only in an intellectual form, the memory of the sufferings of those who were murdered by German hands ... If we were to brush aside this Benjaminian legacy, our fellow Jewish citizens and the sons, daughters, and grandchildren of all those who were murdered would feel

---

[8] Daniel Goldhagen, *Hitler's Willing Executioners* (New York: Alfred A. Knopf, 1996). See also Habermas's speech upon the occasion of the awarding of the German Democracy Prize to Goldhagen in 1997, "On the Public Use of History," in Habermas, *The Postnational Constellation*, tr. Max Pensky (Cambridge, MA: MIT Press, 2001), pp. 26–37.

themselves unable to breathe in our country."[9] Public remembrances and commemorations of the suffering of victims – through artistic as well as historical representations, in public rituals and public places, in school curricula and mass media – play crucial roles in transforming traditions and in determining what will or will not be passed on to future generations. Whether or not past evils are kept present in public consciousness, whether or not their victims are still mourned, Habermas continues, are central elements of who "we" (Germans) are and who "we" want to be. For recognizing past evil as integral to German history, as issuing "from the very midst of our collective life" – rather than as marginal or accidental to it – "cannot but have a powerful impact on our self-understanding … and shake any naive trust in our own traditions."[10] It is, in fact, an essential ingredient in any genuine effort to re-form national identity *in full awareness* of the horrors that issued from its previous formation.

The unity of this "we" is, to be sure, by no means given: it is some-thing that has to be continually shaped and reshaped in the public sphere. For in the politics of public memory there is typically a poly-phony of voices, emanating from a diversity of "subject positions": the voices of victims and perpetrators, of resisters and collaborators, of those directly involved and those who were born later, of different regions and cultures, races and classes, political ideologies and religious convictions, and so forth.[11] In a democratic context, this means that

---

[9] This passage appears in an earlier (1987) article with the same English title as Habermas's address at the award ceremony for Goldhagen (see n. 8), "On the Public Use of History," in *The New Conservatism*, pp. 229–240, at 233. It hardly needs mentioning that with the appropriate substitutions of "American" for "German" and "African American" for "Jewish," this sentiment might be directed toward the US situation as well – but with at least three very important differences. First, today German Jews number in the tens of thousands, while African Americans number in the tens of millions, so shaping an American "we" inclusive of the descendants of the previously excluded is a task of a significantly different order than forming an inclusive German "we." Second, like most Europeans, Germans still tend – albeit with growing opposition – to think of themselves as belonging to an ethnocultural nation, whereas the American nation – at least since the decline of Anglo-Saxonism – generally understands itself to be multiethnic and, increasingly, multicultural. Finally, the United States fought a civil war over slavery.

[10] Habermas, "On the Public Use of History," in *The Postnational Constellation*, pp. 45–46.

[11] On the notion of a "subject position," see Dominick LaCapra, "Representing the Holocaust: Reflections on the Historians Debate," in Saul Friedlander (ed.),

representations of the past may be publicly contested from perspectives that are linked to conflicting understandings of the present and orientations toward the future. And in the resultant dialectic of past, present, and future, debates over what happened and why interpenetrate with differences of interest and concern, conviction and attitude, experience and hope among the various participants.[12] This is so in the German debates and, as we shall see, even more so in the American – where the immense presence of the descendants of slaves in the body politic gives the idea of solidarity with the victims of history a different political edge than it has in Germany, and where Southern views of slavery, the Civil War, Reconstruction, and their aftermath managed to gain a hegemony unlike anything to be found in the defeated Germany.

Another issue in the *Historikerstreit* was the extent to which historical scholarship can and should inform the politics of memory in the public sphere by, among other things, introducing an element of objectivity into what might otherwise become simply a matter of power. To be sure, the ideas of "objectivity" in question were, for the most part, "postdeconstructive" rather than foundationalist.[13] It was generally agreed that narratives and interpretations are not simply dictated by facts; that their construction is always informed by the historians' questions, interests, standpoints, temporal positions, and the like; and that there is no absolute divide between facts and interpretations, but rather a continuous spectrum. However, the latitude for reasonable disagreement is palpably different at different points in the spectrum. As one moves in the "factual" direction, the constraints imposed by the evidence – documents, eyewitness reports, quantitative data, and so forth – significantly narrow the range of reasonable disagreement. The critical use of such sources by the community of historical scholars results in the elimination of many proposed interpretations, as the factual claims and presuppositions germane to them are submitted to critical scrutiny – as happened, for example, with the "Auschwitz lie" and the "Lost Cause" view of the Civil War. For though historical judgment is unavoidable, it is exercised in critical dialogue with a

---

Probing the Limits of Representation (Cambridge, MA: Harvard University Press, 1992), pp. 108–127.

[12] Carlos Thiebault elaborates this dialectic in the democratic politics of memory in "Nombrar el mal: Sobre la articulación pública de la moralidad," in M. Herrera and P. De Greiff (eds.), *Razones de la Justicia* (Universidad Nacional Autonoma de Mexico Press, 2005), pp. 151–176.

[13] LaCapra uses this term in "Representing the Holocaust," p. 111.

community of historians that can and often does achieve something approaching unanimity with regard to how the available sources bear upon the plausibility of this or that interpretation.[14] And, as Saul Friedlander, Carlo Ginzburg, Jürgen Habermas, and others have argued concerning the historians' debate over the Holocaust, if non-foundationalist practices of objectivity and truth were not possible, there would be no lies, and might would make right, from which there could be no appeal to the evidence of historical inquiry.

The question of objectivity raises moral and ethical as well as epistemic issues; representations of the past can be faulted not only for their lies, distortions, or half-truths, but also for the unfairness they show and injustice they do to the victims of history. This can be seen, for instance, in the use, misuse, or nonuse a historian makes of the victims' own testimonies and narratives, in how she or he "negotiates" the relationships among the competing "micronarratives" of perpetrators, victims, and onlookers, and between them and her or his own "macronarrative."[15] And the results of those negotiations have to be submitted to the scholarly community at large, where they will be renegotiated in the light of other judgments of fairness and ethical-political senses of solidarity. This becomes especially pressing when the descendants of victims live among "us" and experience disrespect for past suffering as a failure of solidarity in the present. As historical scholarship intersects with ethical-political debates about who "we" are and want to be as a people, about what is really in the common good and general interest, questions of doing justice to the victims of the past interpenetrate with questions of inclusion and exclusion in the present. Pablo De Greiff has put this point as follows: "we have an obligation to remember what our fellow citizens cannot be expected to forget," in the normative sense of what we cannot reasonably expect them to forget.[16]

What are we to make *politically* of these efforts to come to terms with the past? It is impossible to weigh their effects on West German political culture with any precision. There is no doubt in anyone's mind that the changes have been considerable. But how much of that is due to the external imposition of a democratic constitutional order and international

---

[14] This is a point argued by Martin Jay in "Of Plots, Witnesses, and Judgments," in Friedlander (ed.), *Probing the Limits of Representation*, pp. 97–107.

[15] This is the terminology of Martin Jay in the essay cited in the previous note.

[16] In a discussion of "the duty to remember": "El deber de recordar," in *Razones de la Justicia*, pp. 191–221.

pressure on its internal affairs, how much to the German "economic miracle" and widespread prosperity, how much to countless other factors not directly connected with the *Aufarbeitung der Vergangenheit*, as Adorno called it, is difficult to say. On the other hand, we do have two strong comparative indicators of the political-cultural importance of publicly dealing with the Nazi past: Austria and East Germany. In Austria, which after the war represented itself as the passive victim of German aggression, there were never more than superficial gestures in that direction. And the results have been clear for all to see. Though it too is democratic and prosperous, its politics has been haunted by specters of its Nazi past. At the end of the 1980s, for instance, when Kurt Waldheim was elected President *after* it was disclosed that he had lied about his wartime past – he had joined the German Army in 1938 and later served with units that were involved in war crimes in Yugoslavia and Greece – and *in spite of* the anti-Semitic overtones of his campaign, the return of the repressed was unmistakable. And under Jörg Haider, the Austrian Freedom Party rapidly rose to prominence in the 1990s, regularly garnering about one-quarter of the popular vote and eventually joining in a ruling coalition with the conservative Austrian People's Party. That it could do so on the basis of an anti-foreigner platform and accompanied by an only partly veiled anti-Semitic rhetoric elicited shocks of recognition in the rest of Europe. By contrast, West Germany's neonationalist and xenophobic Republican Party, under Franz Schönhuber, enjoyed a comparatively brief rise at the end of the 1980s and to only a fraction of the height.

Yet closer to home, the fall of the Berlin Wall in 1989 and the hasty unification of East and West Germany in 1990 provide another comparative perspective. For unlike the Federal Republic of Germany, the German Democratic Republic dealt only superficially with its Nazi past. The official legitimation of the postwar communist regime as the triumph and rule of anti-fascist forces supposedly made that unnecessary. And after unification, it was the Stalinist and post-Stalinist past that occupied public attention. But here, too, the return of the repressed was unmistakable. The anti-foreigner violence that exploded in the early 1990s and the generally xenophobic character of East German political culture made it clear that they had never worked through their Nazi past. It is, of course, true that after 1990 the process of reshaping an enlarged national identity for Germany as a whole was accompanied by widespread symptoms of political-cultural backsliding, including surges of neonationalism and xenophobia, and troubling appearances of anti-Semitism. But the worst of that came in the early 1990s, when the Christian Democrats exploited the conflict potential generated by the vastly altered and deeply asymmetrical political situation to put the issues of asylum, immigration, and "guest workers" at the top of the public agenda; and even then, it was much worse in the East than the West. In the West, the spontaneous popular protests against anti-foreigner violence, the rising opposition to nativist politics, and the continuing hold on the public mind of a civic nationalism defined by the liberal and democratic principles of the Basic Law made clear how great the discontinuities with the past had become. This is not to say that Germany has fully "mastered" its Nazi past; there is ample indication that this is certainly not the case. It is only to say that the politics of memory practiced there since the 1960s has had a profound effect upon its political culture and national identity.

II

Using the process of coming to terms with the past in postwar Germany to gain another perspective on the politics of the memory of slavery in the USA might seem, on the face of it, to be a stretch. After all, it has been a century and a half since the end of slavery, and there have already been several rounds of intense public debate concerning it, in varying political circumstances, from post-Civil War Reconstruction to the post-World War II civil rights movement. And yet, as historians of professional and public history have made clear, the politics of memory on this subject went badly from the time that 4 million, mostly penniless, propertyless, jobless, and illiterate former slaves were set adrift in the post-Civil War South. After a brief, fiercely contested period of Reconstruction ending in 1877, the price paid for reunion was the reestablishment of white supremacy in the states of the former Confederacy.[17] As it has sometimes been put, the South lost the war but won the peace. And part of winning the peace was a reversal of the usual rule that victors in war get to write the history: the professional and public history of slavery, the Civil War, and Reconstruction were

---

[17] See Eric Foner, *A Short History of Reconstruction* (New York: Harper & Row, 1990); and David W. Blight, *Race and Reunion* (Cambridge, MA: Harvard University Press, 2001).

dominated by pro-Southern, anti-black perspectives until after World War II. Only since the rise of the postwar civil rights movement has that hegemony been overturned among professional historians (A); but central issues remain unresolved in public historical consciousness (B).

A. One might suppose that with the founding of the American Historical Association in 1884, racist historiography would have waned as professional historians began to replace their amateur predecessors. But prior to World War I, "scientific" views of race in America were, as we saw in the previous chapter, largely based on "scientific" – biological, anthropological – racism. And historiographic "impartiality" in post-Reconstruction America took the form of avoiding "partiality" against the antebellum South in the interest of sectional reconciliation.[18] Especially after the generation of historians who had living memories of the war and Reconstruction was displaced by generations who didn't, the aim of building a national community of professional historians, free of sectional conflict, motivated the negotiation of a consensual version of slavery and its aftermath. And abetted by the pervasive racism of the period – in the North and West as well as in the South, and across the boundaries of social class and political party – professional historians did in fact manage to achieve a high degree of historiographic agreement along racist and nationalist lines. This included a romanticized version of antebellum plantation life with softened images of slavery, a depiction of abolitionists and Radical Republicans as extremist agitators, and an account of the outrages of Reconstruction, replete with Southern white "scalawags," grasping Northern "carpetbaggers," and impudent black freedmen – that is, just the sorts of views that were disseminated to the nation at large in Thomas Dixon's fictional *The Clansman* (1907), D. W. Griffith's film version of it, *The Birth of a Nation* (1915), Claude G. Bowers' popular history of Reconstruction, *The Tragic Era* (1928), and countless other widely received portrayals.

In this process of historiographic consensus formation, there was considerably more give on the Northern side than on the Southern. One reason for this was the pervasive racism of Northern historians in this period, fostered by the rise not only of "scientific" racism and social

---

[18] See Peter Novick, *That Noble Dream* (Cambridge University Press, 1988), chap. 3, "Consensus and Legitimation." The remarks on the historiography of slavery that follow draw on Novick's account.

Darwinism, but also of American expansionism, Anglo-Saxonism, and consciousness of the white man's "civilizing mission."[19] Another was the large number of Southern historians working in the North and the virtual absence of Northern historians employed in the South.[20] Thus there were "no southern centers of pro-northern historiography to compare with [William A.] Dunning's Reconstruction seminar at Columbia, which attracted scores of southern students, who under Dunning's direction turned out a stream of studies" that dominated Reconstruction historiography for decades.[21] And Southern historians employed in the South worked under very strong constraints to hold to the received version of slavery and its aftermath. Black historians dissented, to be sure, but their work was marginalized in the profession by the white mainstream – John Hope Franklin was the first black historian to receive a regular appointment at a white institution, in 1956 – and was consigned to non-mainstream venues, particularly the *Journal of Negro History* founded in 1916.[22]

In the interwar period, especially in the 1930s, this ruling consensus, while remaining dominant, came under increasingly sharp attacks from different corners of the rapidly expanding ideological spectrum – not only from racial egalitarians, black and white, but also from Northern and Southern liberals, and from Marxists and other left intellectuals.[23] There were a number of influences at work here – the new antiracist anthropology and post-Mendelian genetics, which challenged scientific racism; the repellent harshness of Southern racism as epitomized in the numerous lynchings; the critical interpretive frameworks provided by left political and social thought; and the rise of a new generation of dissident historians, North and South. But despite the breakdown in consensus, no alternative synthesis appeared until after World War II. Thus, the overtly racist views of slavery propounded in the extremely influential work of Ulrich B. Phillips had no effective competitors and were still being incorporated into best-selling textbooks like that

---

[19] See chapter 3 for relevant details.
[20] Included among the former was Woodrow Wilson, who was born in Virginia in 1856 and grew to adulthood during Reconstruction.
[21] Novick, *That Noble Dream*, p. 78.
[22] One exception to this rule was an article by W. E. B. Du Bois, "Reconstruction and Its Benefits," which appeared in the *American Historical Review* 15 (1910): 781–799.
[23] See Novick, *That Noble Dream*, chap. 8, "Divergence and Dissent."

coauthored by Samuel Eliot Morison and Henry Steel Commager in 1930, with numerous subsequent editions.[24] Similarly, the dominant view of Reconstruction propounded by Dunning and his students – who represented it as a regime of humiliation imposed on the prostate South by vindictive radicals and valiantly resisted by the knights of the Ku Klux Klan – came under attack but was not displaced, and it informed public consciousness through incorporation into popular fiction, film, and history. Again, the views of black historians, some of whom were now Harvard-trained professionals, were disregarded by most orthodox historians of the South – and that includes the views advanced by W. E. B. Du Bois in his monumental *Black Reconstruction* (1935).[25]

Despite the continuing dominance of the racist orthodoxy, however, the underlying consensus among historians gave way in the interwar years to a conflict of interpretations. And the new anti-racist synthesis toward which dissident historians began pointing in the 1930s finally took shape and achieved dominance after World War II. The horrors perpetrated by the Nazis under the banner of racial superiority and inferiority, the decline of scientific racism and social Darwinism, the worldwide breakup of colonial empires, the exigencies of international competition during the Cold War, and the rise of the civil rights movement gave wind to the writings of younger, heterodox historians who were formed in the interwar years. Works by historians of that generation, North and South, who were committed to racial equality began to

[24] S. E. Morison and H. S. Commager, *The Growth of the American Republic* (Oxford University Press, 1930). Novick cites the following passage (*That Noble Dream*, p. 229): "Sambo, whose wrongs moved the abolitionists to wrath and tears ... suffered less than any other class in the South from its 'peculiar institution' ... There was much to be said for slavery as a transitional status between barbarism and civilization." On p. 350, n. 46, Novick reports that in the 1950s, "Protests by Negro students and others at the City College of New York were ultimately successful in ending the use of [this text] in classes because of its racist characterizations of Negroes."

[25] W. E. B. Du Bois, *Black Reconstruction in America, 1860–1880* (New York: Atheneum, 1935); reprinted with an introduction by David Levering Lewis in 1992. In the concluding chapter of that work, "The Propaganda of History," Du Bois provided an impassioned overview of post-Reconstruction historiography, including then current textbooks: "This chapter, therefore, which in logic should be a survey of books and sources, becomes of sheer necessity an arraignment of American historians and an indictment of their ideals" (p. 725). The story of slavery, the Civil War, Reconstruction, and post-Reconstruction the historians present "may be inspiring, but it is certainly not the truth. And beyond that it is dangerous" (p. 723).

appear in the 1950s and by the close of the 1960s had completely transformed the *historiography*, but not yet the public memory, of slavery, the Civil War, Reconstruction, and post-Reconstruction.

B. The politics of the *public memory* of slavery and its aftermath was already in full swing in the 1880s and 1890s, driven by many of the same forces that drove historical scholarship and in much the same direction. The memory of the Civil War was particularly contested, for the meaning conferred on that great conflict in the nation's past was perceived to be closely connected with competing visions of the nation's future. In the end, "race" lost out to "reunion."[26] The demands of sectional reconciliation were met by figuring the Civil War as a fight between valorous brothers, while leaving the slavery and emancipation that were its cause and outcome in the shadows. This configuration also presented fewer obstacles to the reestablishment of white supremacy in the South, which generally met with less and less resistance as racism intensified in all regions of the country, and the Republicans, in order to hold on to their Northern white constituency, increasingly distanced themselves from the politics of racial equality. By the time of the fiftieth anniversary of the battle of Gettysburg in 1913, the central public commemoration could be staged as a "Great Reunion" among thousands of white veterans from both armies, with scarcely a mention of the Emancipation Proclamation, whose fiftieth anniversary also fell in that year. As the *Baltimore Afro-American Ledger* summed up the situation at that time: "Today the South is in the saddle, and with the single exception of slavery, everything it fought for during the days of the Civil War, it has gained by repression of the Negro within its borders. And the North has quietly allowed it to have its own way."[27]

The last line proved to be an underestimation of the situation. That same year, the newly inaugurated Woodrow Wilson, in collaboration with the newly elected, Southern Democrat-dominated House and Senate, initiated a policy of racial segregation in federal government agencies, a policy that eventually expanded, especially under the New Deal, to include most federally sponsored programs in employment, training, and housing, among others, as well as in federal prisons and,

---

[26] See Blight, *Race and Reunion*.

[27] July 5, 1913. Cited in D. Blight, "Quarrel Forgotten or a Revolution Remembered?" in D. Blight and B. Simpson (eds.), *Union and Emancipation* (Kent State University Press, 1997), p. 175.

as previously, in the armed services.[28] That is to say, from that point until the 1950s or 1960s, federal agencies were not only a prime locus of racial segregation but also enforcers of the "separate but equal" dispensation and propagators of it throughout the land. And, as W. E. B. Du Bois noted in 1935, a segregated society required a segregated historical memory: there was a "searing of the memory" in America by white supremacist historiography and a public consciousness that had "obliterated" the black experience and the meaning of emancipation.[29]

Given the enormous shift in the historiography of slavery and its aftermath since the 1960s, one might expect, especially in the wake of the civil rights movement, a similar shift to have taken place in public memory. And there have, to be sure, also been important changes in the latter; but those who study popular uses of history have repeatedly noted a significant gap between academic and public historical consciousness of these matters. "Generally Americans believe that slavery was a Southern phenomenon, date it from the antebellum period, and do not think of it as central to the American story." They are generally ignorant of the fact that "by the time of the Revolution it had become a significant economic and social institution in every one of the thirteen colonies and would remain so in every region of the new nation well into the nineteenth century."[30] Moreover, many think of legally institutionalized racial oppression as ending with emancipation and know rather little about racial relations in the post-Reconstruction South; and most are quite ignorant of institutionalized racism in the rest of the country – for instance, of the roles it played in the formation of the American working class in the nineteenth century, in structuring immigration policy and citizenship law throughout US history, and in the policies and programs of the federal government in the twentieth century.[31] With the German discussions in mind, one might be tempted to say that

---

[28] See Desmond King, *Separate and Unequal: Black Americans and the US Federal Government* (Oxford University Press, 1995).

[29] The phrases in quotes come from the last chapter of Du Bois, *Black Reconstruction in America*, pp. 725 and 723.

[30] James Oliver Horton, "Presenting Slavery: The Perils of Telling America's Racial Story," *The Public Historian* 21 (1999): 21. He refers, for instance, to the fitting out of slave ships in New England and the financing of the slave trade by New York and Pennsylvania merchants.

[31] See David R. Roediger, *The Wages of Whiteness: Race and the Making of the American Working Class* (London: Verso, 1999); Matthew Frye Jacobson,

though the US *Historikerstreit* concerning slavery and its aftermath effectively ended, at least in regard to fundamentals, in the 1960s and 1970s, the public *Aufarbeitung der Vergangenheit* has only just begun.[32]

A number of different reasons are offered for the lag in public historical consciousness. To begin with, there is a clear popular preference for history that confirms rather than confronts positive portrayals of the nation's past. Thus in public memory, the "master narrative" of American history remains largely unshaken: "a national history teleologically bound to the Founders' ideals rather than their reality," an "inexorable development of free institutions and the expansion of political liberty," in which racial slavery and oppression are treated as regional "aberrations – historical accidents to be corrected in the progressive upward reach of the nation's destiny."[33] And then there is the appalling state of history instruction in the public schools: "much of the best and latest scholarship never reaches high-school students because most high-school history courses are taught by teachers with inadequate training in history … In Louisiana, 88 percent of the students who take history in high school are taught by teachers who have not even a college minor in history. In Minnesota, the proportion is 83 percent, in West Virginia 82 percent, in Oklahoma 81 percent, in Pennsylvania, 73 percent, in Kansas 72 percent." Similarly, in Maryland, Arizona, South Dakota, and Mississippi, the percentages are 70 percent or greater.[34] Nor is this failure generally remedied at the post-secondary level: US history courses are not required, even for liberal arts degrees, in more than four-fifths of the colleges and universities. But the most frequently mentioned reason for the gap is the continuing volatility of race relations: talk about racial injustice in the past is typically

Whiteness of a Different Color: European Immigrants and the Alchemy of Race (Cambridge, MA: Harvard University Press, 1998); Rogers M. Smith, *Civic Ideals: Conflicting Visions of Citizenship in U.S. History* (New Haven: Yale University Press, 1997); and King, *Separate and Unequal.*

[32] This is not to deny the continuing disagreements among professional historians of race, which Novick recounts in *That Noble Dream*, pp. 469–491; it is only to say that the white-supremacist historiography that was hegemonic from the end of Reconstruction through World War II is no longer a viable option.

[33] Nathan Irwin Huggins, *Black Odyssey* (New York: Vintage Books, 1990), p. xii.

[34] Horton, "Presenting Slavery," p. 23. Jonathan Zimmerman summed up the situation in an op-ed piece for the *New York Times*, July 11, 2001: "Across the country, about 54 percent of history students in grades 7 to 12 are taught by teachers who have neither a major nor a minor in history" (p. A21).

experienced, by both blacks and whites, as being also about the present, and reacted to accordingly. This is not only the case in the South, though the heightened activism of Southern heritage groups has exacerbated the difficulties there;[35] it holds for whites across the country, and for blacks as well.[36] In short, relations to the passions and interests of the present are integral to the politics of the memory of racial injustice and have to be addressed as such.

Like Germany and so many other countries, the USA too has a past that is still present, that refuses to pass away. It is just this continuing presence of the past that the politics of public memory seeks to address. This type of cultural politics is, of course, not new. It is practiced every day by public historians, museum curators, artists, writers, journalists, and others in mass communication; it is a familiar element of local and national politics; and it has historically resulted in various forms of institutionalized memory. I am attempting here only to delineate more sharply and underline more emphatically its irreplaceable role in US political life. Until legal, institutional, normal, everyday racism is publicly and widely understood to have been *integral* to US history and identity as a nation, Americans will likely continue to encounter major obstacles to developing the degree of transracial political solidarity required for democratic solutions to the forms of racial injustice that are its continuing legacy. Without a developed awareness of the sources and causes of US racialized practices and attitudes, Americans will likely continue to find it extremely difficult even to carry on reasonable public discussions of racially inflected problems, let alone arrive at just and feasible solutions to them.

The United States has, of course, historically been a land of immigration, and that complicates the politics of memory considerably. The diversity of subject positions in US society is marked not only by the

[35] The ongoing controversies about the public use of the Confederate flag are obvious indications of this. There are many others. Horton ("Presenting Slavery") relates that when John Latschar, park superintendent at Gettysburg National Battlefield, suggested in a public lecture that the Civil War may have been fought over slavery, "the Southern Heritage Coalition condemned his words, and 1,100 postcards calling for his immediate removal flooded the Office of the Secretary of the Interior" (p. 26).

[36] As the simmering volatility of race during the recent (2008) presidential election indicates. The wisdom of preserving the memory of slavery has long been debated among black intellectuals, by Alexander Crummell and Frederick Douglass, for instance, as by Booker T. Washington and W. E. B. Du Bois.

differences of class, age, gender, and so forth found in any society, and by black/white racial differences and North/South sectional differences. It also includes positions connected with the conquest, settlement, and expansion of America, and with the policies and practices of US immigration. What does the politics of memory mean, for instance, to the large numbers of recent immigrants from Asia and Latin America whose cultural memories take them back to other worlds? I cannot even begin to sort out these immense complications here; but I do want to argue that the responsibility to come to terms with the past of slavery and segregation is borne by the political community as a whole, regardless of ancestry. This is so not only because the horrors perpetrated were generally state-sanctioned and frequently state-implemented, that is to say, were corporate evils for which there is corporate responsibility; nor only because naturalized citizens who expect to share in the inherited benefits of a continuing enterprise must also share in its inherited liabilities. It is also because immigrant groups, whatever their prior background, unavoidably become members of the same racialized polity to which all US citizens' futures are tied. More specifically, the black/white polarity has fixed the geography of the color-coded world to which successive waves of immigrants have had to adapt; there is no comprehending the bizarre ethnoracial categories into which they have been and still are forced apart from that polarization and its effective history. This is not at all to deny that Americans of diverse origins have their own histories to relate and their own politics of memory to pursue. It is merely to suggest that the history of slavery and its aftermath has formed a template for those histories, that they have been shaped by it, and that their fates have been inextricably entangled in the racialized politics that is its legacy.

This broad and deep diversity of subject positions is sure to be reflected in the democratic politics of public memory – in rival narratives, conflicts of interpretation, and other forms of cultural-political contestation. There is no need for unanimity here, for one substantive version of the American past to which all parties subscribe; but if there is to be public communication across differences, citizens do have to see themselves as members of the same political project, defined in part by overlapping interpretations of constitutional rights, principles, and values. This is not a matter of returning to pure origins or foundations; there can be no reasonable doubt that the United States' foundations were fractured from the start. But it is also not a matter of simply condemning them, or burying them forever under heaps of criticism. It was, after all, the common motley of religious and philosophical ideas that was used to justify both slavery and abolition, both segregation and its dismantling. The politics of memory has to identify those deep tensions and ambivalence in Americans' political-cultural heritage and trace the ways in which ideas implicated in injustice could, upon critical reinterpretation, serve as resources for attacking it. It has to comprehend how black Americans struggling for freedom and equality were able to invoke putatively universal rights and principles and argue that they were being betrayed – how, in Judith Butler's formulation, they could "seize the language of the universal and set into motion a 'performative contradiction,' claiming to be covered by it and thereby exposing the contradictory character" of hegemonic formulations.[37]

Successive waves of immigrants have also been able to tap into that political-cultural heritage to gain a place for themselves in American society. However, because of the polarized force-field of racial relations pervading it, they did so not only by tapping into the critical potential of universalistic ideals but also by making strategic use of their dominant, exclusionary interpretations.[38] An inclusionary politics of memory would today have to be conceived as a multiracial, multiethnic, multicultural dialogue aiming not at unanimity but at mutual comprehension, mutual recognition, and mutual respect. Anglo-assimilationism is in its death throes; the idea of a mosaic of self-enclosed subcultures is a non-starter; what is left to us, it seems, are versions of an interactive and accommodative diversity of forms of life, with an overarching democratic political culture that leaves room for ongoing contestation,

---

[37] Judith Butler, *Excitable Speech* (New York: Routledge, 1997), p. 89. See also, Patricia J. Williams, "Alchemical Notes: Reconstructing Ideals from Deconstructed Rights," in R. Delgado and J. Stefancic (ed.), *Critical Race Theory* (Philadelphia: Temple University Press, 2000), pp. 80–90; and Smith, *Civic Ideals*.

[38] As Dilip Gaonkar has elaborated in conversation, this tension presents peculiar problems for those contemporary "model minorities" who, unlike earlier European immigrants, get reracialized not as white but as "Asian American," thus marking another dimension of the American racial topography. The other side of their higher standing in some spheres (e.g. education, employment) is their marginalization in others (e.g. politics, culture). For such minorities, understanding America's racialized past would seem to be particularly important to comprehending and transforming their own situation. See, for instance, Claire Jean Kim, *Bitter Fruit: The Politics of Black–Korean Conflict in New York City* (New Haven: Yale University Press, 2000).

critique, and reinterpretation of its basic principles and values.[39] For this to come to pass, however, African Americans must be able to participate as equal partners in public life and public discourse. But this means that much will have to change in the massively unequal conditions of life and politics that have historically muted their voices.[40] So we seem to be caught again in a familiar circle.

In the concluding section, I want to take a brief look at one way a politics of public memory might help us to break out of it. To forestall possible misunderstandings: I am certainly *not* claiming that the politics of memory exhausts the politics of race. The furthest thing from my mind is to deny the importance of social-structural factors, group interests, social dominance, or the like. Nor do I harbor the slightest doubt that psychodynamic and socio-psychological factors are especially virulent in this domain. Nor, as I hope my discussions of the dialectic of past, present, and future in sections I and II have made clear, do I think that the past can be separated off, either in theory or in practice, from the present and future. My selective focus on historical consciousness is for analytical purposes only.

III

Politics in America has been racialized from the start; and even after the successes of the civil rights movement, race remains – as the vicissitudes of the Obama campaign indicated – one of "our nation's most difficult subject[s]."[41] On the one hand, there has been an extensive liberalization

---

[39] See J. Habermas, "Struggles for Recognition in the Democratic Constitutional State," in *Multiculturalism*, ed. Amy Gutman (Princeton University Press, 1994), 1–7–148; and Robert Gooding-Williams, "Race, Multiculturalism, and Democracy," *Constellations* 5 (1998): 18–41.

[40] Even today, shockingly large numbers of African Americans are effectively disenfranchised by one means or another. For instance, in 2004 about one black male in seven was legally disenfranchised through felony conviction. (See J. Manza and C. Uggen, *Locked Out: Felony Disenfranchisement and American Democracy* [Oxford University Press, 2007].) On the general sources and significance of "deliberative inequalities," see James Bohman, *Public Deliberation* (Cambridge, MA: MIT Press, 1996), chap. 3, and J. Bohman, "Deliberative Democracy and Effective Social Freedom: Capabilities, Resources, and Opportunities," in J. Bohman and W. Rehg (eds.), *Deliberative Democracy* (Cambridge, MA: MIT Press, 1997), pp. 321–348.

[41] Donald R. Kinder and Lynn M. Sanders, *Divided by Color* (University of Chicago Press, 1996), p. 11. I draw on empirical material provided by Kinder and Sanders

of white attitudes toward racial equality since the 1950s. The great majority of whites are now opposed *in principle* to segregation and discrimination against blacks and in favor of integration, equal opportunity, and freedom of choice in employment, schooling, housing, and the like. On the other hand, when it comes to government policies and programs meant to implement these principles, agreement breaks down. So, to begin with, we have to try to grasp the nature and sources of this discrepancy. There is substantial empirical evidence indicating that among the most important sources of disagreement on such matters is the degree of "racial resentment": the greater the resentment whites feel toward blacks, the greater the likelihood they will be opposed to racially inflected remedial measures.[42] As noted earlier, since the 1950s biological racism has increasingly given way to a kind of ethnocultural racism expressed in psychological and cultural stereotypes.[43] The view that blacks suffer disproportionately from character defects of various

in the analysis of racial politics that follows. For a broader survey of views on the role of race in American politics, see the collection *Racialized Politics: The Debate about Racism in America*, ed. D. O. Sears, J. Sidanius, and L. Bobo (University of Chicago Press, 2000).

[42] This is the view of Kinder and Sanders: "On equal opportunity in employment, school desegregation, federal assistance, affirmative action at work, and quotas in college admissions, racially resentful whites line up on one side of the issue, and racially sympathetic whites line up on the other. Racial resentment is not the *only* thing that matters, but *by a fair margin racial resentment is the most important*" (Kinder and Sanders, *Divided by Color*, p. 124, emphasis in original). For an alternative view that places perceived group positions and interests at the center of the politics of race, see Lawrence Bobo, "Racial Beliefs about Affirmative Action: Assessing the Effects of Interests, Group Threat, Ideology, and Racism," in Sears *et al.* (eds.), *Racialized Politics*, 137–164. For another version of the social-structural approach that stresses the role of race in stratification hierarchies, see Jim Sidanius and Felicia Pratto, *Social Dominance: An Intergroup Theory of Social Hierarchy and Oppression* (Cambridge University Press, 1999). Admittedly, to the extent that the politics of race is driven by the protection of group interests or the maintenance of social dominance, it would be less susceptible to amelioration by a politics of memory; beliefs in racial superiority/ inferiority would be secondary factors – *merely* ideological justifications for existing inequalities in the distribution of material and symbolic resources – whereas the line I pursue gives some independent force to such beliefs. It seems probable that all of these factors, and more, are at work in our racialized politics and that effective political action in this domain will have to address all of them. My characterization of these opposing positions is indebted to Derrick Darby's discussion in "Blacks and Rights," *Law, Culture, and the Humanities* (2006): 420–439.

[43] Not completely, of course, as the hubbub around *The Bell Curve* by Richard J. Herrnstein and Charles Murphy (New York: Free Press, 1994) indicates.

sorts appears to be quite widespread among whites.[44] And this fits with the equally widespread view that the socioeconomic disadvantages of African Americans are largely the result of their possessing too little of the crucial economic-individualistic virtues – motivation, self-discipline, hard work, and the like – that enabled Irish, German, Italian, Jewish, and other minorities to overcome prejudice and work their ways up. On this view, too many blacks prefer to depend on government handouts rather than trying to make it on their own, thus adding to the list of missing virtues "independence" and "self-reliance." There is, of course, a great deal of variation in opinion among whites on these matters, with a significant proportion rejecting altogether this line of reasoning and the stereotypes on which it depends. And even within the majority that accepts them, there are wide variations in the strength with which they are held and, presumably, their susceptibility to influence by evidence, argument, and experience. But there is no doubt that, overall, what George M. Frederickson called "the black image in the white mind" is still a major determinant of views on racial policies.

Two other important factors are whether discrimination is believed to be a thing of the past, and whether the history of slavery and segregation is taken to be a major cause of the inequalities African Americans suffer under at present. Most blacks answer no to the first and yes to the second, and in fact prominently cite these factors in justifying policies aimed at remedying racial inequalities; whereas most, though by no means all, whites do the opposite.[45] And that difference is consequential: the beliefs that racial discrimination has been eliminated and that "the playing field is now level," but that blacks, owing to weaknesses of culture and character, persist in seeking handouts, and that they thereby claim and receive unfair advantages over whites, are further ingredients in the racial resentment syndrome of attitudes that is such a strong indicator of views on racial policies. There are other important elements, some so improbable that one hesitates to introduce them, but at the same time so often noted that one can't simply ignore them. Orlando Patterson reports them as "misperceptions": "Only

---

[44] Kinder and Sanders, *Divided by Color*, chap. 5.

[45] *Ibid.* A similar divide is reported by Sears, Sidanius, and Bobo in *Racialized Politics*, pp. 9–16, drawing upon the extensive survey analyses of Howard Schuman, Charlotte Steeh, Lawrence Bobo, and Maria Krysan in *Racial Attitudes in America: Trends and Interpretations*, rev. ed. (Cambridge, MA: Harvard University Press, 1997).

31 percent of Euro-Americans believe that Afro-Americans have less opportunity to live a middle-class life than they do, compared with 71 percent of Afro-Americans [who believe this]. Most extraordinary of all, 58 percent of Euro-Americans think that the average Afro-American is as well off or better off than Euro-Americans in their income and housing condition."[46]

Even these sketchy remarks may be sufficient to identify one important contribution that a politics of the memory of slavery and segregation might make to the larger politics of race in our society. Persistent racial injustices cannot be addressed by government action without significant support from whites. Opponents of such action are able to tap into, and simultaneously add to, a large reservoir of racial resentment by representing proposed policies as violations of the basic principles and values of American individualism and thus as promoting undeserved and unfair advantages for blacks at the expense of non-blacks. In the give and take of a democratic public sphere, it is typically the case that complex issues can and will be interpreted, contextualized, framed – or "spun" – in different and competing ways. And there is a lot at stake in which frame predominates in public discourse, for that determines the definition of the problem, decides what is central and marginal to it, and circumscribes its justified and feasible resolutions. In the case at hand, effectively recontextualizing the racial issues of today as the latest chapter in the continuing story of slavery and its aftermath could be an important means of countering attempts to tap into the reservoir of racial resentment and of diminishing that reservoir itself. But for that to happen, the general level of historical consciousness in the public culture would have to be much higher than it is.

Let me illustrate this general approach by sketching in broad outline one explanatory narrative that is critical to contemporary debates about racial inequality, in that it seeks to account for the formation and persistence of the urban black ghettos that figure so centrally in the etiology of racial disparities.[47] What has to be explained is the fact that

---

[46] Orlando Patterson, *The Ordeal of Integration* (Washington, DC: Civitas, 1997), 57.

[47] The sketch offered here draws on the work of Douglas S. Massey and Nancy A. Denton, *American Apartheid: Segregation and the Making of the Underclass* (Cambridge, MA: Harvard University Press, 1993), and King, *Separate and Unequal*. I do not wish to imply that this narrative is uncontested; it would have to be defended in public debate; but that is precisely what is required to raise historical consciousness in a democratic public sphere.

"black [residential] segregation is not comparable to the limited and transient segregation experienced by other racial and ethnic groups, now or in the past. No group in the history of the United States has ever experienced the sustained high level of residential segregation that has been imposed on blacks in large American cities."[48] The bare essentials are as follows. From the end of the Civil War to the start of World War I, roughly one-half million blacks migrated to the North. Before 1900, however, nothing like urban black ghettos resulted. Ghettoization began with the "great migration" that accompanied accelerated industrialization and urbanization, and the outbreak of war, in the first part of the twentieth century. From 1910 to 1940, roughly 1.8 million blacks migrated from South to North and from farm to city. The reaction of Northern whites to this rising tide of black arrivals was a marked upsurge in hostility, violence, and exclusion. "[L]evels of residential segregation between blacks and whites began a steady rise ... [and] by World War II the foundations of the modern ghetto had been laid in virtually every Northern city."[49] If urban black ghettos were already taking shape by 1940, during the next three decades they acquired many of their contemporary characteristics. From 1940 to 1970 roughly 4.5 million blacks migrated from South to North. Through the 1940s they were moving to urban areas with rather fixed and limited supplies of housing, and ghetto expansion proved to be difficult. During the 1950s and 1960s, by contrast, there was a boom in residential housing construction and a rapid suburbanization of the white middle class, who deserted the inner cites in increasing numbers. The combination of white suburban flight and continuing black migration (nearly 3 million during these two decades) led to a massive increase in the size of the ghettos. Between 1950 and 1970 the percentage of blacks more than doubled in most large Northern cities, while the index of "residential dissimilarity" (the segregation measure) remained extraordinarily high. Blacks and whites lived in almost wholly separate neighborhoods, and in increasingly separate worlds.

This brief survey of a few important dates and figures outlines a process but offers no real explanation for it, other than a passing

---

[48] Massey and Denton, *American Apartheid*, p. 2. On p. 49 they point out that by 1970 the *lowest* level of spatial isolation observed for blacks in *any* major city, North or South, was greater than the *highest* isolation indexes *ever* recorded for *any* other groups in *any* American city!

[49] *Ibid.*, pp. 30–31.

mention of white racial prejudice. In addition to the aggregate effects of unorganized actions ranging from home sales to random violence and spontaneous riots, important factors in the formation of the black ghetto from 1910 to 1940 included: organized communal violence that drove blacks, particularly integrated elites, out of white areas and into the emerging black ghettos (e.g. bombings, targeted violence, white race riots); the formation of "neighborhood improvement associations" to maintain the residential color line (e.g. through lobbying for zoning changes or boycotting businesses and real estate agents that served blacks); the implementation (typically through such associations) of "restrictive covenants" (enforced by the courts until 1948) excluding blacks from purchasing specific properties; the activities of local real estate boards in maintaining residential color lines, supported by official policies of the National Association of Real Estate Brokers;[50] and the refusal of most white-owned banks to make home loans to black applicants.

For my purposes, however, the salient factor was the expanded role of the federal government in promoting racial segregation, which was due in no small measure to the disproportional power of Southern Democrats in Congress. Desmond King provides a detailed account of how segregation and discrimination were institutionalized in the federal system after 1913, and of how the federal government became one of the principal instruments for propagating them throughout the country, especially through its segregated programs of assistance and training, including those of the New Deal:

In the decades before the Civil Rights Act of 1964, the Federal government used its power to impose a pattern of segregated race relations among its employees and, through its programs (such as housing and employment services), upon the whole of American society well beyond the Mason-Dixon line. This pattern structured the relationship between ordinary Black Americans and the US Federal government – whether as employees in government agencies, inmates or officers in Federal prisons, inductees in the Armed Services, consumers of federally guaranteed mortgages, job-seekers in USES [United States Employment Service] offices, or visitors to National Parks in

---

[50] Until 1950, the code of ethics of the National Association stated, "a Realtor should never be instrumental in introducing into a neighborhood … members of any race or nationality … whose presence will clearly be detrimental to property values in that neighborhood" (cited in *ibid.*, p. 37).

which the facilities were segregated (or often non-existent for Black Americans). In all these instances, segregation did not imply just separation but also profound racial inequality.[51]

In particular, the federal programs and agencies created to increase home ownership were at the same time mechanisms for excluding blacks and thus blocking a, if not the, principal avenue of wealth accumulation in the American middle class.[52]

The Home Owners Loan Corporation (HOLC), which introduced the widespread use of long-term mortgages with uniform payments, also initiated and institutionalized the practice of "redlining" black areas, that is, of routinely assigning them the worst ratings (coded red) of risks associated with loans in various neighborhoods. In this way, HOLC "lent the power, prestige, and support of the federal government to the systematic practice of racial discrimination in housing."[53] And HOLC practices became the model for other credit institutions, private as well as public. Thus, during the 1930s and 1940s private banks relied heavily on HOLC procedures, and even on its "Residential Security Maps," in designing their own "redlining" procedures. Moreover, the HOLC rating system decisively influenced the discriminatory underwriting practices of the Federal Housing Administration (FHA) and the Veterans Administration (VA), which, during the 1940s and 1950s "completely reshaped the residential housing market of the United States ... Loans made by the FHA and the VA were a major impetus behind the rapid suburbanization of the United

---

[51] *Separate and Unequal*, p. 4. For supplementation and continuation of this story, see Ira Katznelson, *When Affirmative Action Was White* (New York: W. W. Norton, 2006), which details the discriminatory character of the sweeping social programs under both Roosevelt's New Deal and Truman's Fair Deal, including the social security system, unemployment compensation, worker's compensation, and the minimum wage. Southern Congressmen purposefully excluded agricultural and domestic workers from these programs, as the areas in which most blacks were employed. They also ensured that the GI Bill of Rights, which massively expanded opportunities for returning soldiers to attend college, receive job training, start businesses, and purchase homes, among other things, was implemented to the enormous disadvantage of black veterans.

[52] Arguments for reparations often single out the black/white wealth gap – currently estimated to be about 1:6 – as a key inequity, the linking of which to past racial discrimination would justify remedial action. The approach I am sketching incorporates that gap in an expanded narrative.

[53] Massey and Denton, *American Apartheid*, p. 52.

States after 1945."[54] The overall effect of these discriminatory lending and underwriting practices was not only to lock blacks into ghettos, but also to dry up the flow of capital into those areas, which led to steep declines in property values and widespread patterns of deterioration.

And that brings us to another chapter in the formation of the urban black ghetto, as we know it today: "urban renewal." During the 1950s and 1960s, local officials, representing the interests of middle- and upper-class urban whites, sought relief for troubled cities from the federal government and received it in the form of federal funds for urban renewal, that is, for purchasing, clearing, and redeveloping slum properties, while relocating their inhabitants to public housing. These programs were used by local elites "to carry out slum clearance in growing black neighborhoods that threatened white business districts and elite institutions. ... As a result, projects were typically built on cleared land within or adjacent to existing black neighborhoods ... The replacement of low-density slums with high-density towers of poor families also reduced the class diversity of the ghetto and brought about a geographic concentration of poverty that was previously unimaginable ... This new segregation of blacks – in economic as well as social terms – was the direct result of an unprecedented collaboration between local and national government."[55]

By the time of the urban riots of the 1960s, black isolation in all major American cities was significantly greater than that of any other ethnic group. And the systematic disinvestment in black communities – aided and abetted by federal agencies – as well as the concentration of high-density housing projects within them – constructed by local authorities under federal programs – brought about an intersection of race and class that was not only unparalleled but self-perpetuating. In that situation, the economic upheavals of the 1970s – the long and deep recession, the decline in manufacturing, the suburbanization of employment, and the expansion of the low-wage service sector for unskilled workers – seriously undermined the capacity of ghetto inhabitants to support the formation of families.[56]

---

[54] *Ibid.*, p. 53. The 1939 FHA *Underwriting Manual* states, "if a neighborhood is to retain stability, it is necessary that properties shall continue to be occupied by the same social and racial class" (cited by Massey and Denton, *American Apartheid*, p. 54).

[55] Massey and Denton, *American Apartheid*, pp. 55–57.

[56] A very influential analysis of this process was provided by William Julius Wilson, *The Truly Disadvantaged: The Inner City, the Underclass, and Public Policy* (University of Chicago Press, 1987). Massey and Denton's analysis differs from Wilson's by making residential segregation the key variable. For a more widely diverging view of

One does not have to be a sociologist to appreciate the profound, and until now unbreakable, connection between the geographic concentration of poverty in urban black ghettos and the deterioration in them of educational facilities, employment opportunities, health care delivery, the security of person and property, and so on. Residential segregation "systematically undermines the social and economic well-being of blacks ... [It] concentrates poverty to build a set of mutually reinforcing and self-feeding spirals of decline into black neighborhoods ... The damaging social consequences that follow from poverty are concentrated as well, creating uniquely disadvantaged environments that become progressively isolated ... from the rest of society."[57] Moreover, residential segregation concentrates and amplifies the negative effects of economic downturns, so that black neighborhoods suffer a disproportionate share of the socioeconomic deprivation caused by such slumps.

In these and other ways, the urban black ghetto is a nodal point of the causal nexus that helped create and perpetuate an urban black "underclass." The historical-sociological account of the rise and reproduction of the former helps explain the existence and persistence of the latter – including the deep cultural and psychological alienation from mainstream America, which neoconservative intellectuals and, unfortunately, many of their fellow citizens point to as causes rather than effects or reciprocal causes/effects of black deprivation. Blaming the victims of hypersegregation for the culture of hypersegregation is getting the causal story backwards. And now, it appears, those ghettos and that underclass are self-reproducing, linked in a causal feedback loop of race and poverty; for racially defined residential segregation has a massive, negative impact upon employment opportunities, family formation, the quality of education and other public services, crime, the availability of home and business loans, and electoral power, among many other things.

This narrative sketch of the origins and development of existing patterns of residential segregation could, of course, be supplemented by overlapping and intersecting narratives about racial discrimination in other major sectors of American life, such as labor markets, educational institutions, and criminal justice systems. A corresponding public understanding of existing racial inequalities as an intergenerational

these and other matters, see Stephen and Abigail Thernstrom, *America in Black and White: One Nation, Indivisible* (New York: Simon & Schuster, 1996).
[57] Massey and Denton, *American Apartheid*, p. 2.

effect of the US's history of racial injustice would likely make a difference in the judgments of many citizens as to whether proposed measures are "deserved compensation" for discrimination or "unfair advantages." For even those generally committed to the idea of racial equality normally have to be persuaded that a particular racial policy is in truth a fair and proportionate remedy for the effects of clear and persistent injustice. And it is difficult to see how that could happen on a significant scale without a serious upgrading of public memory to provide the necessary background for public justifications of a historical sort. There is, then, a political need for historical consciousness-raising.

I shall not review here the various forms of cultural politics peculiar to the field on which public memory is contested. But in closing, I would like at least to mention one proposed vehicle of public memory: reparations claims.[58] In my view, one of the strongest arguments for the class-action lawsuits favored by the Reparations Coordinating Committee and others is that, in present circumstances, they might prove to be an effective means of igniting a "national conversation on race." On the other hand, there are a number of weighty considerations against taking this path, including the hostile political reaction it is likely to elicit in broad segments of the population. To date, one of the major stumbling blocks has been the tendency of the courts to dismiss such suits on grounds of the lack of standing of the descendants of slaves, the expiration of the statute of limitations, and the like. If no way can be found around these legal barriers, the politics of reparations is unlikely to gather the steam needed to effect the needed change, either symbolically or materially. For this and other reasons, many theorists and activists advocate class-based rather than race-based policies to deal with urban poverty. But public support for such policies is also affected by their racial subtext and the willingness of political opponents to exploit it. So it is difficult to see how an effective political response to urban poverty

---

[58] Of course, reparations are usually also aimed at materially remedying the continuing harms of past injustice. On the role of reparations in coming to terms with the past generally, see the invaluable *Handbook of Reparations*, ed. Pablo De Greiff (Oxford University Press, 2006). Among the recent monographs on the subject of reparations for slavery and segregation, see Roy L. Brooks, *Atonement and Forgiveness* (Berkeley: University of California Press, 2004), and John Arthur, *Race, Equality, and the Burdens of History* (Cambridge University Press, 2007), both of which stress the symbolic dimension of reparations. I stress the material dimension in "Coming to Terms with the Past, Part II" (see n. 3 above).

could be mounted and sustained without directly addressing the workings of racial resentment. It remains to be seen whether a black president can help the US break out of this circle.

Among nonblack Americans, the political will to deal with the catastrophic situation of the urban "underclass," particularly the millions of "truly disadvantaged" blacks living in inner-city ghettos, has proven too weak to resist the politics of racial resentment waged so effectively since the 1960s. Strengthening that political will requires diminishing the reservoir of racial resentment drawn upon in framing issues of racial policy. I have argued that a politics of the public memory of slavery and segregation is one way of contributing to that. In any case, as with *Vergangenheitsbewältigung* in Germany, it may well be the best way to assure that the descendants of the victims will be able to "breathe" more freely in the United States.

PART TWO

5 | *What may we hope? Reflections on the idea of universal history in the wake of Kant*

The philosophy of history is now widely believed to be extinct. How could anyone take seriously the idea of progress in the wake of the bloodiest century on record, in the faces of its 100 million victims? If the temptation to indulge in this genre of thought should prove too strong to resist, one might look instead to *Verfallsgeschichten* of Nietzschean or Heideggerian provenance. But it would be best if we learned to resist the temptation altogether, perhaps through assembling postmodernist reminders of the conditions of impossibility of grand metanarratives or postcolonialist reminders of the massive injustices the latter were used to underwrite, or through a Benjaminian remembrance of and solidarity with the countless, voiceless victims of "progress." And if this proves insufficient, we might recall the long-standing epistemological and methodological objections to the philosophy of history in its classical variations. The institutionalization and expansion of academic history and empirical social research, which were already underway as Hegel and Marx fashioned the culminating works of that genre, eventually rendered it infeasible.

Marx's materialist turn away from philosophy as the medium in which to comprehend history and society was subsequently continued in directions that were incompatible with the residual Hegelianism of his own constructions. To be sure, general accounts of the sociocultural development of the species as a whole did not thereby disappear; rather, they assumed the altered form of macrohistorical theories of social change – from Durkheim and Weber to Parsons and Habermas. But even such empirically based, "postmetaphysical" forms of grand metanarrative have become questionable. For one thing, the sheer mass and diversity of data, theories, methods, interpretations, and the like overpopulating all the relevant disciplinary and subdisciplinary fields of inquiry lend to the idea of constructing a universal history or unified theory of the entire species an air of hubris, if not megalomania. For another, hermeneutic reflection has taught us that theoretically generalized, historical accounts are themselves historically situated, that they belong to history rather than transcending it. Thus, social-theoretical pretensions to a contemplative grasp of the whole of history from some point of view outside or above it are no more credible today than were Hegel's philosophical ambitions later in the nineteenth century.

And yet, as the excited reception of works like Francis Fukuyama's *The End of History* indicates, the genre refuses to disappear without a trace.[1] The idea of the unity of the human race was always more than a mere idea: even in its early Christian versions, it reflected the realities of the Roman Empire; in the heyday of the philosophy of history, from the mid-eighteenth to the mid-nineteenth century, it echoed the early modern proliferation of European encounters with non-European cultures; and the connection of evolutionary theories of society with the age of empire is as evident as that of development and modernization theories with the post-World War II international order.[2] But the pace and extent of globalization in recent decades, the breathtaking compression of lived space and time – made possible by the revolution in information and communication technology and made irresistible by the expansion and intensification of global capitalism – have lent to this unity a pressure of reality beyond anything that preceded it. We can scarcely avoid thinking in global terms about the possibilities and necessities, consequences and side effects, opportunities and risks of these accelerating changes in the conditions of human life. Indeed, it has typically been in such periods of epochal change, experienced crisis, and heightened anxiety that grand theorizing about history has proved most irresistible – in the dying days of the Roman Empire, at the time of the first bourgeois revolutions, in the throes of the industrial revolution, and during the cataclysmic first-half of the

---

[1] Francis Fukuyama, *The End of History and the Last Man* (New York: Free Press, 1992). A wide-ranging symposium on Fukuyama's "end of history" thesis was organized by Danny Postal in 2006 for the *Open Democracy* website: www.openDemocracy.net.

[2] Anthony Pagden, *Lords of All the World: Ideologies of Empire in Spain, Britain, and France, c.1500–c.1800* (New Haven: Yale University Press, 1995); Mike Hawkins, *Social Darwinism in European and American Thought, 1860–1945* (Cambridge University Press, 1997); and Nils Gilman, *Mandarins of the Future: Modernization Theory in Cold War America* (Baltimore: Johns Hopkins University Press, 2003).

twentieth century. And that is not surprising, for thinking about universal history has typically been carried out, if often only tacitly, *in praktischer Absicht*, as Kant put it, in a search for practical orientation.[3]

It should also come as no surprise, then, that the flood of contemporary works on globalization are characteristically practical rather than contemplative in orientation, and as concerned with the future as with the past. For what alternative is there, in the final analysis, to the historically informed diagnoses of the present with an eye to practically possible futures that have been so much a part of modern consciousness? This appears to be an irrepressible and irreplaceable mode of thought. And if that is so, we might do well to reexamine its classical forms and remind ourselves once again of the strengths that made "grand metanarratives" so broadly influential and of the weaknesses that buried them in disrepute. The *propaedeutic* reflections that follow are offered in the belief that the postmodern dismissal of the genre was overhasty and has tended to clear the intellectual field for the neoconservative ideologists who now dominate it. The trenchant criticisms of universal-historical thinking accumulated over the past century point instead, I shall suggest, to chastened and decentered ways of going about it: modest hopes for troubled times.

I shall begin by (I) briefly reviewing the philosophy of history (a) before, (b) in, and (c, d) after Kant, and then offer (II) some thoughts on the "dialectic of progress" in those philosophies and in the general theories of social change that succeeded them. Section III takes up the singular failure of morals and politics to keep pace with the rapid development of the means of power in the modern period. The general burden of these sections is to sort out what is living and what is dead in developmental-historical thinking and to get a bit clearer about the costs and benefits of "progress." The chapter concludes with (IV) a few tentative remarks on the contemporary discourse of global modernity from the perspective of the preceding critical-historical reflections.

---

[3] In his early work, Jürgen Habermas regarded critical theory as a kind of empirically informed philosophy of history with a practical intent. I discuss this in *The Critical Theory of Jürgen Habermas* (Cambridge, MA: MIT Press, 1978), pp. 126–136.

I

My point of reference for these reflections is the Kantian idea of universal history discussed in chapter 2.[4] Kant not only appropriated, while transforming, the main lines of the philosophical theology of history that had dominated in the West since Augustine; he not only distilled and crystallized the new ways of thinking philosophically about history that were taking shape in the eighteenth century; and he not only opened some of the more important paths that universal-historical thinking would subsequently follow; but he also presented a view of such thinking as a mode of empirically informed, practically oriented, reflective judgment which, I shall suggest, provides a better indication of what might still make sense today than do the more extravagant views that followed.

(a) Prior to the Enlightenment, biological metaphors structured thinking about development, from the cyclical theories of the ancient Greeks to the natural histories of the eighteenth century. The central metaphor was that of growth as a natural process, that is, as a natural course of development. This was clearly central to the Greek notion of *physis*, and it remained central to the conceptions of natural history in the eighteenth century. Closely associated with the idea of a natural process of development – from the acorn to the oak, from the neonate to the adult – was the idea of gradual, continuous, irreversible change that was directional, cumulative, and toward some end state. For each distinct type of living being, the natural path of development and end state were intrinsic to its very nature, as were the principal forces driving development. On this model, then, however dependent the process of growth was on a supportive environment, its path, end state, and moving forces were immanent to the thing growing.

The ancients understood this model also to explain processes of degeneration and decay, which were no less natural than those of generation and growth. Various forms of this cyclical model of growth and decay dominated thinking about human history in the millennium before Augustine. It did not disappear from Christian thinking about history in the next millennium, but was integrated into the then dominant understanding of history as a grand narrative of creation, fall,

---

[4] A number of Kant's essays on history are collected in *Kant: Political Writings*, ed. H. Reiss, tr. H. B. Nisbet (Cambridge University Press, 1991).

redemption, and the final days before the end of the world and the Last Judgment. The uniform paths of development inscribed in the very natures of things were now understood to be part of God's plan of creation, that is, part of an overall design with an overall purpose. And human history took on the character of an epic of salvation that was singular, universal, and in its main plot line non-cyclical. God's plan for creation and His governance of the world, divine providence, were especially concerned with these matters.

This is essentially the combination that Kant inherited late in the eighteenth century, but with some important intervening changes. For one thing, the modern conceptions of natural law and natural history had somewhat altered the notion of development. On the one hand, modern natural law theory stressed our rising above nature through the use of reason, paradigmatically in the trope of a social contract that subdues the state of nature through free and rational agreement. On the other hand, eighteenth-century natural history adjusted the ancient idea of a natural course of development to fit with the spirit of modern natural science: natural history was a scientific study of the laws and causes governing natural processes of development, not only in biological but also in social entities. After Rousseau incipiently historicized the Hobbesian–Lockean transition from the state of nature to the social contract, historical thinking was left with the problem of how to close the gaps now possible between the *empirical* accounts of natural history and the *normative* demands of natural law. Kant's response to this problem, in terms of the development of reason in history, became paradigmatic for the generations that followed.

Perhaps the most important change in developmental thinking in the early modern period concerned precisely the character of this growth of reason. Beginning in the seventeenth century with the "quarrel between the ancients and the moderns," and driven by the modern sciences of nature, the idea of a growth of knowledge without limit came increasingly to dominate developmental thinking. When the growth of knowledge was linked to the prediction and control of natural processes, it promised a limitless expansion of our mastery over nature. And when it was linked to processes of enlightenment, it promised a gradual diminution of the power of prejudice, superstition, blind custom, and unreflected tradition, and a continuous increase in the practical power of reason. Kant attempted to transform and integrate all of these aspects of prior developmental thinking into a systematic teleology of nature and history, that is, he sought to combine modern natural law and natural history with a post-Newtonian account of natural purpose and a rationalized account of providential history.

(b) Kant presented his idea of universal history as an answer to one of the three fundamental questions he posed in the *First Critique*: What may I hope? – as refracted through a fourth, anthropological question he posed in the *Logic*: What is man? So refracted, the question concerned the possibility of humanity realizing the highest good in history, in the form of a cosmopolitan world order and a global ethical community. In the *Critique of Practical Reason* and elsewhere, Kant discussed hope for the highest good from the perspective of morality, in terms of an otherworldly union of virtue and happiness, and thus in connection with a practically rational faith in God and personal immortality.[5] But in his scattered essays on history and in the *Critique of Judgment*, he took up the question of this-worldly hope from a socio-historical perspective, in connection with the development of culture, law, and morality.[6] And in the *Religion* he brought both perspectives to bear, discussing the highest good in terms of overcoming radical evil in individual and social life.[7] That is to say, Kant was not willing, as were Augustine and many succeeding Christian thinkers, to leave the earthly city of man to the forces of inevitable degeneration and decay, while reserving any hope for lasting peace to an otherworldly city of God. If the morally obligatory pursuit of justice in this world was to make sense, the end commanded had to be possible of attainment, at least by way of ongoing improvement of the "glittering misery" that passed for civilization.

It is this universal-historical hope for amelioration of the human condition that I want to consider here. Of course, in Kant this hope is, in the end, bound up with a practically rational faith in a just God, the Lord of nature and history, whose plan for both includes, as its ultimate end (*letzter Zweck*), the perfection of all our rational capacities, and as its final end (*Endzweck*), the gradual realization of an ethical

---

[5] I. Kant, *Political Writings*; Kant, *Critique of Practical Reason*, in *Practical Philosophy*, ed. and tr. M. J. Gregor (Cambridge University Press, 1996), pp. 133–271.

[6] I. Kant, *Critique of the Power of Judgment*, tr. P. Guyer and E. Matthews (Cambridge University Press, 2000).

[7] I. Kant, *Religion within the Boundaries of Mere Reason*, tr. G. di Giovanni (Cambridge University Press, 1996), pp. 39–215.

commonwealth, the Kingdom of God on earth. This moral teleology is the Kantian version of the moment of theodicy that inhabits and animates the philosophy of history from Augustine to Hegel; and it is that moment, above all, which has become incredible. The business of *justifying* the horrors of history by pointing to the unfolding of reason, the steady march of progress, or an anticipated happy ending now strikes most of us as implausible. And the more recent tendency to reduce this to some sort of political justification – for instance, in terms of the global triumph of socialism or of liberal capitalism – strikes many of us as even less plausible. In any case, the present reflections start from the premise that it can be no part of thinking about the global present in terms of the universal-historical past and with an eye to a practically projected future that we try to *justify* the historical record of humankind's horrific inhumanity by pointing to desirable outcomes, or in any other way.

(c) In his metanarrative of the development of reason, Hegel endeavored to get beyond Kant's metaphysical dualism and unmediated subjectivism; and the price he was willing to pay was very high. His lectures on the philosophy of world history did not overcome the eighteenth-century genre but outdid it – with claims "that reason governs the world," that it is "the substance" of history and "the power" animating it, and thus that the aim of philosophical inquiry into history is "to eliminate the contingent," any "external necessity" originating in "causes which are themselves no more than external circumstances."[8] Later theorists of modernization as rationalization generally eschewed philosophical idealism for a variety of more empirically based theories. However they sometimes agreed with Hegel on one key point: that there are internal logics to some cultural developments, which must be captured in any adequate account of sociocultural transformation. Thus Max Weber was concerned to spell out the *Eigengesetzlichkeiten* of the cultural spheres whose rationalization he was studying; and Jürgen Habermas has tried to articulate the "developmental logics" underlying the cultural learning processes he reconstructs. But unlike Hegel, and like most social theorists since, they regard rationalization processes, whatever their inner logics, as empirically conditioned all the way down.

---

[8] G. W. F. Hegel, *Lectures on the Philosophy of World History: Introduction*, tr. H. B. Nisbet (Cambridge University Press, 1993), pp. 27–28.

Another central element of Hegel's idealist immanentism is his particular appropriation of the Greek model of development as growth. The law of life, he reminds us, is that the germ or seed has to develop all that is in it potentially; and this potentiality is more than mere possibility, for it harbors both the power and the path of its own self-development. His version of this influential metaphor places freedom at the center of historical development, such that an *an sich* free being gradually, internal-logical step by internal-logical step, unfolds its essential being *für sich*. He thereby also continues the tradition dominant since the Greeks of placing political formations at the center of human development: the state is where a particular community's consciousness of freedom manifests itself in institutional form. Unlike Kant and later cosmopolitan theorists, however, Hegel locates the overcoming of national particularity not in a transnational rule of law but in the international struggle for power: *Weltgeschicht' ist Weltgericht.*[9] This opposition is, of course, still very much alive in the contemporary discourse of global modernity, as is another feature of Hegel's developmentalism.

Hegel ascribed to cultural development a more important role than most politically oriented developmentalists before him. In his view, forms of the institutionalization of freedom develop together with forms of the consciousness of freedom, such that the political institutions of a community are accompanied by cultural self-understandings they are taken to embody. Especially in the cultural forms of "absolute spirit" – art, religion, and philosophy – existing institutional forms of "objective spirit" are thereby represented as full and final realizations of freedom. But this is a claim against which they can and will be measured – and before the fully developed form of the state is realized, inevitably found wanting. Thus, there is a negativity inherent in reflexivity. Overcoming an outmoded stage of development requires a "determinate negation" by institutional forms that measure up to the level of critical consciousness attained; forms of political organization that fail to do so are inherently unstable. When similar lines of thought appear in contemporary discussions of globalization, it is usually with an emphasis on the empirically conditioned character of such developments, cultural as well as institutional.

---

[9] G. W. F. Hegel, *Elements of the Philosophy of Right*, tr. H. B. Nisbet (Cambridge University Press, 1991), p. 371.

Marx led the way in this regard. Though world-historical processes of development did tend, in his view, toward the full unfolding of human rational capacities, what ultimately drove them belonged rather to the "external circumstances" that Hegel wanted to eliminate than to the internal development of the spirit. "From the start," Marx insisted, "the 'spirit' is afflicted with the curse of being 'burdened' with matter."[10] More emphatically, "life is not determined by consciousness, but consciousness by life"; consequently, "philosophy as an independent branch of knowledge loses its medium of existence" and has to give way to the materialist theory of history.[11] Post-Marxian social theorists have generally acknowledged the need to bring "material circumstances" centrally into the explanation of cultural developments and shared the view that what drives historical change is not the unfolding of reason itself but changes in the mode of production, political struggles, and a variety of other such "material factors." At the same time, most have distanced themselves from the remnants of Hegel's dialectic in Marx's theory of history – and thus from the residual necessity and providentiality in his account of the inexorable development of productive forces and the eventual arrival of a classless society.

Marx's turn to a medium other than philosophy, viz. political economy, was at the same time a turning away from the traditional focus of the philosophy of history on the political domain. Hegel had broadened that focus to include cultural developments, among other things; but Marx, like thinkers of the Scottish Enlightenment before him, explicitly placed the history of "civil society" at the center. And "grand theorists" of social change since Marx have, in one way or another, usually viewed the development of forms of political organization in conjunction with developments in other dimensions of social life, the economic and cultural prominent among them. The contemporary discourse of global modernity largely follows them in this regard – even though the prominence of economic globalization as a driving force can make it seem that Marx was describing our world more directly than his own: the world market that he envisioned as ruling over the fortunes of peoples like some ancient fate has only now become an inescapable reality of daily life in every corner of the globe. Nevertheless, the cultural and political

[10] Karl Marx, "The German Ideology: Part I," in Robert C. Tucker (ed.), *The Marx–Engels Reader* (New York: W. W. Norton, 1978), pp. 146–200, at p. 158.
[11] *Ibid.*, p. 155.

aspects of globalization are hard to ignore, as the reactions and responses thereto become increasingly articulated and organized. And those who, like Marx, continue to insist on the irresistible logic and dynamics of economic development tend today – in one of history's ironic turns – to be ideologists of neoliberalism rather than socialism. To be sure, Marx combined the theoretically grasped necessity of developmental processes, which he naturalistically appropriated from Hegel's contemplative view of history, with a practical orientation toward history more reminiscent of Kant. But he failed coherently to integrate the two perspectives – that is, the "iron laws" of his developmental perspective with the political agency of his practical perspective.

(d) In this respect, I want to suggest, Kant's insistence on the primacy of practical reason makes him more of a contemporary than either Hegel or Marx, both of whom expressed theoretical disdain for moral perspectives on history, Hegel in metaphysical terms of the "cunning of reason" and Marx in scientistic terms of economic "laws of motion." There is another respect in which Kant is more of a contemporary than Hegel or Marx: he explicitly rejected the possibility of *theoretically* grasping history as a whole, whether in the mode of Hegelian self-transparency or in that of Marxian economic determinism. History was a domain of human action and thus shot through with the unpredictable expressions and effects of free agency. The aim of *universal* history was to give systematic unity to the totality of events in this domain, an undertaking that far outran the capacity of the empirical-theoretical sciences to produce well-founded "determinant judgments." It was, Kant argued, rather a task for "reflective judgment," which strove to construct a general interpretation of history that was consistent with, but necessarily went beyond, the mass of determinant judgments available from empirical inquiry of all sorts. In my view, some such postmetaphysical and postempiricist, practically oriented and methodologically interpretive approach to the tasks of universal history is a more viable option today than more strongly theoretical approaches descended from Hegel, Marx, or the evolutionary theories that succeeded them.

In the later nineteenth century, and partly in reaction to Hegel's idealist transformation of the Kantian synthesis, developmental theory took a naturalistic turn. Modeled once more on biological paradigms, theories of social evolution were keyed not to the internal logic of cultural development but to the internal differentiation and growing complexity of quasi-organic social systems. Understood as the natural evolution of such systems, societal development could then be reconstructed from a purely objectivist perspective as advancing through a sequence of structurally defined stages.[12] Toward the end of the century, typological models were displaced by specifically Darwinian conceptions of social evolution. But the temporary dominance of social Darwinism already faced serious challenges in the early twentieth century, not only from advances in evolutionary biology itself but also from functionalist approaches to cultural anthropology.[13] Later in the twentieth century, functionalist perspectives were integrated into a social-evolutionary framework by Talcott Parsons and others, yielding a neoevolutionist synthesis that became for a time the dominant paradigm.[14] In the post-World War II period, it served as the general framework for theories of development and modernization;[15] and it has more recently been expanded, especially by Niklas Luhmann, into a general systems theory that covers virtually the entire range of social and cultural phenomena.[16] The integration of structuralism and functionalism into a system-theoretical approach makes it possible to build analogues to key elements of the theory of biological evolution into theories of sociocultural evolution: self-regulating, boundary-maintaining, social systems have to adapt to hypercomplex environments to survive, which requires a heightening of their own internal complexity. Thus, structural and functional differentiation and the integration of functionally specified subsystems are understood as adaptive responses to environmental pressures, adaptations that are necessary for system survival. When problems arise that overburden the functional capacity of a social system, it either develops so as to expand that capacity or it fails.

As I shall suggest below, some features of this way of theorizing development as functional adaptation are useful for thinking about the pressures and constraints that globalization processes place on national and international institutions of all sorts. However, it cannot stand on its own as an

---

[12] Robert A. Nisbet, *Social Change and History* (Oxford University Press, 1975), chap. 5.

[13] See chapter 3.

[14] Leslie Sklair, *The Sociology of Progress* (London: Routledge & Kegan Paul, 1970), part two.

[15] See chapter 7.

[16] N. Luhmann, *The Differentiation of Society*, tr. C. Larmore (New York: Columbia University Press, 1982).

account of sociocultural development, for the analogy with biological evolution is an imperfect one, which becomes evident when one presses the question of the social equivalents for mutation, genetic populations, and the survival of individual organisms. One aspect of development, in particular, seems to find inadequate expression in the neoevolutionist synthesis: development as cultural learning. This aspect, which dominated the philosophy of history from the Enlightenment to Hegel, was subsequently reworked by "grand" social theorists and integrated with accounts of institutional change. They sought thereby to capture the developmental interplay between "internal" and "external" factors, variously conceived, rather than to eliminate one in favor of the other. Thus, for example, Max Weber was concerned to spell out the *Eigengesetzlichkeiten*, or inner logics, of the cultural spheres he studied and to connect their rationalization with the spreading institutionalization of purposive rationality in major domains of social life; and Jürgen Habermas has attempted to articulate the developmental logics underlying cultural learning processes and to connect the corresponding "rationalization of the lifeworld" with the functional rationalization of the economy and the state.[17] While this type of approach does retain the idea that some cultural developments are cumulative and directional and can be rationally reconstructed as learning processes, those processes themselves, and the institutional uses to which they are put, are thoroughly contingent: cultural learning occurs only under particular empirical conditions and gains institutional embodiment only in particular historical circumstances. Moreover, the consequences of such processes for human well-being, however defined, will vary with the concrete conditions under which they occur. In this respect, such approaches are quite different from schemes in which developmental advance itself serves as the basic standard of evaluation for change, as was the case, in quite different ways, with Hegel and Marx, nineteenth-century evolutionism, and much mid-twentieth-century modernization theory.

II

A key element in the transformation of classical, cyclical notions of development into modern, progressive notions was the paradigmatic

[17] *From Max Weber*, ed. H. H. Gerth and C. W. Mills (London: Routledge & Kegan Paul, 1970). Jürgen Habermas, *The Theory of Communicative Action*, vols. I, II, tr. T. McCarthy (Boston: Beacon Press, 1984, 1987).

status ascribed to the growth of knowledge. Cognitive development – directional, cumulative, and apparently limitless – was variously understood to be the core of a process of enlightenment that would finally emancipate humankind from the chains of ignorance, superstition, and prejudice; the motor of a general progress of the human spirit encompassing morality and politics as well as the arts and sciences; the vehicle of an ever-increasing mastery over nature and society and thus of growing human happiness; and the main catalyst for the progress of civilization and reordering of human life. But there were dissenting voices from the start. Thus Rousseau's pessimistic view of the relation between ethical life and advances in the arts and sciences was published almost simultaneously with Turgot's optimistic view. Later in the century, conservative critics of the French Revolution maintained that "progress" in individualism, egalitarianism, secularism, and the like meant social disintegration and disaster. With the onset of the massive dislocations caused by the industrial revolution, doubts concerning progress became commonplace. And during the expansion and acceleration of industrialization in the second half of the nineteenth century, pessimism about progress received its classic theoretical formulations. The assumed ties between reason, truth, morality, and happiness were called into question. Enlightenment optimists had not anticipated the ways in which what Nietzsche called "the will to truth" could turn back upon and challenge the very ideals of reason, including truth itself. Nor had they anticipated the ways in which the spread of forms of rationality suited to technological, strategic, and organizational practices – Weber's *Zweckrationalität* – might undermine the sociocultural conditions of individual autonomy and lock us up in an "iron cage" of our own making.[18] In the twentieth century, scientific and technological progress became even more ambiguous in its consequences, both intended (e.g. weapons of mass destruction) and unintended (e.g. global warming). Indeed, growing consciousness of the inherent risks associated with technological advances (e.g. genetic engineering) has rendered the assumed connection between the growth of knowledge and the rational "mastery" of nature and society – let alone the connection between such mastery and happiness – increasingly problematic. In

---

[18] Max Weber, *The Protestant Ethic and the Spirit of Capitalism*, tr. T. Parsons (London: Allen & Unwin, 1974). See also Max Horkheimer and Theodor Adorno, *Dialectic of Enlightenment*, tr. E. Jephcott (Stanford University Press, 2002).

these ways and others, then, progress in knowledge seems to have led not only to religious disenchantment, as Enlightenment thinkers expected, but to the disenchantment of reason and progress as well.[19] Given that the advance of knowledge itself – not only in science and technology, but also in history and the human studies – is difficult to deny, the real problems for progressive thought arise when cognitive advances are connected too quickly with improvements in other aspects of human existence, at the limit with the quality of human life as a whole.

The inherent ambivalence of progress has often been traced back to the very mainsprings of development, especially to deeply rooted features of the human condition, individual and social. Thus, in the eighteenth century, the motors of progress were sometimes said to be "man's" natural self-love, self-interest, fear of harm, pride, ambition, greed, or the like, in combination with his need and desire to live in society and with the conflict and competition that inevitably result. Kant's "unsocial sociability" is representative in this regard. And like a number of other developmental theorists at the time, he resolved the tension between the egocentric character of these motor forces and the social character of his idea of progress through postulating a favorable concatenation of unintended consequences. His version of the private vices/public virtues figure of thought was, as we saw, the teleology of nature and history that served as a stand-in for divine providence in his philosophy of history. In some places, Kant wrote as if the highest legal-political good, a cosmopolitan order under a global rule of enforceable law, could come about wholly as the consequence of self-interested actions, that it could be achieved even by a "race of devils," if only they were sufficiently rational. In other places, he suggested the need for a morally motivated pursuit of justice, if the highest legal-political good was to be achieved or, once achieved, to be sustained.[20] But he was quite clear that at least the highest *moral* good in history, the formation of an

---

[19] The relation of modernization to secularization in general, and to religious disenchantment in particular, is, to be sure, still contested. See the recent discussion by Charles Taylor, *A Secular Age* (Cambridge, MA: Harvard University Press, 2007).

[20] See the discussion of these two paths to "perpetual peace" by Henry Allison, "The Gulf between Nature and Freedom and Nature's Guarantee of Perpetual Peace," and Paul Guyer, "Nature, Morality, and the Possibility of Peace," both in H. Robinson (ed.), *Proceedings of the Eighth International Kant Congress*, vol. I.1 (Milwaukee: Marquette University Press, 1995), pp. 37–49, 51–69.

ethical commonwealth or Kingdom of God on earth, could only be the work of morally motivated actors joining together to promote the triumph of good over evil.

With the transition of developmental thinking from the philosophy of history to social theories of macrohistorical change, the teleology of nature and providentiality of history had to go. Moreover, morality lost the otherworldliness it had acquired in Kant and came back to earth: it was historicized by Hegel and naturalized by Marx, Durkheim, Weber, and the social-theoretical tradition generally. But developmental thinking retained many of its problematic features. Thus at the very point of transition Marx retained a teleo-logic of history in the form of natural-historical laws of economic development that led inexorably to a classless society. That enabled him to bridge the gap between the ever-changing forms of exploitation, domination, and struggle that moved history along and its final happy ending; but it also reproduced the tensions between the practical-political and natural-historical perspectives already evident in Kant. And Marx's proposed resolution thereof – that, while political action could not affect the laws of motion of history, it could hasten the arrival and reduce the birth pangs of its final stage – has generally been viewed as an unhappy compromise.

To some degree, such tensions have been reduced by the tendency of more consistently postmetaphysical theories of social change to be less immanentist and to assign a greater role to historical contingency and political action. Thus, for example, in the dominant forms of post-World War II development and modernization theory, the need for action by political elites, national governments, and developed countries is not a theoretical embarrassment but a practical necessity. On the other hand, tensions between political aims and automatic processes persist in influential contemporary approaches – such as neoliberalism and systems theory – that fundamentally question the ability of complex societies to steer themselves in the medium of politics. Moreover, the ambivalence of progress has become, if anything, an even more pressing problem. Once the guarantee of a happy ending is removed, the reckoning of costs and benefits is principally a matter of life and death, well-being and misery, happiness and suffering, fulfillment and frustration. This is even clearer when the notion of development as progress is disaggregated and applied only to particular aspects of society; when the consequences and side effects of such limited developments are viewed as empirical questions; and when the summary evaluation of their desirability is treated as a practical-political question to be answered by those who have to live with them.

While the ambivalence of modernization has repeatedly been remarked, the ways of accounting costs and benefits and the resultant balance sheets have differed greatly. To begin with, rapid modernization has usually been accompanied by a widespread sense of loss, the experience of a familiar world being torn asunder. When one considers, even superficially, what sociocultural modernization involves, this appears to be unavoidable. Increasingly individualized and self-directed forms of life; abstract and more formal modes of association, coordination, and social integration; increasingly reflexive and critical appropriations of tradition; and the like, by their very nature entail the transformation of traditional ways of life. In more and more domains of action, inherited schemes of interpretation and evaluation, expectation and expression can no longer be taken for granted and relied upon: members are no longer sure what is going on, what they can count on, how one does things, or even who one is. Unsurprisingly, then, a loss of guidance for action and orientation in life, a sense of rootlessness and emptiness have been constant accompaniments of sociocultural modernization.

If one simultaneously brings into play the systemic aspects of modernization that Marx, Durkheim, and evolutionary sociologists have emphasized, the costs mount up. The differentiation of functionally specialized subsystems of action entails by its very nature that more and more domains of action are transferred from traditional modes of coordination – for example through inherited status and ascribed roles – to formally organized, media-steered modes – for example markets and bureaucracies. The world of work becomes increasingly "rationalized," instrumentalized, and disembedded from traditional beliefs and practices, norms and values. The fragmentation of life grows, subcultures of expertise proliferate, and the intuitive grasp of how things hang together dissipates, as material reproduction becomes increasingly dependent upon "counterintuitive" modes of functional integration.

Observations of this sort have long been the stuff of sociology, which has been preoccupied with modernization processes from the start. But, as noted, the accounting schemes applied to such observations have differed considerably. Thus, in the wake of the French Revolution, many conservative critics argued that modernization amounts to disintegration and ought to be resisted. While Marx agreed that it was destructive of traditional modes of social integration, he disagreed that it could be resisted or, supposing *per impossibile* it could, that it should. Capitalist modernization, he insisted, wiped away the *Dreck* of traditional forms of life and ultimately made possible an emancipated, post-scarcity, truly human form of life. Half a century later, influenced by Nietzsche's scathing portrait of the "last men," Weber depicted the advent of a world inhabited by "specialists without spirit and sensualists without heart," a world in which increased productive power and capacity for organization did not bring the greater freedom and happiness that earlier thinkers envisaged, but lives of increasingly limited autonomy and increasingly empty pleasures. There was, in his view, no hope of choosing what was to be, but only of enduring what had to be – of unblinking, unbending, individual self-reliance amidst the modern ebb tide of meaning and freedom.[21]

Jürgen Habermas has recently offered a differentiated accounting of costs and benefits.[22] To begin with, (a) the disruption of traditional ways of life and the sense of profound loss that comes with it are unavoidable concomitants of modernization. This is true as well for (b) the fragmentation and distantiation that inevitably accompany increasing functional differentiation and formal organization. These costs have to be weighed against the benefits that modernization brings, not only through the enhanced power of material reproduction that generally comes with functional differentiation, but also through the heightened individualization, autonomy, and reflexivity that cultural rationalization brings, as well as through the spread of legal-political systems based on individual rights and democratic self-determination. There are, presumably, few moderns who would, if they could, return to lives of ascribed statuses, roles, and identities; of unquestioned and unquestionable bodies of belief and practice; of inherited and enforced values and lifestyles – and, in any case, those who would can't.

There is another type of ambivalence inherent in societal development that is akin to the entwinement of good and evil we saw in some

---

[21] *The Protestant Ethic and the Spirit of Capitalism*; and *From Max Weber*.
[22] In *The Theory of Communicative Action*. See also his *Communication and the Evolution of Society*, tr. T. McCarthy (Boston: Beacon Press, 1979); *The Philosophical Discourse of Modernity*, tr. F. Lawrence (Cambridge, MA: MIT Press, 1987); and *The Postnational Constellation*, tr. M. Pensky (Cambridge, MA: MIT Press, 2001).

modern philosophies of history: (c) the intensified suffering that often accompanies functional differentiation. Thus, for example, the formation of hierarchical systems of authority and eventually of a differentiated state undoubtedly brought a heightened capacity for administration and planning by comparison to kinship-based societies; but it also escalated relations of hierarchy, domination, and repression. And the differentiation of market-based economies usually increased productive capacity; but it often also amplified dependence, exploitation, and inequality. These types of suffering can be, and have been, somewhat ameliorated by the growth of democratic forms of government and the expansion of state-sponsored social services and protections. Nevertheless, as the travails of globalization once again make clear, such trade-offs between a society's "adaptive capacity" and its members' well-being mean that developmental and ethical perspectives on social change may well diverge at key points, and that is a relevant consideration in the discourse of global modernity.

Habermas further identifies (d) costs of Western modernization that he attributes to its capitalist character rather than to its character as modernization. Whereas the "mediatization of the lifeworld" – the anchoring of formally organized systems of action in the lifeworld by way of institutionalizing "delinguistified" media like money and administrative power – is an integral feature of societal modernization, the "colonization of the lifeworld by the system" results from an imbalanced modernization propelled onwards by processes of capital accumulation.[23] As central to the latter, he singles out the ever-increasing scope and intensity of what Marx identified as the commodification of life relations, as well as of what Weber described as their bureaucratization. Without going into detail, the general idea is that a good deal of the painful damage inflicted upon the lifeworlds of modern and modernizing societies – much of the alienation and anomie, individual psychopathologies and collective identity crises, loss of freedom and withdrawal of legitimation – are due to the increasing penetration of systemic mechanisms, such as money and power, into every nook and cranny of daily life. This, Habermas argues, distorts the symbolic reproduction of the lifeworld and impedes the successful replacement of traditional forms of social integration by more individualized, autonomous, and reflexive

---

[23] *The Theory of Communicative Action*, vol. II, esp. chaps. VI and VIII.

modern forms. The result is often destruction without replacement, or with replacements that are unstable in the long run. On his accounting, this type of cost is ultimately dysfunctional for the maintenance of the social system as a whole. His proposed remedy is a rebalancing of modernization that gives a significantly larger role to democratic processes aimed at "self-limiting" control of the economy and state.

For much of the world, however, the depredations of capitalist modernization have gone beyond the figurative colonization of the lifeworld by the system to (e) the real colonization of both lifeworld and system by foreign powers. The forms of disruption and loss, abstraction and dislocation mentioned above are amplified and intensified when modernization is imposed from without. In many parts of the world and for much of the modern period this has meant: at the point of a gun, or gunboat, or helicopter gunship. Today it also means: under the threat of exclusion, marginalization, subordination, or even dissolution. Neoliberal globalization seems to leave non-Western societies no choice but to modernize to survive, and to do so on terms largely set by the demands of capital accumulation in former colonial powers and, recently, in rapidly developing regional powers. In this regard, one can say that the convergence thesis regarding historical development – that it leads, by its very nature, to basically the same cultural and societal forms – has never been and never will be tested, for only Western modernization was endogenous. And the especially high costs of forced modernization in other parts of the world have been as evident as they have been lasting. As things now stand, "taming" the still "wild" global economy may well require some global functional equivalent for the rise of the modern, regulatory and redistributive, nation-state that domesticated the raw capitalism of the earlier nineteenth century. But it is not at all clear yet what new forms of global governance might look like, let alone how they could be achieved and stabilized, or to what extent they would allow for democratic participation.

After the horrors of the twentieth century, the most keenly felt deficiency of modern progress may well be (f) the evident gap between massive advances in the available means of power – technological, economic, political, military – and the failure to develop effective normative structures – moral, legal, political – to contain and direct those powers onto paths of peace and justice.

III

For Kant, morality was both the key to the final end of history and itself
fundamentally non-historical, indeed non-empirical. This perplexing
combination did not long trouble universal-historical thought, for morality was soon brought back to earth by Marx and subsequent social
theorists. But the developmental-historical problems Kant tried to
address with his nature/freedom dichotomy have persisted, albeit in
altered forms. Like a number of other eighteenth-century thinkers,
Kant saw human progress as the largely unplanned emergence of
good from evil, an unintended (by human beings) consequence of the
play of instincts and interests. The gradual cultivation and civilization
of the human race, especially the establishment of republican forms of
government based on the rule of law, were themselves largely the result
of antagonism meeting antagonism, interest meeting interest – at best,
of enlightened self-interest. But like Augustine before him, he considered an "earthly peace" founded only on contingent concatenations of
"self-love" to be inherently unstable. Thus he was ambivalent to the end
about what role morality, and especially a moral politics, had to play in
achieving and maintaining a cosmopolitan rule of law. It was clear to
him, however, that all such achievements of civilization would remain a
"glittering misery" in the absence of moralization. Thus, especially in
the *Religion*, he emphasized the emergence of a purely moral religion
with a non-authoritarian church to nourish and propagate it as essential
to attaining the final end of history. What was required was a turning of
individual hearts from evil to good, the foundation of a worldwide
ethical community unifying those so reborn, and the pursuit of a
moral politics to transform a civilization based on self-love into a kingdom of ends, in which each willed the good of all.

Hegel, by contrast, denied the exceptional status of morality in Kant's
sense; he radically historicized ethical life (*Sittlichkeit*) as a whole. Marx
went much further, naturalizing morality and ethical life as, at bottom,
distorted reflections of class-ridden modes of material reproduction. To
fill the role in history occupied by Kant's notion of moral politics, Hegel
relied on the more or less automatic efficacy of reason in history, using
world-historical individuals as vehicles, and Marx on the more or less
automatic working of economic laws of motion, creating revolutionary
classes as agents of transformation. But once faith in the inner-logical
unfolding of reason and the revolutionary transformation of productive

relations dissipated, historical thought seemed to be left with only the contingent play of particular interests to drive history, with no plan of nature or divine providence to ensure its happy outcome. In opposition to this type of Hobbesian reductionism, sociological theorists from Durkheim to Habermas have repeatedly addressed what they took to be a theoretical need for some independent account of normative development, and in a variety of ways. Talcott Parsons, for instance, disputed the self-sufficiency of instrumental action and argued that social integration required the institutionalization and internalization of shared norms and values. Related disagreements arose in political theory – for instance, between those who understood democratic procedures primarily as a way of aggregating particular interests and those who understood them primarily as a way of expressing common values or deliberating on the common good. And the central issues have remained very much alive: whether a society based only on self-interest is a stable, or even possible, formation; whether, if possible, such a society could achieve anything more than a glittering misery; and whether it is possible to achieve or maintain "perpetual peace" or a cosmopolitan rule of law on this basis. To be sure, at the level of world society, the shared values and norms that figure so centrally in the republican tradition seem, at best, to thin out to the kind of abstract morality embodied in human rights conventions. But it is doubtful that even such *minima moralia* could be achieved and sustained on a purely instrumental basis. On that basis, we could reasonably hope, it seems, only for ever-changing configurations of the "balance" of international power – which has just brought us a century of devastation without equal.

Having reason to hope for something more than this means refusing the reduction of human action to instrumental action and of modernization to the institutionalization of instrumental rationality. As noted, the main way of doing so theoretically has been to construct historicized and naturalized accounts of what Kant was appealing to when he invoked morality as a countervailing force to self-interest – as Durkheim did, for example, with his conception of "collective consciousness," and George Herbert Mead did with his "generalized other." Habermas has sought to develop this approach by conceptualizing instrumental action as only one aspect, albeit a central and pervasive one, of communicative action. Starting from a multidimensional conception of social interaction – which also attends to its normative, evaluative, expressive, and emotional aspects – he goes on to construct a multidimensional account of social development, in which "postconventional" forms of morality, law, and politics play irreducible and irreplaceable roles. Without going into the details of that account, it might be noted that moral universalism is there understood to be embodied in the basic-rights foundation of modern law, and autonomy in the self-rule conception of modern democracy.[24] At least to this extent, then, we get a naturalistic reconstruction of the important role that Kant assigned to his non-naturalistically conceived structures of moral consciousness in the spheres of law and politics.

But what of the other role he described as the rise and spread of a purely moral religion, that is, the overcoming of self-interest as the dominant force structuring individual and social life? For Habermas, this takes the form of a requirement that cultural transmission, social integration, and the socialization of new members of a society must reliably reproduce moral and ethical attitudes, orientations, and dispositions that can serve as preconditions of substantive legal rights and effective political democracy.[25] The quality of public culture, in particular of political culture and the democratic public sphere, depends on it. But it is just such processes of "symbolic reproduction" that many critics of capitalist modernization claim are being systematically corrupted and distorted in the contemporary world. In Habermas's terms: the more that empirical tendencies point in the direction of an expanding "colonization of the lifeworld" by an increasingly global economic system, the more the prospect of cosmopolitan justice appears to be a merely utopian hope. To the extent that traditional modes of cultural transmission, social integration, and socialization are undermined by capitalist modernization, without giving rise to viable, communicatively rationalized, posttraditional modes; that functional differentiation and systemic modernization outpace cultural rationalization and political democratization; and that political cultures and public spheres, which could be resources for containing such colonization, are themselves increasingly colonized – in ways that were already anticipated in the 1940s by Horkheimer's and Adorno's account of the mass-culture industry, and by Schumpeter's account of democratic politics as

---

[24] J. Habermas, *Between Facts and Norms*, tr. W. Rehg (Cambridge, MA: MIT Press, 1996), chap. 3; Jeffrey Flynn, "Habermas on Human Rights: Law, Morality, and Intercultural Dialogue," *Social Theory and Practice* 29 (2003): 431–457.

[25] Habermas, *Between Facts and Norms*, chap. 8.

basically geared to procuring mass loyalty for competing political elites – the idea of progressive politics having history on its side loses much of its power. At best, it seems, a longer-term perspective on the development of normative structures might sustain a weak hope that the current ravages of capitalist modernization may abate, that the problems besetting neoliberal globalization will induce the institutionalization of forms of communicative rationality that foster human rights, democratic governance, social justice, and multicultural dialogue rather than undermine them. As Kant noted, a "moral politics" in pursuit of cosmopolitical justice only makes sense on the basis of hope. But is this kind of weak hope sufficient?

The shift in Christian philosophy from predominantly cyclical to epical conceptions of development worked a fundamental transformation in Western thinking about history. It came to be represented as a scene of the radically new: the messianic moment, the second coming, the millennium. These religious ideas of an objective meaning and final end of history, and even the representation of the final end in millenarian terms, survived the secularization of the philosophy of history in the eighteenth and nineteenth centuries. Utopian projections of a wholly transformed future remained its stock in trade from Condorcet to Marx and beyond. But today, it seems, the idea of a radical utopian break has largely lost its credibility and the surviving forms of "gradual utopianism" have been radically desublimated: development as the improvement of legal-political and socioeconomic conditions posits no objective meaning of history, no final end, no perfection, no complete emancipation or fulfillment. There has, of course, also been strong resistance to this somber closure of the disenchanted mindset, and not only from political revolutionaries and religious millenarians. Many find unbearable, as Walter Benjamin did, the thought of history's countless victims being nothing more than stepping stones along the path of development, and of hope being contracted to the accumulation of gradual improvements; they try to keep alive the radical hope for a disruption of the continuum of history that would rescue some meaning for past suffering. But for most secular thinkers, messianic hopes without God are no more convincing than revolutionary hopes without the Proletariat. And so, the spectrum of hope in developmental thinking today tends to run from straightforwardly non-normative conceptions of increasing functional capacity (e.g. systems theory); through restrictedly normative conceptions of increasingly marketized societies (e.g. neoliberalism); to more robustly normative conceptions of increasing global justice (e.g. cosmopolitanism). Theorists of this last persuasion typically link their normative conceptions to empirical accounts of sociocultural development showing that, while such modestly utopian hopes never come close to predictions, they do amount to more than empty possibilities. In Kantian terms, one might say that their interpretations of universal history are meant to ground "reasonable" hopes for practically "feasible" futures, hopes that are supported by basic patterns of development and tendencies of contemporary history. And as with Kant, they typically represent these normatively characterized futures as having to be approached step by step, based on what is practicable at any given time.[26]

Kant represented the *ideal* of cosmopolitical justice as a *Völkerstaat*, a federation of national republics, under the rule of *Weltbürgerrecht*, or cosmopolitan law. But he conceded in "Perpetual Peace" that this ideal could not be realized in his day, owing mainly to the unwillingness of nation-states to surrender their sovereignty to any binding, supranational form of organization.[27] And so he proposed the "practicable" goal of establishing a *Völkerbund*, or voluntary league of nations, as a step on the way to that distant goal. Similarly, cosmopolitan theorists today think in terms both of overarching normative ideals and of practically feasible steps. Practical-political projections of feasible futures are, it appears, all that is left of "reasonable hope" once our confidence in divine providence, in the power of reason to realize itself, and in iron laws of historical motion has been shaken. Such projections are thoroughly contingent – subject to empirical conditions, unpredictable events, and shifting tendencies – and only conditionally realistic – dependent upon, among other things, whether political actors effectively pursue them. Short of invoking some equivalent to Kant's faith that God will make good our deficiencies if only we do what is morally required of us, there seems to be no practical alternative to politically shaping and pursuing agendas of progressive change with reasonable chances of success. No doubt, to some this will seem less a politics of hope than a politics of disappointment.

---

[26] J. Habermas, "The Kantian Project and the Divided West," part IV of Habermas, *The Divided West*, tr. Ciaran Cronin (Cambridge: Polity Press, 2006), pp. 113–193.

[27] J. Bohman and M. Lutz-Bachmann (eds.), *Perpetual Peace: Essays on Kant's Cosmopolitan Ideal* (Cambridge, MA: MIT Press, 1997).

IV

What lessons for the contemporary discourse of global modernity can we draw from this brief retrospective on universal-historical thinking before, by, and after Kant? In the way of a very partial and preliminary response, I shall conclude this chapter by proposing three basic "facts" of global modernity that strike me as fundamental to thinking sensibly about universal history, indicating briefly what may follow from them.[28]

1. The first, which I shall call *the fact of cultural modernity*, is a variation of sorts on the Hegelian theme of growing reflexivity. The participants in the global discourse of modernity find themselves in similar positions with respect to the cultural resources at their disposal. In fact, the recent course of discussion suggests that representatives of historically oppressed and excluded groups are quite often more adept with the weapons of critique than their opposite numbers: the virtuosos of reflexivity in our time come disproportionately from such groups. But the capacity for critical reflection is not merely a matter of individual virtuosity; it is bound up with social and cultural conditions that undergo historical change. In modern societies conditions are such as to provide increased institutional, cultural, and motivational incentives for reflective modes of argumentation and critique. Forms of specialized discourse, transmitted and developed within specialized cultural traditions and embodied in differentiated cultural institutions, present enduring possibilities of discursively thematizing various types of claims and of productively assimilating the results of critical reflection upon them. It is, among other things, the extent to which, and the manner in which, modes of reflective discourse have been institutionalized and the requisite cultural and motivational conditions for them have been met that distinguish posttraditional from traditional cultural spheres. And it is important to recognize that this heightening of reflexivity informs and structures the contemporary discourse of global modernity itself. For instance, all the various participants in that discourse – post- and antimodernists as well as diverse modernists – take for granted the

---

[28] I am using the term "fact" here in roughly the same way that John Rawls used it in *Political Liberalism* and elsewhere to refer to basic features of modern life (such as "the fact of reasonable disagreement concerning the meaning and value of life"), in the light of which social and political theory must proceed, if they are to be at all "realistic."

possibility of reflectively questioning received beliefs and values, of gaining critical distance from inherited norms and roles, and of challenging ascribed individual and group identities. Even arguments for the superiority of premodern traditions are not themselves traditional arguments but the traditionalistic arguments of hyperreflexive moderns. One can argue against these basic features of posttraditional culture only by drawing upon them; and this is a good indication that they are practically unavoidable presuppositions of contemporary discourse.

A fuller reconstruction of the pragmatics of our discursive situation could make clearer at least where our discussions have to start. And that itself could have important implications for the discourse of modernity. This discourse turns on what we, the participants, can and cannot make sense of, render plausible, justify, refute, effectively criticize, conceive of as alternatives, and so on. If there are constraining preconditions built into our discursive situation itself, they will in turn constrain the range of reasonable options. Now, it is precisely our historically, sociologically, and anthropologically schooled understanding of the diversity of worldviews, among other things, that fuels the discourse of modernity. Hence we are constrained, on pain of incoherence, to regard any worldview which remains largely untouched by the second, historicist enlightenment – that is, which does not reflectively comprehend itself as one possible interpretation of the world among many others – as deficient in that respect, as not evincing adequate awareness of something that we know to be the case. There is no going back on the experiences of cultural change and pluralism we have had, nor unlearning what we have learned from them about the variability of forms of life and views of the world. From within the (critical-reflective) discourse of modernity, which begins precisely at that point, we cannot sensibly argue against that.

There are other general presuppositions of contemporary discourse with which one might, perhaps, coherently take issue, but with respect to which the burden of proof on the critic is so great as to be prohibitive. For instance, in our cultural-historical situation it would be difficult-bordering-on-impossible to produce a warranted denial that there has been a significant learning process underway in regard at least to our scientific understanding of nature and our technical ability to manipulate it, and that modern societies have learned to pursue the interest in prediction and control more effectively by differentiating it out from other concerns. (Practically living out that denial would, of course, be even more difficult.) But this means that from where we – participants in the discourse of modernity – must start, some differences in beliefs will be more than mere differences, precisely because we can only make sense of them as the results of learning.

I have been speaking primarily of beliefs, but it is also important to note that our assessments of norms and values cannot remain unaffected by what we regard as learning in more narrowly epistemic domains. Traditional value systems are intimately interwoven with beliefs about how the world is. That is why the learning processes associated with names like Galileo and Darwin could have such a profound impact on normative and evaluative elements of modern life. To put the point somewhat crudely, certain premodern ethical views could be publicly justified only by appeal to beliefs that are no longer tenable. Since the reasons we regard as warranting evaluative and normative judgments have to be compatible with what we have learned in other domains, whole classes of reasons for acting are no longer available to us. In such cases it is *kinds* of reasons that have been devalued, that have lost their discursive weight, and not just specific claims resting on them. This is what appears to have happened, for instance, with justifications of unequal treatment by appeal to the "natural" inferiority and unfitness for self-rule of women, blacks, non-Europeans, or other categories of human beings. Fundamental inequalities that could once be justified by appeals to beliefs about the world that are no longer tenable are hard put to find substitute justifications capable of withstanding critical-reflective scrutiny. Moreover, the discourse of global modernity itself is structured by a pragmatic presupposition of normative symmetry, which requires treating all participants with equal respect. The tension between that presupposition – with its attendant train of ideas of impartiality, toleration of differences, and so forth – and ethical views constructed around basic inequalities is evident and inescapable. This too enormously increases the burden of proof on anyone who would discursively defend such views. Though the elimination of broad classes of reasons does not by itself settle questions of right and wrong, good and bad, better and worse, the scope of reasonable disagreement gets considerably narrowed. As a result, the norms and values that could stand up to criticism and be upheld in free and open discussion is by no means coextensive with the spectrum of what has historically been, or is now actually, valued or required. But it is also not uniquely determined. One of the things inhabitants of cultural modernity have learned about values, for instance, is that reasonable people can reasonably hold different conceptions of the good, that there is no one way of life suited to all individuals and groups. And this acknowledgment has forced us to rethink enlightenment universalism from the perspective of multiculturalism.

2. To these sketchy remarks about the fact of cultural modernity, I want to add a few equally sketchy remarks about what I shall call *the fact of societal modernity*. The circumstances of global modernity, in which all contemporary societies willy nilly find themselves, confront them with an array of basic problems they have to resolve if they want to survive – for instance, problems concerning how to relate to an increasingly integrated global market economy; how to administer an increasingly complex and functionally differentiated society; how to accommodate ethnic, cultural, and religious diversity in a single, coherent set of social institutions; how to maintain political unity and legitimacy in the face of it, and so forth. From this perspective, many modern institutions appear to be not simply results of the peculiarities of Western history and culture but responses to macrohistorical challenges of a general nature, which include those arising from the ever-deeper immersion of all societies in transnational flows of capital, commodities, technology, information, communication, and culture.

Consider, for example, the legal institutions and practices that are widely regarded as emblematic of Western modernity. Sociologists of law broadly agree that modern law must have many of the general features it has in order to fulfill the functions it fulfills, that there are no viable functional equivalents for its formality, positivity, reflexivity, individuality, actionability, and the like. Thus, for instance, the fact that positive law issues from the changeable decisions of legitimate authorities loosens its ties with traditional ethics and makes it more suitable as a means of organizing and administering complex and changing modern societies. This requires in turn that the enactment, administration, and application of the law themselves be legally institutionalized; law becomes reflexive. And since modern law, as a positive, reflexive, and therefore fungible "steering medium," can no longer be legitimated solely by appeal to inherited beliefs and practices, there is a need for new forms of legitimation. That need is compounded by the facts that cultural pluralism limits the authority of any one tradition and that rights-based conceptions of individual citizenship increase the pressure for political participation. One could go on in this vein. The general thought is that the functions and forms of modern law are generally tailored to one another. Because any contemporary society, whatever its cultural traditions, will find it difficult to do without the former, it will find it correspondingly difficult to do without some version of the latter.

Similar lines of thought could be elaborated for other aspects of societal modernization; and together they pose an issue that Charles Taylor has formulated in general terms as follows: assuming that some degree of convergence in economic, governmental, and legal institutions and practices is an unavoidable feature of a globalized modernity, what kinds and degrees of divergence remain possible and desirable? In particular, how much room do such modernizing tendencies leave for deep cultural differences?[29] Multiculturalists note that different starting points for the transition to modernity are likely to lead to different outcomes, and thus that new forms of modern society are likely to evince new forms of difference. This is, of course, already true of Western modernity: Swiss society is clearly different from Spanish and Swedish society, not to mention American and Japanese society. And yet they are too similar to satisfy some multiculturalists who are concerned with broader and deeper differences in ideas and beliefs, outlooks and attitudes, values and identities, practices and institutions, than these societies evince. To the question of how much and what kinds of difference we have good empirical and theoretical reasons to expect or to pursue, there is clearly no generally accepted answer. But one might well conjecture that it is less than those theorists envision. They usually concede that market economies and bureaucratic states are inescapable features of modern societies, and that with them come expanded spheres of instrumental action, as well as increased industrialization, mobility, and urbanization. They typically also regard science and technology as something all modern societies have to take on, as well as general education and mass literacy. We could add to these the legal forms I mentioned above, together with the legal cultures that support them, and a host of other changes that also appear to be irresistible for modern societies: decline of the agricultural mode of

---

[29] Charles Taylor, "Two Theories of Modernity," in Dilip Gaonkar (ed.), *Alternative Modernities* (Durham, NC: Duke University Press, 2001), pp. 172–196; and *Modern Social Imaginaries* (Durham, NC: Duke University Press, 2004). I discuss Taylor's views in "Imaginaires sociaux et modernités multiples," *Philosophiques* 33:2 (2006): 485–491.

life that has defined most of humanity for much of our recorded history; functional differentiation and specialization of occupational and professional roles; diversification of outlooks, attitudes, and lifestyles; pluralism of belief systems, value commitments, and forms of individual and group identity; institutionalized growth of secular knowledge understood as fallible and susceptible to criticism and revision; spread of mass media and of mass-mediated popular culture; and, of course, ever-deeper immersion in transnational flows of capital, commodities, technology, information, communication, and culture. And we may want also to consider changes that most participants in the discourse of modernity find desirable, but concerning which empirical tendencies are not as unambiguous: the decline of patriarchal, racist, and ethnocentric stereotyping and role-casting, and of other "natural" hierarchies of this sort; the inclusion, as equals, of all inhabitants of a territory in its legal and political community; and the existence of public spheres that allow for open exchange and debate.

Taken together, these facts of cultural and societal modernity suggest that the scope of deep divergence possible and desirable in today's world may be somewhat more constricted than many multiculturalists suppose, especially if we take into account the very dense internal relations and causal connections between societal changes and the cultural patterns that are too often treated as swinging free of them. Cultural and institutional developments do not belong to different *orders* of reality. This is only an analytical distinction between *aspects* of social reality, and it can take us only so far. In reality, institutional structures are anchored in shared cultural practices, and cultural practices are structured by institutional forms. This interdependence becomes crucial to the discourse of modernization because, as we well know, structural changes have cultural presuppositions – so that if they are externally imposed or hastily adopted they often disintegrate or transmute – and they generally entail significant, unforeseen, and often unwanted cultural consequences. On the other hand, cultural modernization can make certain traditional institutions unsustainable, at least in their traditional forms, and may make certain modern institutions unavoidable.

3. Notwithstanding the facts of cultural and societal modernity, however, a global discourse of modernity carried on at a critical-reflective level simultaneously opens up *an inexhaustible, ever-shifting horizon of possibilities for reasonable disagreement*. Consider only a

few evident features of such discourse. Not only claims to universal validity have to stand up to transcultural scrutiny but claims to progress as well, for they implicate claims to improvement. Representing a given cultural change as the result of a learning process, for instance, implies that it offers a superior way of dealing with some domain of experience. Thus, for a certain range of problems there is little doubt that the history of the natural sciences and associated technologies can be represented as a progressive learning process. The same can be said for the history of historiography and other human studies in the modern period – at least in general, for when it comes to specifics, as we know, there is more than enough room for disagreement. However, even if the progressivist interpretation of a particular innovation proves to be superior to competing accounts, there still remains the rather different question of what to make of it, that is, what place a given innovation should have in the life of a society, whether and how it should be institutionalized. Thus, for instance, classical social theorists generally agreed that scientifically based technologies of production and instrumentally effective modes of organization represented developments of our rational capacities to cope with certain domains of problems. But they disagreed considerably in their assessments of how those developments had been incorporated into advanced capitalist societies via markets and bureaucracies. Obviously, now that issues of this kind are being debated in a diversity of societies, with a diversity of traditions, and in a diversity of circumstances, one would expect a diversity of views; for they centrally involve matters of well-being, variously understood, and on such matters unanimity is highly unlikely.

The same holds for "structural-functional" modifications generally. There is little doubt that some societal developments – for example market economies, bureaucratic administrations, or, more abstractly, the differentiation and integration of functionally specialized subsystems of action – generally increase the power or functional capacity of complex societies; that is, other things being equal, societies with them are better able to cope with certain types of problems than societies without them. But these societal developments are open to contestation in ways that cultural developments *as such* – as distinct from the place they should have in the life of a society – are not. Wholesale critiques of cultural modernity by cultural moderns always risk incoherence or bad faith, for we cannot but draw upon its resources in criticizing it: there is no extramundane standpoint available to us from which we could set modern culture as a whole at a distance. On the other hand, rejecting power-enhancing functional innovations may be perfectly coherent: there need be no *conceptual* confusion involved in wanting to live without markets or bureaucracies. Of course, *in practice*, in the type of world we live in, going without developments of this sort runs the risk – not of incoherence but – of impotence, of being dominated and exploited by others in ways that undermine a population's well-being even more than would likely result from undertaking the transformation in question. Obviously, the choices a society faces are quite different if it is situated (today) in a nexus of neoliberal globalization dominated by neoimperial powers or, as some hope (one day), in a more law-governed, cosmopolitan world order.

Together, then, these three facts of global modernity open up a space for reasonable disagreement about what is progressive and what is regressive in capitalist modernization. I shall conclude with a few, brief, general, and no doubt controversial remarks about that space.

(a) As noted above, disagreements about what *place* either cultural or societal innovations should have in the life of a specific society cannot be decided simply by demonstrating that a given transformation represents a developmental advance, either of "rational capacity" or of "functional capacity." Once the demands of theodicy and teleology are stripped from developmental schemes, such advances no longer carry the imprimatur of divine providence, ends of nature, or the cunning of reason. Furthermore, the perfection of species capacities, for its own sake, can no longer serve, as it did for Kant and many of his developmentalist successors, as an ultimate sanction of historical progress, no matter how bloody. The issues under discussion in practical discourses concerning the desirability of institutionalizing specific innovations in specific societies have directly to do not with species perfection but with what participants judge to be in the best interests of everyone affected by those changes, including those not yet born who will have to live with the consequences of present decisions. In practice, these sorts of discussions unavoidably implicate the different values, goods, and identities of those involved, and thus can often be brought to a conclusion only through negotiation, compromise, accommodation, voting or the like – that is, through something short of consensus.

At the same time, one has to keep in mind that developmental advances are deemed to be such because of the enhanced capacity they bring to deal with certain types of problems. And improving our ability to cope with the world bears directly on our pursuit of well-being, at least under most interpretations thereof. So judgments concerning the development of functional capacity are by no means irrelevant to practical discourse; but neither are they decisive. One also has to keep in mind that genuine cultural developments, in contrast to particular institutionalizations of them, normally can be blocked only by maintaining a closed society in which threats to established views from that quarter are forcibly excluded or repressed. Those who have understood the cultural developments will usually find any defense of such a society that rests on incomprehension of them unpersuasive – and any defense that rests on comprehension of them sinister. It is worth noting that cultural learning and societal problem solving sometimes converge on the same institutional changes, which reflect both enhanced rational capacity and enhanced functional capacity at once. Consequently, such changes can be defended as developmental advances, as superior to what came before, both normatively and functionally. Many argue, for instance, that this is the case with the democratic rule of law, that is, that modern subjects formed in modern cultures eventually demand basic legal protections and rights, including rights of political participation, and increasingly refuse legitimacy to governments that deny them. And some even argue projectively that this holds true for global governance as well: that a cosmopolitan rule of law with institutionalized forms of democratic publicity, accountability, representation, and participation is the only rationally defensible *and* practically effective form of world order in a globalized modernity.[30]

(b) Because interpretive standpoints are, as Weber long ago noted, themselves located in the stream of historical life, they bring with them not only cognitive but evaluative presuppositions (*Wertbeziehungen*).[31] This means that our knowledge of the historical-social world is value-laden in a stronger sense than is our knowledge of the physical-biological world, for it reflects not only the epistemic values of a mode of rational inquiry, but also, and unavoidably, particular values of the sociocultural locations from which it is pursued. This suggests that in the discourse of modernity, claims to "objectivity" will have to be

---

[30] For instance, Habermas, *The Postnational Constellation*; David Held, *The Global Covenant* (Cambridge: Polity Press, 2004); and James Bohman, *Democracy Across Borders* (Cambridge, MA: MIT Press, 2007).

[31] M. Weber, *The Methodology of the Social Sciences*, ed. and tr. E. Shils and H. Finch (New York: Free Press, 1949).

defended on normative and evaluative as well as on narrowly cognitive grounds. And it is generally recognized today that "ethical" questions concerning competing goods, values, identities, and the like usually do not admit of universal answers. Moreover, as considerations of the right and the good are normally entwined in matters of law and politics, justice claims are susceptible to contestation from many of the same angles as interpretive and evaluative claims generally.[32] In short, the space for reasonable disagreement that social-theoretical accounts permit – no matter how rich they may be in empirical data – is extensive and multidimensional. This is true even for claims regarding objective constraints and possibilities. As we know very well, from policy debates for instance, such claims are strongly influenced by interpretive and evaluative standpoints that reflect political commitments; and they also involve political will, so that judgments of impossibility may be expressions of an unwillingness to take action. To acknowledge all of this is not to say that there are no better and worse arguments in this area, but only that there will often be no one right answer. Nor is it to deny that developmental considerations of the sorts, cultural and societal, discussed above figure importantly in such arguments; but at a critical-reflective level of discourse, developmental claims are too blunt an instrument to settle cultural disagreements by themselves. For one thing, even when there is widespread agreement that a given innovation is an improvement on what came before, the structural features that characterize it in developmental terms will typically be of such a general and abstract nature as to allow for an indeterminate variety of concrete realizations.

(c) In the global discourse of modernity, all participants are in principle operating at the same discursive level, which means that any culture or society talked about is entitled to talk back – for instance, to challenge the theorist on his or her own presuppositions, procedures, standards, assessments, and so forth. In short, normative symmetry makes any epistemic or evaluative claim about culture or society essentially contestable.[33] One thing that will be especially subject to

---

[32] I discuss the entwinement of the right and the good in "Legitimacy and Diversity: Dialectical Reflections on Analytical Distinctions," in A. Arato and M. Rosenfeld (eds.), *Habermas on Law and Democracy: Critical Exchanges* (Berkeley: University of California Press, 1998), pp. 115–153.

[33] This is my translation of Habermas's discourse model into the domain of intercultural dialogue.

disagreement is whether a proclaimed end-point of development or "end of history" is really such or is, instead, itself in need of *Aufhebung*, of being superseded. For it certainly makes good sense to doubt that modernity as it has developed in the West and through its relations with the rest of the world is a perfect ending to the story of human development. Moreover, the modernization of formerly colonized parts of the globe cannot simply replicate that pattern for the obvious reason that it was predicated upon treating the non-Western world as a resource base for Western development. Of necessity, then, local adaptations of modernization processes will produce alterations and innovations, elaborations of modernity in very different circumstances.[34] And it would be baseless to deny that these will often be improvements, from which others can learn, including societies whose development was premised upon imperialism. Learning how best to be modern in a world in which "we are now all moderns" will require going beyond Eurocentric modernity by going forward, that is, by superseding it both in theory and in practice. While universalism certainly does not become superfluous in such a setting, it entails intercultural discussion and negotiation of the universals we have to bring into play in shaping our common human lives, ongoing contestation of their meaning in practice. Establishing common ground in and through public discourse and political practice across national and cultural boundaries is essential to constructing the kind of global order that might make the future less of a slaughterhouse than the past.

It is not unreasonable to hope for the advent of a cosmopolitan world order in which all human beings receive equal respect and consideration. But such an order is unlikely to emerge as a fortuitous side effect of the self-interested actions of global economic, political, and military actors. However dependent it undoubtedly is on the favorable confluence of unintended consequences and enlightened self-interest, its realization also requires, as Kant would remind us, that it be consciously pursued as a moral-political goal. We may reasonably hope for it, then, not only because it is a possible future, but also because it is one that we can and should try to bring about.

---

[34] Partha Chatterjee, *The Nation and Its Fragments* (Princeton University Press, 1993).

6 | Liberal imperialism and the dilemma of development

Interrogating the tension in liberal thought between norms of equal respect and theories of sociocultural development is critical to understanding the relations of modern Europe to the rest of the world. From the settlement of the Americas and the formation of the East India and Royal African Companies in the seventeenth century to present-day neoimperialism, European (and later, American) dominion over non-Europeans has repeatedly been justified with conceptions of development, enlightenment, civilization and progress, which were deployed to reduce the cognitive dissonance between liberal universalism and liberal imperialism. At the same time, as we have been made increasingly aware by postcolonial scholarship, many of the classical liberal theorists were deeply involved with colonial affairs and constructed their political philosophies with a view to them.

In what follows, after (I) assembling a few scattered reminders of this involvement and briefly recalling the systematic formulation of the dilemma of development by Kant, I shall (II) examine the form that dilemma assumed in the detranscendentalized atmosphere of Mill's utilitarianism and basically retained thereafter. Two contrasting ways of dissolving the dilemma will be reviewed and rejected in sections III and IV, leading to the conclusion that it cannot be theoretically eliminated but may, perhaps, be politically displaced to a predicament with which we have to come to terms. Section V will consider some conditions for doing so.

I

John Locke, who was an original shareholder in the Royal African Company when it was chartered in 1672, had earlier (1669) coauthored the Fundamental Constitutions of Carolina, which legally recognized Negro slavery, and later (1682) participated in their revision, which retained the slavery article unaltered.[1] In addition to serving as Secretary to the Lords Proprietors of the Carolina Colony (1669–1675), he also served as Secretary and Treasurer to the English Council for Trade and Foreign Plantations (1673–1674) and as Secretary to the English Board of trade (1696–1700). His rationalizations of the enslavement of Africans and the expropriation of Native-American lands drew upon a narrative of development from the state of nature to political society. In the state of nature, such as obtained in Africa and North America, each is guarantor of his own life, liberty, and possessions; and when attacked, threatened, or resisted in the pursuit of his interests, each may resort to force, which might then legitimately result in conquest, enslavement, or expropriation. Most famously, Locke declared America to be a "vacant land" occupied only by nomadic savages, who had failed to heed God's command to cultivate the earth and Nature's law that conferred ownership upon those who did so – and hence a land morally and legally open to appropriation. "God gave the world to men in common; but … He gave it to the use of the industrious and rational (and labor was to be his title to it)."[2] This contrast between the idle, irrational, "wild Indian" wandering the "uncultivated waste" of America and the industrious, rational, civilized planter harvesting its bounty dominates Locke's repeated references to America and its indigenous peoples in the *Second Treatise* and gives figurative expression to his view of the general development of human forms of life from nomadic hunting and gathering to settled agriculture, for "in the beginning all the world was America."[3]

Locke's involvement with, detailed knowledge of, and liberal apologetics for England's Atlantic empire was later equaled, if not surpassed, by the Mills in their connection with East Indian affairs.[4] James Mill was engaged by the East India Company in 1819, became

---

[1] There is a large literature on the relationship of Locke's liberalism to English colonialism. See, for instance, the discussions of this in James Tully, *An Approach to Political Philosophy: Locke in Contexts* (Cambridge University Press, 1993); Barbara Arneil, *John Locke and America: The Defense of English Colonialism* (Oxford University Press, 1996); and David Armitage, *The ideological Origins of the British Empire* (Cambridge University Press, 2000).

[2] John Locke, *Two Treatises on Government*, ed. Peter Laslett (Cambridge University Press, 1993), *Second Treatise*, p. 291.

[3] Locke, *Second Treatise*, p. 301.

[4] From the extensive literature on this connection, see, for instance, the discussions in Eric Stokes, *The English Utilitarians and India* (Oxford University Press, 1959);

its Chief Examiner in 1830, and remained with it for the rest of his life. Indebted both to Bentham's utilitarianism and Scottish Enlightenment conceptions of development, he retained only superficial traces of their respective criticisms of colonialism. England's dominion in India was, he granted, generally against its own best interests; but it did serve the best interests of the indigenous population: "If we wish for the prolongation of an English government in India ... it is for the sake of the natives, not of England ... Even the utmost abuse of European power is better, we are persuaded, than the most temperate exercise of Oriental despotism."[5] This was in keeping with Mill's characterization of Indian society as barbaric and of Indians as incapable of self-government – a characterization informed by a scheme of development that flattened Scottish Enlightenment stadial theories onto the plane of utility and reduced the number of importantly different developmental stages to a binary opposition: barbarism versus civilization. The imposition of British rule on backward India was then justified in terms of a tutelary duty to assist it, through colonial administration, in passing from its social childhood to social maturity.

James's son, John Stuart, who was also employed by the East India Company for most of his adult life and rose to be Chief Examiner in his last year there, subsequently imported this idea of progressive colonial dominion into the core of his classical formulation of liberal values – hence the sudden admonition in the introductory chapter of *On Liberty* that its principles are "meant to apply only to human beings in the maturity of their faculties" and not to "those backward states of society in which the race itself may be considered as in its nonage."[6] As to the latter, "despotism is a legitimate mode of government in dealing with barbarians, provided the end be their improvement and the means justified by actually effecting that end."[7]

Lynn Zastoupil, *John Stuart Mill and India* (Stanford University Press, 1994); Uday Singh Mehta, *Liberalism and Empire* (University of Chicago Press, 1999); and Jennifer Pitts, *A Turn to Empire: The Rise of Imperial Liberalism in Britain and France* (Princeton University Press, 2005).

[5] Cited from Mill's review of *Voyages aux Indes orientales* in Pitts, *A Turn to Empire*, p. 125.

[6] J. S. Mill, *On Liberty*, ed. E. Rapaport (Indianapolis: Hackett Publishing, 1978), pp. 10–11.

[7] *Ibid.*, p. 10.

I shall have more to say of J. S. Mill's views on these matters in section II. Here it is important to note that, though the use of developmental schemes to justify illiberal practices toward non-Western societies has been characteristic of the mainstream of classical liberal theory, it is not present in all streams of liberal thought; there are others characterized rather by a deep ambivalence toward, or even an outright rejection of, colonialism.[8] Nor, as we shall see in sections III and IV, does the tension between universalism and developmentalism trouble only liberal thought. Given this diversity of views, it seems to me an oversimplification to argue, as many recently have, that imperialism is constitutive for liberalism *as such*, especially since the critiques advanced by anticolonial liberals have typically appealed to liberal values. On the other hand, it is undeniable that the mainstream of liberal thought, running from Locke through Mill to contemporary neoliberalism, has continually flowed into and out of European–American imperialism, and that ideas of sociocultural development have been integral to that connection. Developmental thinking has proved to be rather adaptable and thus quite serviceable in rationalizing the various truncations of universal rights and obligations that colonial domination and exploitation required. Moreover, the putatively scientific status of theories of development has lent a naturalistic aura to socially constructed hierarchies, thus deflecting moral assessment and political critique. In this and other ways, the refraction of liberal ideals in the medium of developmental theory has made it rhetorically possible to combine universalism in principle with Eurocentrism in practice.

As we saw in chapter 2, the inherent tensions between moral universalism and developmental hierarchy were already recognized and given sharp systematic expression by Kant. From the *moral-legal standpoint* of practical reason, he repeatedly denounced contemporary forms of European imperialism and their purported justifications. At the same time, from the *anthropological-historical standpoint* of reflective judgment, he argued that the only way to make sense of human history was in terms of the gradual diffusion of an asymmetrical development centered in Europe. The tensions that arose from his uncompromising adherence to both standpoints are a defining characteristic of the

---

[8] See, for instance, Sankar Muthu, *Enlightenment and Empire* (Princeton University Press, 2003); and Jennifer Pitts's discussions of the Scottish Enlightenment and Jeremy Bentham in *A Turn to Empire*.

Kantian world picture. He lived with the tensions because he believed he could not do otherwise: morally speaking, the fundamental principles of equal dignity, respect, and consideration dictated that we pursue a global kingdom of ends, in which everyone recognized everyone else as an end in him- or herself; but anthropologically speaking, the development of our rational nature resulted from the play of our unsocial sociability, with vastly inequitable outcomes. What I am calling the dilemma of development is evident in this construction: the path Kant projects toward the "moral destiny" of humankind is marked, even prepared, by mutual conflict and uneven development, which, from the start of the modern period, has meant European dominance and non-European assimilation. As a result, historical events and tendencies that are unacceptable from a moral-legal perspective often prove to be functional from a developmental perspective, as a means to the perfection of our rational nature. Thus war, conquest, oppression, inequality, exploitation, and the other great evils of the human condition, which are morally despicable, have served as valuable spurs to the development and spread of culture and civilization. In the larger scheme of things, "this splendid misery is bound up with the development of the natural predispositions in the human race, and the end of nature itself, even if it is not our end, is hereby attained."[9]

As we shall see, this dilemma of development can be variously transformed but cannot easily be eliminated from the liberal world picture. It haunts liberalism even when ethics is naturalized and well-being is reinstated as its final end; when the teleology of nature and theodicy of history are no longer theoretical concerns; and when history and anthropology are viewed simply as forms of empirical inquiry – as a closer look at the thought of John Stuart Mill will make clear.[10]

---

[9] I. Kant, *Critique of the Power of Judgment*, ed. P. Guyer, tr. P. Guyer and E. Matthews (Cambridge University Press, 2000), p. 299.

[10] I shall be referring primarily to Mill's writings from the years just after the Great Uprising against the British in India (1857), the end of the East India Company, and the institution of direct imperial rule by the British government: *On Liberty* (*OL*: 1859); "A Few Words on Non-Intervention" (NI: 1859), in *Essays on Politics and Culture*, ed. G. Himmelfarb (Garden City, NY: Doubleday, 1962), pp. 396–413; "Civilization" (C: 1836; rev. ed. 1859), in *Essays on Politics and Culture*, pp. 51–84; and *Considerations on Representative Government* (*CRG*: 1861), (South Bend, IN: Gateway, 1962). References will be given in parentheses in the text by abbreviated titles and page numbers.

II

As explained in chapter 2, Kant dealt with the tension between the universality of law and morality, on the one hand, and the unevenness of sociocultural development, on the other, by appealing to "rational" faith and hope in the workings of Divine Providence. He could avoid a moral-political choice between the imperial rule of what he saw as less developed by more developed societies and the self-rule of underdeveloped societies condemned to lasting inequality and subordination, because he could believe and hope that the hidden hand of God/Nature-in-history would guide human affairs toward the "ultimate end" of history and the "moral destiny" of humankind. As this sort of progressive eschatology of history lost its credibility, Kant's specific way of defusing the dilemma between liberal universalism and liberal imperialism ceased to be an option. Thus, the more naturalistic resolution to the dilemma offered by John Stuart Mill in the context of nineteenth-century British imperialism became more typical of the justifications of colonialism within progressive liberal thought until the advent of the postcolonial condition following World War II.[11]

Mill did not appeal to divine providence or to a teleology of nature and history; and he placed general well-being at the center of moral and political theory. At the same time, he transfigured the baser motives for imperial conquest and exploitation into the noble motives of a civilizing mission and a benign paternalism, which was for the good of those subject to it, whether or not they realized it. The *superior force* of European societies, which made empire a real possibility, was thereby combined with their putatively *superior character* to make the case for imperial dominion. Such power-backed paternalism, while admittedly despotic, was at the same time progressive and thus was superior to the indigenous forms of self-rule found in less developed societies, which, while no less despotic, were evidently less progressive. As Mill plainly put it, there are conditions of society in which "there being no spring of spontaneous improvement in the people themselves, their almost only hope of making any steps in advance depends upon the chances of a

[11] See Karuna Mantena, *Alibis of Empire* (Princeton University Press, forthcoming), for qualifications of this generalization having to do with the shift from ethical to sociological conceptions of imperial legitimacy in the closing decades of the nineteenth century.

good despot. Under a native despotism, a good despot is a rare and transitory accident; but when the dominion they are under is that of a more civilized people, that people ought to be able to supply it constantly" (*CRG*, 346).

How does he arrive at this view, theoretically speaking? There are several paths, but the main one is marked by his understanding of the basic normative standard of utility: "I forego any advantage which could be derived to my argument from the idea of abstract right as a thing independent of utility. I regard utility as the ultimate appeal in all ethical questions; but it must be utility in the largest sense, grounded on the permanent interests of man as a progressive being" (*OL*, 10). The internal connection between utility and progress is spelled out in the same essay through contrasting liberty with custom. Mill traces a series of links connecting liberty with autonomy, individuality, reason, progress, and the like, on the one side, and on the opposite side, connecting custom with unfreedom, stagnation, and the like. In consequence, the full development of the capacities of the individual and of the species requires individual freedom, while the great enemy of development is conformity to custom, which does not educate any of the distinctive endowments of human beings. In civilized societies, where liberty is given greater scope, each individual becomes "an independent center of improvement," whereas in uncivilized – savage or barbaric – societies, where custom rules, human life becomes stagnant or retrogresses: "The despotism of custom is everywhere the standing hindrance to human advancement, being in unceasing antagonism to that disposition to aim at something better than customary, which is called, according to circumstances, the spirit of liberty or that of progress or improvement ... [T]he contest between the two constitutes the chief interest of the history of mankind. The greater part of the world has, properly speaking, no history, because the despotism of custom is complete. This is the case over the whole East" (*OL*, 67). With this characterization of non-European modes of life as just so many forms of the despotism of custom, which blocks the development of human capacities and frustrates the permanent interests of man as a progressive being, we are close to a justification of colonial intervention and superintendence.

There is, however, a palpable tension in this with other elements of Mill's argument in *On Liberty*. For if self-development and self-improvement are ethically enjoined by his brand of perfectionism, the latter simultaneously proscribes interfering with the liberty of others for their own good: "the only freedom which deserves the name is that of pursuing our own good in our own way"; "mankind are the greater gainers by suffering each other to live as seems good to themselves than by compelling each to live as seems good to the rest" (*OL*, 12). But, Mill explains, this applies only to "human beings in the maturity of their faculties" (*OL*, 9). It does not apply to children or to backward societies, "in which the race itself may be considered in its nonage" (*OL*, 10). For the latter, spontaneous progress is so fraught with difficulties that "a ruler full of the spirit of improvement is warranted in the use of any expedients that will attain an end perhaps otherwise unattainable. Despotism is a legitimate mode of government in dealing with barbarians, provided the end be their improvement and the means justified by actually effecting that end" (*ibid.*). And as Mill emphasizes in other writings from the same period, this civilizing despotism can better be afforded by an already civilized nation with non-self-interested foreign policy aims – such as England – than by indigenous rulers.

Furthermore, the principle of nonintervention in the internal affairs of other sovereign nations, which stands at the center of modern international law, governs, Mill tells us, only relations among civilized nations, not relations between them and uncivilized or barbarous peoples: "The sacred duties which civilized nations owe to the independence and nationality of each other are not binding towards those to whom nationality and independence are either a certain evil or at best a questionable good ... To characterize any conduct whatever towards a barbarous people as a violation of the law of nations only shows that he who speaks has never considered the subject ... [B]arbarians have no rights as a *nation* except a right to such treatments as may, at the earliest possible period, fit them for becoming one" (NI, 406). If this "right" were applied to British rule in India, Mill is confident, there would be no violation. It was at bottom a non-self-interested, civilizing tutelage aimed at reforming economic, political, and educational institutions, so that India – which must once have been capable of self-development before stagnation set in – might some day again take responsibility for its own improvement.

In general, the proper normative standard for evaluating government is the best possible institutions in the existing state of a society, where "best" is to be understood as "most conducive to progress" (*CRG*, 27). Hence the appropriate institutions will differ according to a society's "stage of advancement." More specifically, the form of government must be such that "its operation is favorable, or not unfavorable, to the next step, which it is necessary for them to take, in order to raise themselves to the next level" (*CRG*, 39). Representative government – "the ideal type of the most perfect society" – is suitable only to societies at advanced stages of improvement (*CRG*, 75). As societies range lower in development, other forms of government are preferable, "when the people, in order to advance in civilization have some lesson to learn, some habit not yet acquired, to the acquisition of which representative government is likely to be an impediment" (*CRG*, 79). In some such situations, what is called for is "the government of dependencies by a free state," under the condition, of course, that the rule be in the best interests of the ruled: "this mode of government is as legitimate as any other, if it is the one which, in the existing state of civilization of the subject people, most facilitates their transition to a higher stage of improvement" (*CRG*, 346). Rule by a "good despot" is "the ideal rule of a free people over a barbarous or semi-barbarous one" (*ibid.*). And as colonization was at that time rapidly becoming "the universal condition of the more backward populations" (*CRG*, 347), it was this ideal of good colonial despotism that should govern the relations of the most advanced European nations to the rest of the world, for whom it was typically the best attainable form of government, that is, the most favorable to future development.

Mill's own account of such development is notably thin by comparison to those that came before and after. It is, to begin with, one-dimensional: there is a single axis of development, along which every society can be ranked as more or less advanced. Moreover, the rankings pertain to societies as wholes; all aspects of a society – its art and religion as well as its economics and politics – are held to reflect its general level of development. And these holistic, one-dimensional rankings are further simplified by grouping all differentiations into one overriding binary opposition: civilized versus barbarian (or savage, rude, uncivilized, etc.). Though Mill does sometimes remark on the differences between nomadic and settled societies, between hunting and gathering bands and the great ancient civilizations, between the indigenous cultures of North America and those of China and India, and the like, all such differentiations get reduced to that single dichotomy when he is concerned with colonial relations. Thus, in an essay on "Civilization" written in 1836 and republished with minor revisions in 1859, after enumerating a variety of respects in which societies can be compared, Mill assures his readers that "though these ingredients of civilizations are various ... they begin together, always coexist, and accompany each other in their growth. Wherever there has introduced itself sufficient knowledge of the arts of life, and sufficient security of property and person, to render the progressive increase of wealth and population possible, the community becomes and continues progressive in all its elements which we have just enumerated" (C, 53). And it is just this characteristic of being "progressive in all its elements" that structures the dichotomy between civilized and uncivilized societies. In this he followed in the footsteps of his father, as he did in his low estimation of the degree of civilization in India.[12] Though clearly different from what he called "savage tribes," India was also a stagnant society that was incapable of progressive self-rule and could thus be improved only with outside guidance. And of course, in terms of Britain's relations to its colonies, that is the attribution that counted. One might conjecture that the practical-political perspective of who colonized whom rendered finer theoretical distinctions insignificant; it was the perspective of colonial rule that framed the description and evaluation from the start.

Mill was not entirely clear in identifying the chief motor of progress. At times he accentuated "material" developments – in property relations, in trade and manufacture, in the division and combination of labor, and the like – and at other times "cultural" developments – in the "powers and acquirements of mind," in the diffusion of intelligence, in opinions, habits and social practices, and the like – and quite often, both. But he was clear that race was not the decisive factor; and this distinguished him from many late nineteenth- and early twentieth-century developmentalists.[13] He did not, it seems, reject out of hand the existence of "natural" differences among the "various races of men"; rather, he judged the empirical evidence that they were decisive to developmental differences to be weak in the extreme – especially when compared to the evidence for the developmental significance of the sorts of material and cultural factors mentioned above.[14] The factor he most often singled out for attention, "national character," he clearly

---

[12] J. S. proofread the many volumes of his father's *History of British India* (1817) – when he was 11 years old!

[13] See chapter 3.

[14] See J. S. Mill, "The Negro Question," published anonymously in *Fraser's Magazine for Town and Country* in 1850, in response to an earlier article by Thomas Carlyle (reprinted in *Littell's Living Age*, XXIV, 465–469); and the discussion of Mill's views on "race" by John Robson, "Civilization and Culture

understood in cultural rather than racial terms. In this respect, he anticipated a line of argument favored by many late twentieth-century theorists. Indeed, with his "postmetaphysical" rejection of any theodicy or teleology of history, his replacement of laws of nature and commands of reason with utilitarian considerations of well-being and progress, and his reliance – however defective – on empirical history and the human sciences to make his case, Mill could be said to have anticipated in many respects the approaches to development and modernization that came to dominate after World War II.[15]

As noted, even in the desublimated atmosphere of Mill's postmetaphysical liberalism, the dilemma of development does not disappear without a trace. It surfaces repeatedly in the tension between his basic liberal value of autonomy – "If a person possesses any tolerable amount of common sense and experience, his own mode of laying out his existence is the best, not because it is the best in itself, but because it is his own mode" (*OL*, 64) – and the paternalism underwritten by his developmental reading of Europe's relations with non-European peoples, for whom government by a more civilized people is "as legitimate [a mode of government] as any other" and is in fact "their almost only hope in making any steps in advance" (*CRG*, 346). The tension is further heightened when Mill asserts that the comparative evaluation of different modes of life cannot properly be made from a God's-eye view but only "practically, when anyone thinks fit to try them" (*OL*, 54).[16] Or when he castigates the persecutors of Mormons by declaring: "I am not aware that any community has a right to force another to be civilized ... Let them send missionaries, if they please" (*OL*, 90). Or when he goes so far as to state that "on every principle of morality and justice," Great Britain ought to consent to her colonies separating, "should the time come when, after full trial of the best form of union, they deliberately desire to be dissevered" (*CRG*, 342). But such reservations are regularly outweighed by the worry that non-European societies are ruled by "the despotism of custom," which is irremediably opposed to the "free development of individuality," which is in turn

---

as Moral Concepts," in John Skorupski (ed.), *The Cambridge Companion to Mill* (Cambridge University Press, 1998), pp. 338–371.

[15] I will discuss some of these approaches in chapter 7.

[16] Nevertheless, though he was himself importantly engaged with the governance of India throughout most of his adult life, Mill never deemed it necessary to visit that part of the world.

not only "one of the leading essentials of well-being" but also "a necessary part and condition" of civilization, education (i.e. *Bildung*), and culture (*OL*, 54). Here one must choose, for "the contest between the two is the chief interest of the history of mankind" (*OL*, 67). And though the tension between them cannot be made simply to disappear, it can, Mill thinks, be reduced considerably by the requirement, in regard to the government of dependencies by free states, that a "government of leading strings" is admissible only if it actually "train[s] the people to walk alone" (*CRG*, 42).[17] That is to say, it belongs to the normative ideal of such government – to which Mill supposed Britain's rule of its colonies approximated – that the dominant people seek to advance the development of the subject people, so that the arrangement is temporary: once the immature people is capable of self-rule and self-improvement, it can be treated as an equal member of the community of civilized nations – but not just yet.

III

Whatever the tensions internal to this ideal, it so evidently diverged from the realities of colonial rule that critics had an easy time debunking it. In this Marx was at the forefront. In two articles on British rule in India written for the *New York Daily Tribune* in 1853, that is, at about the time Mill was publishing the views considered above, Marx took it as evident that the East India Company was "actuated solely by the spirit of gain"[18] (June 25, 654). The advancements it fostered in the conditions of life in India were largely the consequences of a basically exploitative relationship. So while they were, as he too believed, necessary to the full development of Indian capacities, they were anything but benign. England had destroyed the entire framework of Indian society for its own purposes and thereby wreaked havoc on traditional institutions, organizations, and communities, and great suffering upon their members. Nevertheless, it remained that England's pursuit of its own self-interest had led to fundamental transformations of Indian life that

---

[17] This remark is made specifically with reference to a type of uncivilized society that is slave-based, but it applies to the governance of other types as well.

[18] I shall be citing articles from June 25 and August 8, 1853, both of which are reprinted in *The Marx–Engels Reader*, ed. Robert C. Tucker (New York: W. W. Norton, 1978), pp. 653–658 and 659–664, respectively. References to them are given in parentheses in the text by date and page number.

were a prerequisite to further progress – "the laying of the material foundations of Western society in Asia" (August 8, 659). England, he assures us, "in causing a social revolution in Hindostan, was actuated only by the vilest interests, and was stupid in her manner of enforcing them. But that is not the question. The question is, can mankind fulfill its destiny without a fundamental revolution in the social state of Asia? If not, whatever may have been the crimes of England, she was the unconscious tool of history in bringing about that revolution" (June 25, 658). In this the British were no different from other capitalist regimes around the globe: "Has the bourgeoisie ever done more? Has it ever effected a progress without dragging individuals and peoples through blood and dirt, through misery and degradation?" (August 8, 662). Covering over naked self-interest with the mantel of a civilizing mission was just one more instance of the "profound hypocrisy" of capitalism (*ibid.*, 663). So, what Mill regarded as a reconciliation of liberal values with colonial practices, Marx called hypocrisy – and in this he was in agreement with most critics of colonialism to the present. What separates him from many of them, however, and particularly from many postcolonial theorists, is the horn of the universalism/developmentalism dilemma he holds on to. Moral judgments are beside the point. The transformation of the world by capitalism is a necessary stage on the way to the full flowering of human capacities in socialism: "When a great social revolution shall have mastered the results of the bourgeois epoch, the market of the world and the modern powers of production ... then only will human progress cease to resemble that hideous pagan idol, who would not drink the nectar but from the skulls of the slain" (*ibid.*, 664).

Today Marx's historical confidence in that "great social revolution," like Kant's rational faith in God's or Nature's plan of history, has largely lost whatever powers of reconciliation it might once have possessed. Thus, as I shall elaborate in section IV, many postcolonial critics have grabbed on to the other horn of the dilemma: morally condemning neoimperial relations while dismissing developmental theory as an ideology of empire. Theorists who still hold on to both horns and try to close the gap between them stand accused by both sides of "profound hypocrisy." And it is by no means easy to avoid that charge without surrendering either universal norms or developmental schemes, the ideological combination of which to justify empire was coeval with liberalism.

As we have seen, the problem arises when universal moral principles – such as those Kant derives from pure practical reason or those Mill derives from considerations of utility – are "applied" to a social reality described anthropologically historically as developing in essential respects. For this purpose, in Kant's formulation, "pure moral principles" have to be "schematized" to take account of relevant differences, if they are to be applied properly, that is, differently in different contexts. As examples of such schematized moral principles, he mentions rules that apply to the treatment of people "in accordance with their differences in rank, age, sex, health, property, or poverty, and so forth," or according to whether they belong to "the cultivated or the crude."[19] Similarly, Mill advises us that, though the "comprehensive science or art of government" yields general principles, the latter have to be applied differently according to "the stage of advancement already reached," for "the one indispensable merit of a government" is that it promote the development of the people governed (*CRG*, 37–39).

But it is not only such "contexts of application" that connected liberal theory to European imperialism; that connection was already forged in its "contexts of origin."[20] The combination of developmentalism with universalism was deployed by progressive liberalism as a justification for empire from the beginning, and not by chance; for the general accounts of history and society that served this purpose were always interpretations from a practically engaged point of view. They reflected the nature of Europeans' contacts with non-European societies from the voyages of "discovery" onwards. And given a hermeneutic standpoint shaped by their growing superiority of force and by their growing confidence in the superiority of their culture and institutions, that is not surprising. The imbalances of power of various sorts formed a context in which the autonomy and equal respect required in theory could not be effectively demanded in practice. As colonial powers usually could not be forced to negotiate differences on equal terms, they were disposed to interpret them in hierarchical and temporal terms. Other societies and cultures became earlier "stages" of development, salient differences from the West became marks of backwardness, and

---

[19] I. Kant, *The Metaphysics of Morals*, in Mary J. Gregor (ed. and tr.), *Practical Philosophy* (Cambridge University Press, 1996), p. 584.

[20] The classic formulations of liberalism postdate the completion of the conquest of Ireland, the founding of the East India Company, and the granting of a charter to Virginia, among other things.

backwardness meant that a society's or culture's time had passed. Correspondingly, the application of liberal ideals could take the form of a temporalizing or, better, temporizing universalism. This produced the familiar "not yet" effect – as in "not yet ready for self-rule," the deferral of equal respect and autonomy until such time as the subjects' needs for education and improvement had been met.[21] From this perspective, when dealing with backward peoples, as with children, it makes no sense to seek the consent of the governed; the most that can be expected is good colonial government – or as Mill bluntly put it, good despotism – that will one day make such consent appropriate. Thus colonial policy, in dealing with institutions and practices that belong essentially to the past, legitimates itself as future-oriented reform. It compensates denial of freedom and equality in the present by issuing a "promissory note" for future freedom and equality – conditional, of course, on the requisite developments actually taking place. The shape of that future is already known: it is, by and large, the present shape of the most advanced societies. What are required now are the use of power for improvement by the colonizers and the acceptance of the (temporary) deferral of self-rule by the colonized. Historically, however, it was all too evident that "good despotism" was always already an ideological cover for domination and exploitation and that "the natives' patience" had always already run out. Against this background, it is not surprising that many postcolonial thinkers today dismiss or deconstruct the very idea of development.

IV

Until relatively recently, and with some important exceptions (e.g. Gandhi), critics of liberal developmentalism have, like Marx, tended to remain within the ambit of developmental thinking, broadly conceived. In the 1980s and 1990s, however, outright rejections of developmentalism became widespread. Various forms of postcolonial thought, often appropriating post-Nietzschean and post-Heideggerian critiques of Western humanism, challenged its fundamental assumptions. From these more radical perspectives, even the received forms of Marxist critique appeared to be modernist tropes oriented to the

---

[21] U. S. Mehta elaborates upon this temporizing effect in *Liberalism and Empire*, pp. 106–111.

ultimate convergence of all societies and cultures. What was needed,
however, was not a new form of critical modernism but "postmodernism," not a better theory of development but "postdevelopment." There
has since been a continual proliferation of postmodern and postdevelopment critiques, of which I shall briefly note only two broad streams,
which in practice often flow together and join other streams.[22]

One, which often uses Foucault's genealogical critique as a point of
reference, sees post-World War II development theory and practice as a
neocolonial regime of power/knowledge meant to succeed the colonial
regime and thus as a central strategy of modern power rather than a
path to emancipation from it.[23] It links "universal reason" internally to
relations of power: what is rational is right for everyone, what everyone
should do, what everyone may be sanctionably expected, even forced,
to do. Through multiple, often tacit, chains of reasoning of this sort,
Western humanist ideals get linked to disciplinary strategies that are
embedded in power relations and aimed at subjugating, normalizing,
and dominating non-Western peoples. As the practical knowledge of
local traditions gets disqualified in the development paradigm, there is a
need for outside assistance from already developed societies and the
international agencies that implement their policies. Vast armies of
officials, planners, and experts are thereby vested with power/knowl-
edge. And given the resultant gradient between expert and local knowledge, development is inherently structured as a top-down field of
action. It is the expert who determines what improvements are needed,
what will be most beneficial to the "target populations," in short, what
is to be thought and what is to be done. The hegemony of "reason" is
thus secured by forces beyond the force of the better argument. The task
of critical analysis in this genealogical mode is to subvert the constitutive Eurocentrism of discourse formations like "development" and

---

[22] For a sampling of diverse lines of critique, see the collections edited by Wolfgang
Sachs, *The Development Dictionary* (London: Zed Books, 1992); Majid
Rahnema and Victoria Bawtree, *The Post-Development Reader* (London: Zed
Books, 1997); and Ronaldo Munck and Denis O'Hearn, *Critical Development
Theory* (London: Zed Books, 1999).

[23] See, for example, Arturo Escobar, *Encountering Development: The Making and
the Unmaking of the Third World* (Princeton University Press, 1995). Earlier on,
Edward Said's very influential work, *Orientalism* (New York: Vintage Books,
1979), drew upon Foucault in analyzing colonial discourse as the intrication of
particular forms of knowledge with particular relations of power.

INVOLVED
complex/
INTHSNO

SAID

"modernization" by revealing their complicity with technologies of neoimperial power.

A second broad stream of postdevelopment critique (in practice, often flowing together with others) is deconstructive in tenor and often in conversation with the work of Jacques Derrida. A guiding thought here is that Eurocentrism has so deeply penetrated not only historical and social scientific modes of inquiry but also political and popular modes of representation that colonial discourse has been able to outlive the death of colonialism itself. Development theory, in particular, is a very deep-seated mindset, and there is no antidote for it but a patient and persistent "decolonization of the mind."[24] Decolonizing the historical and social imaginaries of ex-colonizers and ex-colonized alike requires something different from what even the most humanitarian versions of developmentalism are able to provide; for they attempt only to improve development, to reconstruct development with justice, dignity, democracy – that is, "with a human face." But the development paradigm is *inherently* tied to the project of Western domination and so cannot be remedied by reconstruction. It has, rather, to be ongoingly deconstructed until we have un-learned to think of history in totalizing terms, as a unitary process with a uniform future. The proper tools for this can be found in forms of cultural critique that operate both inside and outside the ambit of Eurocentrism.[25] There is no possibility of thinking outside "the West" altogether; rather, critics can use the alterity and ambivalence that ineluctably inhabits Western thinking about the Other to effect its own deconstruction. For the repeated attempts of colonial and neo-colonial discourse to constitute a totality through exclusion or homogenization of the Other inevitably fail; inassimilable elements ineluctably pervade such discourse, ambivalence is intrinsic to it, and deconstructionist critique can exploit that ambivalence to subvert its authority.[26]

---

[24] As Ashis Nandy, who is, however, no deconstructionist, has famously put it. See his "Colonization of the Mind," in Rahnema and Bawtree (eds.), *The Post-Development Reader*, pp. 168–178.

[25] Robert Young, *White Mythologies: Writing History and the West* (London: Routledge, 1990).

[26] See, for instance, Gayatri Chakravorty Spivak, *In Other Worlds: Essays in Cultural Politics* (New York: Methuen, 1987); and Homi K. Bhabha, *The Location of Culture* (London, Routledge, 1994).

Genealogical and deconstructive modes of discourse analysis, as well as other forms of postmodern and postdevelopment critique, pursue a type of cultural politics aimed at resisting the dominance of Eurocentrism and loosening its hold on the imaginaries of postcolonizers and postcolonized alike. But the question is repeatedly raised: in the name of what are these modes of resistance, transgression, and subversion exercised? If postmodern critique is not to end merely in parasitic forms of discursive dissolution and identification through opposition, it should provide some idea of possible alternatives to liberal and Marxist conceptions of development. And then the grip of modern cultural and institutional forms becomes harder to shake; it proves difficult, if not impossible, to think consistently about social and political reconstruction without drawing upon those forms. And if that is so, we have no alternative but to revisit and rethink our dilemma.

Dipesh Chakrabarty puts the matter this way: "The phenomenon of 'political modernity' – namely the rule by modern institutions of the state, bureaucracy, and capitalist enterprise – is impossible to *think* of anywhere in the world without invoking certain categories and concepts, the genealogies of which … all bear the burden of European thought and history. One simply can't think of political modernity without these and other related concepts … This heritage is now global."[27] That is to say, in consequence of European global hegemony in the modern period, certain forms and matters of thought have become "unavoidable – and in a sense indispensable" (*PE*, 4). They shape scholarship, now also global, in history and the human studies, including the analysis and critique of Western imperialism itself. But though European thought "is now everybody's heritage," it is also "inadequate in helping us think through the experiences of political modernity in non-Western nations" (*PE*, 16). "Provincializing" or decentering Europe thus calls not for rejecting the European thought "to which one owes one's intellectual existence," but for rethinking and renewing it "from and for the margins," which are plural and diverse (*PE*, 16). In particular, the historicist ideology according to which non-Western modernities will merely replicate the Western model, albeit at more or less retarded rates of development, and which still informs development

---

[27] Dipesh Chakrabarty, *Provincializing Europe: Postcolonial Thought and Historical Difference* (Princeton University Press, 2000), p. 4. Cited in the text as *PE*.

theory and practice in most national and international settings, has to be displaced by more pluralistic modes of thinking about past histories and present possibilities.[28]

This suggests that the "inside/outside" predicament utilized by postmodernist thinkers for deconstructive purposes can also serve as the starting point for a reconstructive undertaking: an attempt to elaborate a critical theory of global development, in which the unreasonable, unjust, and undesirable elements of actually existing development – those which owe their establishment and persistence primarily to force and violence, structural and symbolic as well as intentional – are corrected or eliminated, while those which are reasonable, just, and desirable – which evince good reasons, basic fairness, and desirable consequences when examined "from and for the margins" – are retained and revised. In short, we need not choose between the ravages of neoliberal and neoconservative globalization, on the one side, and wholesale rejections of modernization, on the other. Beyond this either/ or lies the possibility of critically reconstructing developmental theory and practice in the interest of collectively organized action toward democratically defined aims of improving the life conditions of the wretched of the earth. For most of human history, most people, everywhere, have lived their lives under conditions of dire poverty, chronic malnutrition, and narrowly constricted possibilities. Science and technology, modern economies and administrations, individual liberties and democratic self-rule have alleviated these conditions of human suffering in some parts of the world.[29] The vast multitudes now living lives of deprivation and oppression do not need to have development of every sort forced upon them; they have not chosen their destitution, powerlessness, suffering, and humiliation. For most, material sufficiency, basic protections, some chance of improving their situations, some voice in the decisions that affect their lives, and the like are intrinsically desirable.

Amartya Sen has captured this thought in his conception of "human development" as the development of people's "capabilities," that is, as a process of expanding their "substantive freedoms" to lead the kinds of

---

[28] For another version of this line of thought, see Partha Chatterjee, *The Nation and Its Fragments* (Princeton University Press, 1993).

[29] Robert William Fogel, *The Escape from Hunger and Premature Death, 1700–2100* (Cambridge University Press, 2004).

lives they value.[30] To this end, having basic rights and some say in important decisions affecting oneself and one's community are essential, for they condition the exercise of all other capabilities. It is this last thought that Jürgen Habermas has sought to elaborate in his discourse theory of democracy, according to which regimes, laws, programs, and policies can be legitimated in the end only through the reasoned agreement of those affected by them in open public discussion.[31] And postcolonial critics of classical development theory have made it abundantly clear that such agreement is not to be expected so long as the equation of human progress with Western modernity serves the wholesale validation of its cultural and social forms. Once that is no longer granted, the value of Western values is no longer "given" but has to be ongoingly interrogated and negotiated in culturally hybrid discourses leading typically to hybrid outcomes.

Notwithstanding their considerable differences in history and culture, as well as in colonial and postcolonial experience, the formerly colonized regions of the world now share the problem of having to "provincialize" or decenter Europe, "the original home of the modern" (*PE*, 42). Moreover, they have to do so under conditions of a global capitalism that engulfs them all. In this situation, it seems, voices "from and for the margins" will be effectively heard only to the extent that the dynamics of capital accumulation are again brought under legal-political regulation and management, this time at a global and not merely national level. Failing that, the poorest and weakest societies will continue to be dominated and exploited, or at best patronized, by the richest and strongest. The now dominant, neoliberal form of globalization undercuts social goals of every kind: it reduces nature, society, and culture to so many "standing reserves" at the disposal of the most powerful economic interests. And postmodern pessimism saps the hope that this situation can be changed for the better through politically organized, collective action, which is the "good intention" behind at least some forms of developmental theory and practice.

---

[30] Amartya Sen, *Development as Freedom* (New York: Alfred A. Knopf, 1999). Note that this formulation encompasses the basic values of personal autonomy and political self-determination, but freed of the asymmetrical restrictions liberalism historically placed on their application.

[31] Jürgen Habermas, *Between Facts and Norms*, tr. W. Rehg (Cambridge, MA: MIT Press, 1996).

V

Where does this leave us with respect to the dilemma of development that Kant identified and analyzed? Our discussion of Mill has made manifest that it did not dissolve along with natural teleology and historical theodicy. Even the naturalization of ethics did not attenuate it, so long as one or another form of species perfectionism supplied the standard for judging "improvement." But another departure from the Kantian paradigm has substantially altered the way we (should) think about the dilemma: the detranscendentalization of our idea of reason and the general recognition of its constitutive embeddedness in language games and forms of life. Human reason is always already "impure," and the universal can only ever be actual as "concrete." In the absence of a Hegelian Absolute, this leaves us, as Gadamer and others have convincingly elaborated, with a multiplicity of forms of embodied reason, the distances between which can only be bridged by hermeneutic modes of communication. For present purposes, this means that we must rethink the dilemma of development from the perspective of the historical and cultural polyphony of communicative rationality. Whatever "unity of reason" there may be in the "diversity of its voices" is not simply given but also has to be achieved.[32] Thus the idea of cultural convergence that underwrote Kant's cosmopolitan hopes will, if those hopes are to survive, have to be complicated by the idea of negotiating cultural differences in the never-ending "struggle over the universal." Neither the arrogance of Enlightenment universalism nor the diffidence of cultural relativism is up to the global challenges that confront us.[33] Once again, we have to think in terms of the unavoidable dialectic of the universal and the particular: if norms of global justice are to be accepted as legitimate on all sides, they will have to accommodate global cultural diversity, and that will require leaving

---

[32] Jürgen Habermas, "The Unity of Reason in the Diversity of Its Voices," in Habermas, *Postmetaphysical Thinking*, tr. W. Hohengarten (Cambridge, MA: MIT Press, 1992), pp. 115–148. I discuss the implications of reason's constitutive embeddedness for critical theory in *Ideals and Illusions: On Reconstruction and Deconstruction in Contemporary Critical Theory* (Cambridge, MA: MIT Press, 1991), and in *Critical Theory* (Oxford: Basil Blackwell, 1994), coauthored with David Hoy.

[33] Anthony Appiah, *Cosmopolitanism: Ethics in a World of Strangers* (New York: W. W. Norton, 2006); Seyla Benhabib, *Another Cosmopolitanism* (Oxford University Press, 2006).

institutional space for the reasonable divergences in interpretation and application that are to be expected.[34] As is evident in the ongoing debates about human rights, agreement on the general validity of norms not only does not preclude but in fact enables debate about their meaning both in general and in particular.

The impurity of reason and the space for reasonable pluralism it opens up also mean that any idea of universal history is essentially contestable. Kant was already aware that general historical schemes constructed through "reflective judgments," however informed they might be by the "determinant judgments" of relevant empirical inquiries, neither attained nor could aspire to the status of rigorous science. Nevertheless, owing to the univocal character of practical reason as he understood it, he could propose a single, overarching metanarrative of the realization of reason in history. From our present perspective, it is clear that the irreducible diversity of hermeneutic standpoints and practical orientations informing interpretive endeavors, however well informed, will typically issue in a "conflict of interpretations" and thus call for dialogue across differences. The historically dominant standpoint of European hegemony and orientation to its civilizing mission can no longer be adopted as a matter of course. Among other things, successful struggles for national liberation following World War II and formal recognition of national equality through the United Nations have meant that sociocultural differences must increasingly be discussed and negotiated rather than assumed a priori to be marks of superiority or inferiority. And this too has rendered developmental schemes essentially contestable – which is not to say arbitrary but, rather, inherently open to reasonable disagreement.[35] This methodological lesson is all the more important for the mainstream of development theory, which followed Mill and Marx rather than Kant in taking itself to be a more or less rigorous empirical science, rather than a practically oriented and empirically informed mode of interpretation. In this regard, the varieties of development theory inflicted upon Third World countries after World War II were typically as smug in their assumptions of Western superiority as the classical theories of progress were during the age of empire.[36]

---

[34] For example, see the special issue of *Comparative European Politics* 5 (2007) on the functioning of different types of norms in transnational contexts.

[35] See the concluding section of chapter 5.

[36] Colin Leys, *The Rise and Fall of Development Theory* (Bloomington: Indiana University Press, 1996). I discuss this in chapter 7.

Methodology is supported here by considerations of morality, law, and politics. One characteristic feature of the tension inhabiting Kant's simultaneous embrace of the functional perspective of anthropological-historical thinking and the normative perspective of moral-legal reasoning is his repeated insistence on the priority of the latter. Thus, the well-known passage in "Perpetual Peace" in which he avers: "nature guarantee[s] that what man *ought* to do by the laws of his freedom (but does not do) will be done by nature's compulsion," so that "the problem of setting up a state can be solved even by a race of devils (so long as they possess understanding),"[37] is closely followed by an appendix in which he proclaims: "A true system of politics cannot take a single step without first paying tribute to morality ... The rights of man must be held sacred, however great a sacrifice the ruling power may have to make."[38] That is to say, political actors should do what is right and leave the rest to God/Providence/Nature. As confidence in providential history waned, however, the split between "right and utility," as Kant termed it, yawned ever larger in international affairs. Pursuing utility in the short run for the sake of right in the long run was the route generally favored by development theory and practice after Mill. But as Chakrabarty reminds us, during the period of decolonization and nation-building following World War II, this hoary structure of deferral became increasingly unstable.[39] The tension between the "not yet" of colonial paternalism and the "now" of anticolonial nationalism was superseded, so to speak, not in development theory, where the tension persisted, but in political practice. The need for mass movements to politicize the peasantry and for mass democracies to grant them full citizenship status engendered the political modernity of subaltern classes and the political displacement of development theories concerning them. A related point could be made concerning the changes in international law since the founding of the United Nations. The formal recognition of new nations in every corner of the world and the globalization of human rights regimes

[37] I. Kant, "Perpetual Peace: A Philosophical Sketch," tr. H. B. Nisbet, in H. Reiss (ed.), *Kant: Political Writings* (Cambridge University Press, 1991), pp. 93–130, at p. 112.

[38] *Ibid.*: "On the Disagreement Between Morals and Politics in Relation to Perpetual Peace," pp. 116–125, at p. 125.

[39] Chakrabarty, *Provincializing Europe.*

have transformed the structure of deferral into what is called in German the *Gleichzeitigkeit des Ungleichzeitigen*, the contemporaneousness of the non-contemporaneous. Struggles for global justice today must proceed on the formal presupposition of the equal standing of all individuals and peoples. Putting that presupposition into legal and political practice is critical to ensuring an effective voice for those who are supposed to be the beneficiaries of development policies and thus for diminishing the ever-present tendencies toward paternalism, benevolent despotism, and worse. More specifically, until the formal recognition of equal standing gets translated into democratic practices – of transparency, accountability, representation, participation, and the like – with a more equitable balance of power, the temptation for liberal progressivism to metamorphose into liberal neoimperialism will likely remain irresistibly great.

The structure of deferral is not the only aspect of the dilemma of development that, while not dissolvable in theory is at least displaceable in practice. Kant held that the functional perspective of historical development was subordinate to the normative perspective of moral duty. Not only was his account of human advancement already constructed with a practical interest in the achievement of our moral destiny, it was meant to be "applied" – not as a predictive tool or a technical recipe but – as a guideline for moral and political practice. In this respect, I think, Kant was closer to the mark than mainstream development theory has since been. The repeated attempts to construct scientific theories of sociocultural development – whether neo-Marxist theories of historical materialism, neo-Darwinian theories of social evolution, structural-functional theories of modernization, or neoliberal theories of globalization – have not only failed badly as theories but have also been harmful in practice. They have tended to inspire top-down, bureaucratic rule by scientifically trained "development experts," which disqualified local knowledge and treated "target populations" as the objects rather than the subjects of life-transforming decisions.

An alternative approach would be to regard the empirical-theoretical analyses provided by developmental studies as tributary to the practical-political deliberation of collective agents seeking to act on such knowledge, including especially those whose condition is supposed to be improved by it. While acknowledging the interpretive and practical dimensions of development theory undercuts its claim to be part of "a natural science of society," it is compatible with understanding it as an empirically informed and practically oriented analytical framework. One could, I think, only accept the former self-description so long as the main participants in the discourse of global modernity generally shared the same hermeneutic standpoint and the same practical orientation, namely the ones dictated by the realities and interests of European imperialism. But what appeared to be advancement from that perspective, usually looked like conquest, set-tlement, enslavement, colonization, imperialism, neoimperialism, or the like from others.

To be sure, the political displacement of the dilemma of development does not eliminate all tensions from it, in particular those arising from the strongly modernist assumptions of democracy, human rights, and the rule of law themselves. These are not cognitively and evaluatively neutral. And they clash with many aspects of non-modern worldviews and forms of life – with viewing social relations in terms of a hierarch-ical complementarity between genders, castes, classes, or the like; with understanding social status in terms of a scale of intrinsic dignity and value; with regarding the established order as "the" cosmologically or religiously anchored, normal and proper order of things; with taking the established structure of social functions to be ontologically rooted rather than contingent and alterable; with judging the diversity of worldviews and forms of life in terms not of reasonable pluralism but of truth and error, good and evil; with rejecting the legitimacy of social arrangements that place limitations on the imperative role of religion in shaping public life; or the like.[40] So the predicament we are left with is marked, at the very least, by a tension between, on the one hand, the preconditions of the modern legal and political forms that underwrite the equal standing and equal voice needed to break the old connection between liberal progressivism and liberal imperialism and, on the other hand, some aspects of the forms of life and social orders most in need of such guarantees. There is no easy exit from this predicament. Kant placed his hope in a gradual "move towards greater agreement on principles ... [that] will lead to mutual understanding and peace" under conditions of global modernity.[41] In a less providential and less

---

[40] Charles Taylor, *Modern Social Imaginaries* (Durham, NC: Duke University Press, 2004).
[41] Kant, "Perpetual Peace," p. 114.

monocultural vein, we may hope at least for a multiplicity of "creative adaptations" to these conditions, as Charles Taylor has put it, drawing on the cultural resources of different traditions and resulting in a degree of overlapping consensus and functional equivalence sufficient to enable global peace and promote global justice.[42]

[42] See his "Two Theories of Modernity," in D. Gaonkar (ed.), *Alternative Modernities* (Durham, NC: Duke University Press, 2001), pp. 172–196.

7 | *From modernism to messianism: reflections on the state of "development"*

Following World War II, many of the same developmental themes that had dominated the theory and practice of imperialism in the nineteenth century reappeared.[1] Of course, there were also important differences. For one thing, the growing differentiation and institutionalization of the social sciences in the intervening years meant that those themes were now articulated and elaborated within specialized academic disciplines. For another, the main field on which developmental theory and practice were deployed was no longer British – or, more broadly, European – imperialism but American neoimperialism. At the close of the war, the United States was not only the major military, economic, and political power left standing; it was also less implicated than European states in colonial domination abroad. The depletion of the colonial powers and the imminent breakup of their empires left it in a singular position to lead the reshaping of the postwar world. And it sought to do so in its own image and likeness, for it saw itself as the exemplar and apostle of a fully developed modernity.[2]

In this respect it was, in some ways, reiterating the self-understanding and self-regard of the classical imperial powers of the modern period. But, in other ways America's civilizing mission was marked by the exceptionalist strain in its political history and culture, which was given an influential formulation by Louis Hartz some fifty years ago.[3] Picking up on Alexis de Tocqueville's observation that Americans were

---

[1] I am grateful to Bill Barnes for making his dissertation available to me: "Development Theory and Ideology: The Triumph of the Modern Middle Class in Theory and Practice," University of Michigan, 1979, together with his comments and his helpful bibliographical advice, which contributed significantly to shaping my discussion in this chapter.

[2] Nils Gilman, *Mandarins of the Future: Modernization Theory in Cold War America* (Baltimore: Johns Hopkins University Press, 2003).

[3] Louis Hartz, *The Liberal Tradition in America* (New York: Harcourt, Brace & World, 1955). As indicated in chapter 3, there is more to the consciousness of American exceptionalism – from the Puritan conviction of being a "chosen

192

"born equal," Hartz elaborated upon the uniqueness of their political experience as follows. Owing to America's settlement by émigrés fleeing the *anciens régimes* of Europe, it never had to undergo a social revolution to arrive at a liberal society. Blessed with an abundance of available land and natural resources, sparsely populated and far removed from the great powers, it was able to develop and sustain a liberal tradition that was not revolutionary but hegemonic. Individual liberty and the pursuit of happiness had a saliency in its political culture that was only enhanced by later waves of immigrants seeking success in a land of opportunity. At the same time, this unbroken and unchallenged liberal tradition entailed a certain narrowness of political discourse and dimness of ideological self-consciousness in comparison to the politics of old Europe, in which liberal and democratic revolutions had first to be won and then to be defended against the forces of feudalism. And that in turn entailed a certain "absolutist" – or, as we might put it today, fundamentalist – quality to the American civil religion. As a result, according to Hartz, Americans had difficulty coexisting with ideological opposition, which was typically perceived as an alien threat and dealt with through avoidance or conversion.

"Americanism" has had a dual life ... [I]t has been characterized by a strong isolationist impulse: the sense that America's very liberal joy lay in the escape from a decadent Old World that could only infect it with its own diseases ... [It] has also crusaded abroad in a Wilsonian way ... Embodying an absolute moral ethos, "Americanism," once it is driven on to the world stage by events, is inspired willy-nilly to reconstruct the very alien things it tries to avoid. Its messianism is the polar counterpart of its isolationism.[4]

Thus, in Hartz's view, America's evangelical impulse to spread the freedom, democracy, and economic opportunity it enjoyed to other societies ran the constant risk of transmuting into an imperialist messianism blinded by the certainty of its own righteousness. And in the half-century since he offered his analysis, the impact of American

---

people," through the triumph of Revolutionary ideals and the "manifest destiny" of continental expansion, to the surge of messianic imperialism at the close of the nineteenth century – but Hartz's emphasis suits the purposes of this chapter. For an influential critique of Hartz's account of American political culture, see Rogers Smith, *Civic Ideals: Conflicting Visions of Citizenship in U.S. History* (New Haven: Yale University Press, 1997), chap. 1.

[4] Hartz, *The Liberal Tradition in America*, pp. 285–286.

national myths on the theory and practice of liberal internationalism has borne him out.

For several decades after World War II, American social science and foreign policy were pervaded by liberal theories of development and modernization, which exercised great influence in such US-dominated agencies as the World Bank, International Monetary Fund, US Agency for International Development, Alliance for Progress, and the like. The spirit behind this incarnation of liberal internationalism was proclaimed by President Truman in his 1949 Inaugural Address: "We must embark on a bold new program for making the benefits of our scientific advances and industrial progress available for the improvement and growth of underdeveloped areas ... The old imperialism – exploitation for foreign profit – has no place in our plans. What we envisage is a program of development based on concepts of democratic fair dealing ... Greater production is the key to prosperity and peace. And the key to greater production is a wider and more vigorous application of modern scientific and technical knowledge."[5]

This mix of material progress (science, technology, and industry as the keys to global peace and prosperity), political idealism (the extension of the "Fair Deal" to the whole world), and purported goodwill (assisting others to better their conditions of life) is characteristic of the earlier phases of postwar development discourse in the US. Moreover, the largely Western-trained leaders of newly and soon-to-be emancipated colonies themselves tended to view the task of nation-building in terms of economic development and social modernization. To that extent, the aims of US foreign policy could converge for a time with the aspirations of many "underdeveloped areas." But the failures of development economics and the widening gap between rich and poor countries soon became evident. The growing disenchantment in Latin America was given theoretical expression in neo-Marxist theories of dependency, which gained increasing purchase across the developing world as the United States escalated its brutal, neocolonial war in Vietnam.

By the 1980s, development and modernization theory had been largely discredited, not only by attacks from the left but also – and increasingly – by attacks from the right. Neoliberal critiques of welfare

---

[5] Harry S. Truman, Inaugural Address, January 20, 1949, in *Documents in American Foreign Relations* (Princeton University Press, 1967).

state programs on the domestic front were accompanied by a shift from modernization to globalization in the international arena. And more recently, neoconservative views combining neoliberalism in economics with liberal interventionism in foreign policy have come to dominate public discourse and political practice. Yet, as I shall argue, the central ideas of development theory have retained their place in scholarly and popular social imaginaries throughout these ideological shifts.

In what follows, I want to reexamine this important but undertheorized strand of the history of the present. After reconstructing (in sections I and II) some main lines of development and modernization thinking in post-World War II America and some elements of the critique from the left, I will then consider (in section III) the neoliberal critique from the right and the conception of globalization that came to dominate in the 1980s and 1990s. Section IV will bring our critical history one step further by examining the neoconservative reprise of American messianism; and section V will offer some concluding thoughts on where this leaves us in regard to thinking about global development today. At every point in the postwar discourse of development, there has been a great *variety* of approaches and critiques on offer; I shall have to confine my remarks to a few of the principal forms and treat even those in very general terms.

I Development and dependency

One formative feature of post-World War II development discourse was its Cold War setting. The West was locked in a geopolitical and ideological struggle for global hegemony with the Soviet Union; and the principal battlegrounds were the vast areas of our planet that had been subjected to various forms of colonial domination and exploitation. The United States, which historically had not been a major colonial center and was now the dominant geopolitical power, was positioned to lead the struggle against communism. Given the entwinement of nationhood and modernization in the "Third World" – so that the nation-state was viewed as the privileged vehicle of modernization, and modernization was viewed as the privileged path to nation-building – a central issue in the struggle concerned the preferred route to modernization in the newly independent states, for the Soviet Union had demonstrated an alternative route: a socialist form of state-directed economic growth rather than the "free trade" capitalism of their former colonial masters.

To be sure, the form of economic development the Western powers opposed to socialism also envisaged an active role for the state. The political-economic ascendancy of social democratic and welfare state models of capitalism after the war, and the perceived successes of such interventionist economic policies as the New Deal and the Marshall Plan, encouraged development theorists in the belief that Keynesian macroeconomics was the key to managing economic growth. It was a presupposition of this approach that national economies were in fact susceptible to state management. And that presupposition had been underwritten by the Bretton Woods Conference in 1944 through the creation of a world trade and finance system under the aegis of the World Bank and the International Monetary Fund, which allowed for state-directed, national economic policy. When this regulated, international system of national economies was dismantled in the 1970s, that presupposition was no longer met, and the route to neoliberal globalization was opened wide. In the immediate post-World War II period, however, the regime of "free trade" established at Bretton Woods was supposed to reflect a convergence of US interests in ensuring free access to markets and resources formerly under colonial restrictions, on the one hand, and postcolonial interests in blazing the shortest possible path to economic growth and modernization, on the other. But that alleged convergence of interests came increasingly into doubt well before the system was transformed in the 1970s. The breakdown of the "development consensus" was already apparent in the fate of the development economics that dominated development theory and practice in the 1950s.

It was no accident that an economic conception of development achieved the primacy it did. No one doubted that improvement of the material conditions of life was a, if not the, significant variable in societal development; and few disputed that increased productivity through industrialization was critical to such improvement. Moreover, by comparison to the other social sciences, economics had a long history as an independent discipline. Thus, it was to be expected that development economists would predominate in such agencies as the World Bank and the US Agency for International Development. In this first phase, then, the focus of developmental theory was on economic growth, particularly as measured by Gross National Product or by GNP per capita, and development practice emphasized policies that favored foreign investment, technology transfer, state management of the economy, and the like. In short, the dominant form of development theory and practice was a kind of global Keynesianism promoting active intervention into national economies to achieve and sustain growth. Subsequently this core conception of development was expanded to include social and cultural variables – as in the "Human Development Index" used by the United Nations Development Program – and to take political participation and the rule of law into account – as in the UNDP "Human Freedom Index."[6] But I will not be tracking such piecemeal expansion here, for toward the end of the 1950s and in the 1960s, development economics was incorporated into a broader, sociological conception of development as "modernization." It is this conception that bears the strongest affinities to the broader views of historical development that we find in the philosophy of history from Kant to Marx and in classical social theory from Durkheim and Weber to Parsons – which is only to be expected, as it was Parsons who elaborated the general theory of action it drew upon. But before shifting the focus to modernization theory, it will be useful for our purposes to take a brief look at a form of neo-Marxist critique that development economics soon encountered, "dependency theory," for it was later directed at modernization theory as well.[7]

The distant ancestors of dependency theory can be found in the theories of imperialism developed earlier in the twentieth century by Hobson, Hilferding, Lenin, Luxembourg, and others to explain the furious scramble for colonies by European powers during the last third of the nineteenth century. A central theme of that discourse had been the need of advanced capitalist economies to resolve their growing internal contradictions and continue the process of capital accumulation by expanding abroad, exporting capital, gaining access to new markets, and the like. A cognate school of neo-Marxist thought was established in the United States after World War II by a group of thinkers around the journal *Monthly Review*, prominently including Paul Baran and Paul Sweezy. At almost the same time, Latin American economists associated with the UN Economic Commission for Latin America – Raoul Prebisch, in particular – were theoretically articulating the growing disillusionment with development theory and practice in

---

[6] Richard Peet, *Theories of Development* (New York: Guilford Press, 1999), chap. 2.
[7] *Ibid.*, chap. 4; and Colin Leys, *The Rise and Fall of Development Theory* (Bloomington: Indiana University Press, 1996), chap. 2.

view of its increasingly evident failure to narrow the gaps between rich and poor nations. Elaborated by other Latin American economists and eventually spread to other parts of the world by theorists like Andre Gunder Frank and Samir Amin, dependency theory criticized development economics for some of the same reasons that Marx had criticized liberal internationalism in his day: it was predatory capitalism in disguise. The idea that non-Western societies were "underdeveloped" for internal reasons – race, custom, culture, tradition, and so forth – and were thus in need of help from the outside, was an ideological coverup of the external causes of misery in the "Third World": precisely the Western conversion of non-Western economies into dependent components of their own, increasingly global economic systems from the fifteenth century onwards. The sustainability of indigenous modes of production in non-Western societies had thereby been undermined. Traditional economies had been restructured as extractive systems producing primary commodities for the industrializing West. In this way, the development of the capitalist world and the underdevelopment of the colonized world were two sides of the same process of capital accumulation, which had been global from the start but by no means even. The economic geography of the planet had been reorganized into centers and peripheries.

Dependency theorists understood the contemporary forms of liberal internationalism articulated by development theory as a continuation by new means of this global exploitation. In theory, national economies in the postwar world were represented as independent units and the trade between them as free and fair; in practice, however, the terms of trade between industrialized countries and primary producers were systematically skewed in favor of the former, for the socially necessary labor time required for industrial goods was much more elastic in relation to technical innovation than that required for primary commodities. As a result, capital – in the form of profits, interest, rents, royalties, and the like – flowed continually to the First from the Third World, which then had to borrow it back to finance its own "development." In reality, what was developed by this system was continuing underdevelopment and dependency. And because it served the interests of powerful states, multinational corporations, and local elites, there was little hope of overcoming structural dependency from within it.

Thus, dependency theorists often promoted an alternative route to development: the de-linking of Third World economies from this system by means of "import substitution strategies." Replacing industrial imports with domestic production under protective tariffs would enable agricultural economies to industrialize and gain a measure of independence. Despite some initial success, however, this alternative route to development proved untenable over time. The high-cost, low-quality output of industrial production in the Third World was generally not competitive with that of the First World; the emphasis on industrialization often led to a deleterious neglect of the agricultural sector; the need for foreign investment in developing industries regularly led to higher levels of indebtedness; and so forth.

According to an important outgrowth of dependency theory, the "world systems theory" elaborated by Immanuel Wallerstein and others, this was not surprising; for there was no possibility of de-linking national economies from the global economy. The world economic system was in fact a single system, of which national economies – or regional economies or economic sectors – could only be interdependent parts. Development could be achieved, if at all, only within this system. And indeed, the success of the state-managed export strategies of newly industrializing countries (NICs) – for example South Korea, Singapore, Hong Kong, Taiwan – since the 1970s demonstrated that it did in fact allow for forms of "dependent development." Consequently, the economic world was not sharply divided into center and periphery, as claimed by dependency theorists; rather, global capitalism allowed for a "semi-periphery" of dependently developing nations. Nonetheless, it remained true that capitalism was an inherently inequitable system predicated upon exploitation. There was no way to "level the playing field" as long as world economic relations were structured along capitalist lines. The only way to do that was to change the system as a whole.

As we shall see, contemporary theorists of neoliberal globalization agree with world system theorists about the impossibility of de-linking from the global economy, but they disagree with them about whether the latter can or should be fundamentally altered. Critics of both have argued that each in their own way – the world system theorists with self-conscious resolution, the neoliberals with unself-conscious irony – evince an economic determinism reminiscent of Marx's political economy, and that both consequently suffer from a blindness to possibilities of political agency. Just as Marxists failed to give due weight to the state management of economic processes characteristic of social democracy and reform liberalism, world system theory and neoliberal globalization theory consistently underestimate the possibilities of legally regulating global markets and politically managing world economic processes.

II Modernization and domination

For our purposes, the most significant theoretical response to the evident inadequacies of purely economic approaches to development was the ascendancy of a general theory of societal modernization in the late 1950s and 1960s. With this, the postwar discussion of development rejoined the tradition of grand social theory and historical sociology descended from Comte and Marx, Durkheim and Weber, which had been occupied above all with the modernization of Europe. The main link to that tradition was, of course, Talcott Parsons, who had been developing a general theory of action since the 1930s, precisely in conversation with such predecessors. From this theoretical perspective, it was evident that the economic system was one, interdependent subsystem of society as a whole, which could be treated separately for analytical purposes but not for practical purposes. There were social, cultural, psychological, legal, and political preconditions and consequences of economic development that had to be attended to both in theory and in practice. One-dimensional, economistic approaches to societal modernization were, therefore, bound to prove inadequate. By contrast, the approach to modernization theory that came to dominate in the 1960s – in the social sciences, in US policy circles, in national and international development agencies, and among Third World elites – was multidimensional and interdisciplinary in character.[8]

Although the modernization-theory approach to development shared many features with approaches articulated a century earlier – for instance, it was holistic, unilinear, and binary (with the earlier backward/civilized dichotomy replaced by traditional/modern or undeveloped/developed) – it benefited from the differentiation and institutionalization of the specialized social sciences in the intervening century. Thus, while some of the same themes and tropes appeared, they were elaborated in much greater detail and were saturated with much more empirical material. Of the myriad strands of modernization theory, it

---

[8] Though I discuss "modernization theory" in the singular here, there were many variants of it; moreover, I consider only a few central tendencies, and those at a high level of abstraction.

will be convenient for our purposes to follow Nils Gilman in focusing on three interrelated strands centered in three institutional contexts: one, in sociology, centered around the Harvard Department of Social Relations (DSR) under Talcott Parsons; a second, in political science, centered around the Social Science Research Council's Committee on Comparative Politics (CCP) under Gabriel Almond and later Lucian Pye; and a third, in foreign policy studies, centered around the MIT Center for International Studies (CIS) under Walt Rostow.[9] But before doing so, it will be useful to get a better sense of its general aims, at least at the start and for most of those involved.

1. In his keynote address to a conference on the problems and prospects of new states, which he delivered in 1959, ten years after Truman's inaugural address, the sociologist Edward Shils characterized the goal of modernization processes as follows: "In the new states, 'modern' means democratic and equalitarian, scientific, economically advanced and sovereign ... [Modernity] is the model of the West detached in some way from its geographical origins and locus."[10] The sociological dimensions of that model were spelled out in a collection that Shils had edited with Talcott Parsons in 1951, *Toward a General Theory of Action*.[11] Building on work that Parsons had done since the 1930s, the contributors elaborated a theoretical approach that combined the emphasis on environmental factors characteristic of post-Darwinian naturalistic theories of society with the stress on rationalization processes characteristic of post-Weberian culturalist approaches, in a construction that also incorporated Durkheimian insights into the functional needs met by differentiated social structures. This "structural-functionalism" provided not only a synoptic framework of analysis and a coordinated agenda of research for social science in general, but an integrated framework for research and policy concerned with modernization processes in particular. The traditional/ modern dichotomy was embedded in Parsons' scheme of dichotomous "pattern variables" (value orientations), and the process of modernization was represented as movement from one pole toward the other. Its path was marked by increasing differentiation between and within specialized subsystems of action, in which changing cultural patterns

---

[9] Gilman, *Mandarins of the Future.*   [10] Cited in *ibid.*, pp. 1–2.
[11] Cambridge, MA: Harvard University Press, 1951. The volume resulted from a DSR faculty seminar sponsored by the Carnegie Foundation.

of value were institutionalized in normative structures and internalized in socialization processes. At the same time, increasing functional differentiation meant growing societal complexity and enhanced adaptive capacity, which meant that more developed societies had a competitive advantage over less developed ones as regards the achievement of societal goals. And given that functional needs were basically similar for all social systems, this superiority in the struggle for survival exerted a pressure toward structural convergence upon developing societies. In consequence, the highly differentiated and adaptive societies of the modern West represented the model and measure of development for the rest of the world.

As applied to the modernization of postcolonial societies in the mid-twentieth century, this meant that the development processes they had begun under colonial regimes could best be completed by adopting Western attitudes, values, practices, and institutions – including market mechanisms and state bureaucracies, industrialization and urbanization, secularization and rationalization, the rule of law and democratization, social mobility and mass education, and so forth. And all this could best be accomplished under the management of strong national states, with the assistance of already developed societies. To be sure, there was always disagreement among modernization theorists as to which factors were most basic to development. But even those who, like Rostow, stressed material factors such as technology transfer and capital investment, subscribed to the multidimensional conceptualization of modern society and to the necessity of interrelated changes in all areas. There were prerequisites and consequences of economic development, as there were of political reform.

2. The type of political reform desired was most often characterized as "democratic." However, from the start this was understood by the most influential theorists less in terms of popular sovereignty than in terms of formal democracy, that is, universal suffrage, regular elections, competing parties, representative bodies, and the like. The recent history of fascism in Europe had made many of them wary of populist politics. And the growing influence in the 1950s of Joseph Schumpeter's 1942 book, *Capitalism, Socialism, and Democracy*, led to widespread acceptance of the "elite theory" of democracy, which conceived it as a legally regulated competition for power among elites. The chief distinguishing mark between modern Western democracies and the "people's democracies" of the communist world was said to be pluralism: a

variety of competing groups were involved in the procedurally legitimate acquisition, transfer, and sharing of power. There was also an
emphasis on the essential role of expertise, particularly of social-
scientifically trained technocrats, in modern government administrations. Democratically legitimated political elites guided by such expertise,
not public opinion, should set policy. This was the sort of democracy
that should be promoted in the Third World as an alternative to communist dictatorship: pluralistic, formal democracies with strong states,
governed by elites with the aid and advice of a variety of experts.
Democratic institutions and procedures of this sort were regarded by
many modernization theorists as the core of political modernization
and thus as integral to societal modernization overall.

The Committee on Comparative Politics, under the leadership of
Gabriel Almond in the 1950s and of Lucian Pye after 1963, laid the
foundations for a new science of comparative politics along these lines.
Drawing on the general theory of action elaborated by structural-
functionalists, particularly on the contributions of Shils, they focused
their efforts on the Third World with a view to America's role as "the
leader of the free world" and the need to counter the threat of global
communism.[12] The work of the Committee was pervaded by the dominant ethos of scientificity, with its emphasis on behavioralism, value-
free inquiry, quantitative measurement, the discovery and testing of
empirical laws, and the like – all framed by and contributing to the
scientific theory of social action. And it generally underwrote the need
for strong postcolonial states to direct the modernization process
through central planning guided by scientifically trained experts.

As we shall see, it was mainly the violent exacerbation of this
authoritarian streak in modernization theory that led to its thorough
discrediting by the 1970s – "mainly" but not "only." From the start,
it was subjected to many of the criticisms of development theory
already mentioned, including those raised by dependency theorists.
Modernization theory was said to be marked by a "blaming the victim"
stress on the internal causes of underdevelopment and a neglect of the
external depredations by European and American imperialism. It
evinced no less inveterate an ethnocentrism than the ideologies of
colonialism; only now an idealized image of the USA served as the
model and measure: modernization = Americanization. And it assumed

[12] Gilman, *Mandarins of the Future*, chap. 4.

(or at least asserted) that US interventions in developing nations were essentially benign – although their targets generally saw them as motivated by self-interest. Moreover, like its predecessors, modernization theory painted the non-Western world with one brush; the binary schemes of traditional/modern and undeveloped/developed classified the very diverse societies in Asia, Africa, Latin America, and the Middle East as one and all traditionalistic and underdeveloped. Together with this unitary starting point went a single end-state: developed modernity in the American style; and a unilinear path of development: a replication of the earlier modernization of the West – though it was never convincingly explained how history could repeat itself under such very different conditions, particularly under the structural domination of the capitalist world system by already modernized centers. Through all the vicissitude of this period, modernizers continued to exude confidence that history was on their side and that they were acting for the benefit of those being modernized – at least in the long run.

3. In the United States, the elaboration of modernization theory was closely linked to the foreign policy aims of the American government. Among its various practitioners were numerous cold warriors – Shils, for instance, in sociology, and Almond and Pye in political science – but nowhere more than in the field of foreign policy studies itself.[13]

The work connected with the MIT Center for International Studies was in general more loosely oriented to democratic values than that by sociologists of modernization or by comparative political scientists. In particular, the Center's leader, W. W. Rostow, had been trained as an economist, and his very influential book, *The Stages of Economic Growth*, though framed by a multidimensional structural-functionalism, was rather more economistic in emphasis than was typical of their work. Moreover, as the subtitle of that book – *A Non-Communist Manifesto* – would suggest, he and his affiliates saw themselves as engaged in a global struggle with communism. In the end, Rostow's deep involvement with the US war in Vietnam – especially as National Security Advisor to President Johnson – would be widely perceived as revealing the true colors of modernization theory and practice generally. For though many of those involved had sincerely entertained democratic hopes for developing countries, and though almost all

[13] *Ibid.*, chap. 5.

had at least paid lip service to democratization as an integral element of modernization, the authoritarian and technocratic strains of elite theory became increasingly salient in the 1960s until, by the end of the decade, talk of freedom and democracy was largely displaced by a stress on order and control.[14]

In part, this shift had its internal grounds, for, as noted above, modernization theory had generally assigned key roles to strong states, political elites, and scientifically trained experts; and modernization practice had largely operated on the paternalistic assumption that the benevolent hegemon knew what was "for their own good." But events on the ground – especially the surge of political instability, revolutionary activity, and military coups in the 1960s – increasingly made even those watered-down commitments to democracy untenable. US foreign policy moved rapidly in the direction of endorsing whichever authorities seemed most likely to maintain order and defeat communist insurgency. Anti-communism became the core of liberal internationalism.[15] In practice, this often meant supporting military coups and repressive regimes; and theorists such as Almond, Pye, and Rostow provided the justification for such policies. Moreover, they did so while apparently remaining within the bounds of modernization theory and drawing upon some of its basic tenets.

For one thing, it had been argued from the start, even by Parsons himself, that there were empirical preconditions to democracy, which had to be in place before it could be successfully established.[16] One needed only to argue that, under the precarious conditions obtaining in the developing world in the 1960s, those preconditions could best be achieved by authoritarian governments, and thus that democracy would have to be deferred until that had been accomplished. It was, then, only a kind of poetic justice when, toward the end of the 1960s, an illiberal critic of mainstream modernization theory, Samuel Huntington, published one of the most influential works on political modernization, which made explicit the concern with order, anxiety

---

[14] Again, I am referring here to some general tendencies and ignoring many individual differences.

[15] Irene Gendzier, *Managing Political Change: Social Scientists and the Third World* (Boulder, CO: Westview Press, 1985).

[16] Seymour Martin Lipset, *Political Man* (Garden City, NY: Doubleday, 1960), offered an influential articulation of this thesis.

over revolution, and obsession with security that were at least implicit in the then prevailing version of liberal internationalism.[17]

Furthermore, many influential modernization theorists had followed Harold Lasswell in arguing that radical political dissent was out of place in a well-ordered, democratic society. This line of thought, reinforced by the "end of ideology" ideology, was elaborated by his students, Almond and Pye, into a full-blown account of the psychopathology of political passion in general and of the passionate resistance to American-led modernization in particular. This left little room for reasonable disagreement with the theory and practice of modernization; ardent opposition was, rather, a symptom of the anxieties caused by rapid change. The normal state of affairs in democratic politics was the disinterest in political matters shown by the contented consumers of mass culture in developed societies, and their trust in the scientifically informed decision-making of their elected officials. In connection with modernization theory, this line of thought was used to assign a passive role to the masses in developing countries and to justify the engineering of mass consent to American foreign policy objectives by authoritarian postcolonial states. That policy was, after all, the result of value-free social science, which trumped the deliverances of any ideology; disagreement with it could only be unreasonable and, if passionate, even pathological. Of course, this line of thought lost much of its plausibility later in the 1960s, when the model democracy itself erupted in passionate protest.

At that time, the model-status of the USA generally became less and less credible: the assassinations of the Kennedys and King, the failures of the War on Poverty, race riots and police riots across the country, Watergate, the disaffection and protest of American youth, and so forth, made its exemplary status as unlikely as the brutality of the Vietnam War did its benevolence toward postcolonial peoples. Criticisms of modernization theory from the left, which had been present from the start but largely ignored, were now amplified by events and gained a broad hearing (as did criticisms from the right, which will be discussed below). As a result, modernization theory had lost much of its plausibility by the early 1970s, when the institutional structures we have been considering – the DSR, CCP, and CIS – either disbanded or

---

[17] Samuel Huntington, *Political Order in Changing Societies* (New Haven: Yale University Press, 1968).

changed the focus of their work. In the Third World, the discrediting of modernization theory meant that the liberal, secular, rationalist, and individualist ethos that informed it also fell into disrepute, as did the putative scientificity and objectivity of the social research that had produced it. The whole package was now widely viewed as a cover for the real interest of the United States in geopolitical hegemony, as well as for the self-interest of the modernizing national elites that colluded with them. Naïve protestations or assumptions of goodwill, which had had some plausibility in the early optimistic phases of modernization, had become incredible.

What had thus come to an unholy end was what James Scott has termed the authoritarian "high modernism" of mid-century development policy.[18] Schemes to improve the human condition, when combined with authoritarian states, regularly lead to disaster, even with the best of intentions. Liberal developmentalism, which deployed state power to effect large-scale improvements in traditional societies, was no exception. Its willingness to impose modern forms on traditional societies – to "force them to be free," as it were – and to push integration into the capitalist world economy at all costs proved to be a license for repressive regimes everywhere.

So once again, the dilemma of development had played itself out; and once more, liberal ideals had succumbed to the realities of power. Many postcolonial critics have since argued that "once more" is more than enough, that it is past time to dismantle developmental thinking once and for all. But before revisiting that suggestion in the concluding section, I want to consider two critiques of modernization theory from the right, which eventually came to prevail in the neoliberal globalization and neoconservative interventionism that later visited their own brands of "development" upon the wretched of the earth.

III Neoliberalism and globalization

Another powerful blow to modernization theory came from a very different direction. Since the time of the New Deal, a number of economists – prominent among them Friedrich von Hayek, Ludwig von Mises, and Milton Friedman – had criticized the basic presuppositions of Keynesianism and argued against state intervention in the economy.

---

[18] James C. Scott, *Seeing Like a State* (New Haven: Yale University Press, 1998).

During the period of postwar economic growth in the 1950s and 1960s, they were largely ignored by the dominant social democratic, welfare state consensus. But the perceived failures of the War on Poverty and other social programs at home, and the increasingly evident failures of development policies abroad, which neoliberal theorists attributed to their Keynesian underpinnings, lent new resonance to these criticisms.[19] The decisive blow came in the 1970s with the breakdown of the regulated system of capital flows and global trade among national economies established at Bretton Woods in 1944. During the international economic crisis following the Arab oil embargo of 1973, the world economy was opened up to the largely unrestricted flow of financial capital. As a result of this and other measures deregulating global markets, the ability of national governments to manage their own economies was significantly reduced. The economic regime to come was signaled early in the 1980s by the policies of Thatcher in Britain and Reagan in the USA. The social-democratic consensus was under severe attack, and not only domestically.

Neoliberal critics of development theory and practice argued that it amounted to an extension of New Deal liberalism across the globe. It sprung from the same confidence in the capacity of government bureaucracies to manage market economies and in the benevolence of political leaders to seek what was best for the people. But that confidence was badly misplaced: governments were constitutionally incapable of displacing markets, and their leaders, particularly in the Third World, were more often than not self-interested and corrupt. Interventionist policies were thus inherently inefficient by comparison to markets, and thus largely counterproductive in respect to both First World economic growth and Third World development, as the world

---

[19] I shall be using the term "neoliberal" in the usual (for scholarly discussions) sense to refer to economic doctrines and policies drawing upon the new classical liberalism of von Hayek and others and the monetarist approach of Milton Friedman and others. In the USA, the public discussion of liberalism is terminologically complicated by a common usage of "liberal" that nearly inverts the traditional meaning emphasizing individual liberty and limited government, which is still dominant not only abroad but also among American political theorists. In this discussion, I shall use "liberal" and its cognates in this traditional sense, unless modified by "reform," "social," or "left," which bring it closer to common usage. To further complicate matters, many of those commonly referred to as neoconservatives in contexts of domestic policy and foreign affairs, hold neoliberal views on economic policy.

economic crisis of the 1970s demonstrated. Once in the ascendant, neoliberals pushed the World Bank, IMF, and other international development agencies to adopt the same sorts of market-oriented policies that were being adopted in Britain and America. By the end of the 1980s, that had largely been accomplished. The new "Washington consensus" increasingly reflected in the policies of major international economic organizations promoted the deregulation, privatization, reduction of state expenditures, fiscal discipline, tax reform, trade liberalization, removal of barriers to foreign investment, and the like that neoliberals demanded. The path had been cleared for a momentous shift from liberal modernization to neoliberal globalization.[20]

The exemplars of development were now the newly industrializing countries (NICs) of the 1970s and 1980s, which, by following export-oriented strategies, had achieved development through successful *integration into* the global economy and not, as dependency theorists had erroneously advised, through de-linking from it. State-based programs were not a shortcut to development but the main obstacle to it; the correct path was market-based globalization. And that was the path now dictated by the principal international development agencies, which offered assistance only on the condition that "structural adjustment programs" were put in place, featuring the sorts of measures mentioned above. (The fact that the NICs typically succeeded not by following the dictates of the Washington consensus but through economic steering by strong states pursuing long-term development strategies did not figure importantly in neoliberal ideology or policy.)

In a restructured global economy organized around free markets, it was up to each nation to pursue its own development. The international division of labor was dramatically changing; the globalization of production and marketing was accelerating; the application of new information and communication technologies had vastly reduced the significance of geography. There was nothing about the structure of the global economy that would prevent any nation from competing successfully for a position within it that would enable it to prosper. If a nation failed to do so, the fault lay with it. It would have to get its

---

[20] Peet, *Theories of Development*, pp. 47–64; David Harvey, *The New Imperialism* (Oxford University Press, 2003), chap. 4; J. Timmons Roberts and Amy Hite (eds.), *From Modernization to Globalization* (Oxford: Blackwell, 2000), part IV. Under the leadership of James Wolfensohn, the World Bank later changed its policy emphasis from "conditionality" to effective government.

economic house in order, in accord with the neoliberal prescriptions of the Washington consensus.

With the breakup of the Soviet Union at the end of the 1980s, a triumphal neoliberalism proclaimed "the end of history," that is, the absence of any real alternative to what it prescribed nationally and internationally.[21] But this replay of "the end of ideology" ideology did not go unchallenged for any longer than the original had. While the failures of development policy in the 1950s and 1960s, and the part played in them by inefficient and corrupt governments, were undeniable, there was little warrant for the neoliberals' unbounded confidence in the workings of the market and their principled opposition to state intervention. The long political struggle to domesticate capitalism in the nineteenth and twentieth centuries was not without cause. Free-market capitalism had proved historically to be horrendously exploitative and had produced vastly unequal distributions of social wealth. There were always weaker and stronger market positions, winners and losers, and consequently gross inequalities and widespread poverty. That had not changed in the 1980s. Now that hard-won controls over the capitalist economy were being dismantled at home and abroad, inequity and immiseration were on the rise.[22] Many weak, impoverished, postcolonial societies were simply unable to compete successfully on these terms. Rather than "catching up," they saw their shares of world trade decrease and their per capita incomes decline, while their indebtedness grew.[23] Thus, in most parts of sub-Saharan Africa, many parts of Latin America, some parts of Asia, and the non-oil-producing parts of the Middle East, the new political economy of development has meant continuing underdevelopment. Many poor nations have become poorer and weaker states even weaker, some to the point of collapse. The gaps between rich and poor have grown larger. For the global economic playing field is by no means level. Its general contours were laid out

---

[21] Francis Fukuyama, "The End of History?" *National Interest* 16 (1989): 3–18.

[22] The unevenness of global development persists; but since the 1980s poverty rates have been on the decline, particularly in Asia, and especially in China – though a majority of the world population still subsists on less than $2 per day, a common measure of poverty. See A. V. Banerjee, R. Bénabou, and D. Mookherjee (eds.), *Understanding Poverty* (Oxford University Press, 2006).

[23] The average per capita income in the thirty-eight least developed countries is currently estimated to be less than $1 per day, the usual measure of extreme poverty. As a result, tens of thousands of children die each day from consequences of severe malnourishment.

by the modern history of colonialism.[24] Societies that entered into
global competition after their economies had been restructured and
underdeveloped by colonial powers were placed at a disadvantage
that many have not been able to overcome. Moreover, the rules of the
"free-market" game are, as usual, heavily skewed in favor of the most
powerful players, who dominate international associations, agencies,
and agreements, from the IMF and World Bank to the G-7 and World
Trade Organization. They have been able, for instance, to maintain
massive subsidies (c. $280 billion in 2005) for their agricultural pro-
duce, to impose trade barriers against "unfair competition" from
underdeveloped nations, and to use intellectual property rights to maintain exorbitant profit margins on key commodities, including many life-
saving drugs, and thus to gain unfair advantage in competition with the
developing world. And they have been able to impose "structural
adjustment programs" that have precipitously reduced the public sectors of developing societies and dangerously weakened the basic social
securities they underwrite, while themselves often disregarding their
own prescriptions.[25]

Where the increase in suffering can't be denied or statistically obfus-
cated, neoliberal apologists sternly advise: "no gain without pain."
Economics is, after all, no longer a "moral science," as it was for their
classical forebears, but an empirical science with iron laws that can't be
bent for political purposes. In the global economy as presently constituted, putatively alternative paths of development are in reality roads to
nowhere: there is one world economy and one general prescription for
becoming a viable competitor within it. If that prescription sometimes
causes pain in the short run, it will pay off in the long run. But the
alleged objectivity of this "value-free" advice has come in for some
heavy criticism. To many it appears to be a not-unfamiliar cover for
what is in reality a political agenda. The shift from Keynesian to
neoliberal policies on the national and international levels was not
simply dictated by laws of economics, as the ruling ideology would
have it. It was the result of organized political mobilization: neoliberals
gained political power in Britain, America, and elsewhere and pushed

---

[24] Ankie Hoogvelt, *Globalization and the Postcolonial World* (Baltimore: Johns
Hopkins University Press, 2001).
[25] Joseph Stiglitz, *Globalization and Its Discontents* (New York: W. W. Norton,
2002).

through significant policy changes in national and international arenas. They were not merely responding to economic realities but shaping them; the growing domination of economics over politics was itself accomplished politically. But once put in place, the globalized market hovers over us, as Marx once put it, "like the fate of the ancients, and with an invisible hand allots fortune and misfortune to men."[26] It can be subdued, if at all, only by the same means that created it: organized political action. From this perspective, the critical question of the present is whether and, if so, in what ways democratic control over capital can be reestablished at the global level.[27] For only insofar as it is possible to subordinate global markets to a new system of national and international regulation will it be economically feasible to pursue social goals. And only to that extent can the narrowly economistic focus of neoliberal development theory be expanded to encompass again concerns with equity, democracy, and social welfare. Failing that, much of the world may be condemned to live in a no man's land between destroyed traditions and unachieved modernity.

IV Neoconservatism and neoimperialism

Development was understood in more directly political terms by the neoconservative policy elites who came to power in 2000 with the improbable (s)election of George W. Bush as the 43rd President of the United States. The term "neoconservative" was first used in the 1970s to designate a group of anti-Stalinist left and liberal intellectuals who had begun migrating rightwards in the 1960s – Irving Kristol, Gertrude Himmelfarb, Norman Podhoretz, Midge Decter, Daniel Patrick Moynihan, Michael Novak, Peter Berger, and Nathan Glazer, among others.[28] Repulsed by countercultural attacks on traditional values and New Left opposition to the Vietnam War, and

---

[26] Karl Marx, "The German Ideology: Part I," in Robert C. Tucker (ed.), *The Marx–Engels Reader* (New York: W. W. Norton, 1978), p. 162. The truth of Marx's dictum was demonstrated once again, with devastating force, by the implosion of global financial markets in 2008.

[27] Jürgen Habermas, *The Postnational Constellation*, tr. Max Pensky (Cambridge, MA: MIT Press, 2001). This is also the perspective of Peet and Leys, in the books cited in notes 6 and 7.

[28] Peter Steinfels, *The Neo-Conservatives: The Men Who Are Changing America's Politics* (New York: Simon & Schuster, 1979); Mark Gerson, *The Neo-Conservative Vision: From the Cold War to Culture Wars* (Lanham, MD:

dissatisfied with the "culture of appeasement" they saw crippling American liberalism, they regarded the 1972 presidential candidacy of George McGovern as symptomatic of all that was wrong with the dominant wing of the Democratic Party and began a rightward migration toward the "Scoop" Jackson wing of the Party or, in some cases, into the Republican Party.[29] That shift was further consolidated during the presidency of Ronald Reagan, when a number of neoconservatives received government appointments – most visibly, Jeanne Kirkpatrick as US Ambassador to the UN. The main source of their increasing influence during the 1970s was their prolific intellectual output, centered around journals such as *Commentary*, in which they attacked détente with the Soviet Union as a failure of nerve and promoted an aggressive brand of anti-communism.[30]

But it was the "second generation" of neoconservatives – such as William Kristol, Richard Perle, Paul Wolfowitz, Joshua Muravchik, Charles Krauthammer, Robert Kagan, I. Lewis Libby, Elliott Abrams, Douglas Feith, and John Bolton, among many others – who completed the turn to the right. They came to intellectual maturity in a world in which a new American conservatism had established itself as an ideological and political force to be reckoned with. The 1970s and 1980s saw not only a proliferation of influential conservative journals but also the formation of a dense network of ideologically conservative think tanks and policy institutes, funded largely by corporations and conservative foundations – all of which gave rise to a flood of books, articles, position papers, draft resolutions, memoranda, speeches, and by the 1990s op eds and talking heads for the mass

---

Madison, 1996); Stefan Halper and Jonathan Clarke, *America Alone: The Neo-Conservatives and the Global Order* (Cambridge University Press, 2004). There is a considerable diversity of views among neoconservatives; once again, my treatment is of necessity selective.

[29] In the early 1970s, Sen. Henry Jackson worked effectively with neoconservatives and major Jewish organizations to address the plight of Soviet Jewry, particularly the barriers to emigration being raised. The success of that effort was a significant factor in consolidating the neoconservative shift.

[30] Though my focus here is on foreign policy, in light of the later affiliation of neoconservatives with neoliberals, social conservatives, and the religious right, it is also worth mentioning their early skepticism concerning Great Society Programs, affirmative action, multiculturalism, and the like, and their abiding interest in the social function of religion.

media, particularly the emerging conservative media empires in cable news and talk radio.[31] And it was the second generation of neoconservatives that forged closer ties to social conservatives and Christian evangelicals, who came broadly to support the neoconservative agenda in foreign and defense policy. The details of this alliance are not of concern here. I am interested, rather, in the ideological background of the "preemptive" National Security Strategy of 2002, the invasion of Iraq in 2003, and the Second Inaugural Address of 2004, in which President Bush announced that "the survival of liberty in our land increasingly depends on the success of liberty in other lands ... America's vital interests and our deepest beliefs are now one."[32] How did the anti-communist liberalism of the first generation of neoconservatives get transformed into the crusading liberalism of the second? Here too I can offer only a few schematic remarks, and again at the cost of unavoidable simplification.

Among the founding generation of neoconservatives, the breakup of the Soviet Union at the end of the 1980s was generally regarded as a confirmation of the stronger anti-communist line they had advocated, the accomplishment of their overriding aim in foreign policy, and an opportunity for the US to adopt a more classically realist policy directed to the nation's "vital interests." For many younger neoconservatives, however, it meant something different: a new round of American messianism, that is, an opportunity to pursue an "idealist" policy of shaping the international environment according to American values.[33] The US now found itself in a position of "universal dominion" in a "unipolar world."[34] And it should take advantage of that situation to launch a

---

[31] Unlike development, modernization, and neoliberal theory, and even the first generation of neoconservatism, second-generation neoconservatism is notably bereft of front-rank theorists. The preponderance of their publishing output, when not sheerly polemical, is devoted to policy and strategy. This may be one reason why so many commentators, in casting about for their intellectual antecedents, have hit upon the improbable figure of Leo Strauss. When confronted with this genealogical hypothesis, Wolfowitz and Perle acknowledged instead their indebtedness to Albert Wohlstetter, who was himself a defense strategist. See Halper and Clarke, *America Alone*, pp. 61–68.

[32] *New York Times*, January 21, 2004, pp. 16–17.

[33] See, for example, Robert Kagan and William Kristol (eds.), *Present Dangers: Crisis and Opportunity in American Foreign and Defense Policy* (San Francisco: Encounter, 2000).

[34] Charles Krauthammer, "Universal Dominion: Toward a Unipolar World," *National Interest*, winter 1989/1990.

democratic crusade, for only thus could it effectively counter the main new threat to world security, the proliferation of weapons of mass destruction in outlaw "weapon states" such as Iraq. That threat called for military intervention and the export of democracy to preserve the peace. Some characterized this new form of liberal interventionism as "hard Wilsonianism," that is, the pursuit of Wilsonian ends with other – military rather than multilateral – means. One can, then, understand the rage among neoconservatives when President George H. W. Bush decided to end the first Gulf War without removing Saddam Hussein.

Second-generation neoconservatives used the interregnum of the Clinton years to develop and promote an alternative, much more aggressive, national security policy, which was focused particularly on the Middle East, and which was subsequently adopted as part of the US "response" to the events of September 11, 2001.[35] The view of international affairs adumbrated in policy statements and public addresses of the period comprises a peculiar mix of "realist" and "idealist" variants of American exceptionalism. On the one hand, unchallengeable military power is said to be fundamental to maintaining national security and international order. And given the nature of the new enemy and the new threat, that power will have to be used preemptively to intervene against despotic regimes that do or may provide terrorists with access to weapons of mass destruction. In a unipolar world, the United States, as the only superpower, will have to assume responsibility for preserving global peace and, when expedient, acting unilaterally to guarantee the security of the "civilized" world

---

[35] The basic outlines of that policy were already visible in the Defense Policy Guidance drafted by Paul Wolfowitz, I. Lewis Libby, and others in 1992, toward the end of the first Bush administration, under then Secretary of Defense Dick Cheney. That draft was never officially adopted; but it was completed and leaked to the press. See Halper and Clarke, *America Alone*, pp. 145–146. The idea of "preemption" was specifically applied to the removal of Saddam Hussein's regime in a 1998 public letter to President Clinton by affiliates of the Project for a New American Century. The signatories included a number of people who later found themselves in positions of power to implement that policy after 9/11: Donald Rumsfeld, Paul Wolfowitz, John Bolton, Richard Perle, and Elliott Abrams, among others. "Letter to the Hon. William J. Clinton on Iraq," January 26, 1998. Available at www.newamericancentury.org/. The PNAC statement of principles in 1997, which was co-signed by Dick Cheney, is available at the same website.

against terrorist "barbarians" and those who support them.[36] On the other hand, moral clarity is essential to survival in this dangerous world. The forces of evil, particularly Islamist radicals, can be most effectively countered by the spread of just those basic values they so violently oppose: freedom, democracy, and human rights. Thus, in the present conjuncture, idealism *is* realism in foreign policy. Regime change, by force if necessary, and nation rebuilding to install American-style, free-market, liberal democracies are, in the final analysis, the most effective response to Islamist terrorism. For "moral truths are the same in every culture," and American values are a privileged expression of just such universal moral truths, which can thus be implemented, with due accommodation for cultural and historical differences, in every society.[37] Iraq is a paradigm case for this approach: the overthrow of tyranny and establishment of democracy there would have a domino effect throughout the Islamic world, and as that happened, the threat of terrorism would recede. So the best way to protect America's interests is to promote American values. And in doing this, the United States cannot allow its hands to be tied by the international norms, institutions, and treaties with which militarily less powerful and morally less clear nations – in particular, the "old Europeans" – seek to restrain us. We must finally get over the "Vietnam syndrome" that has eaten away at national self-confidence for too long. We must, that is, overcome the crippling hesitancy to use military force to accomplish foreign policy aims, which the prevailing misinterpretation of that failure of political will instilled in the national psyche. America must once again assume its proper place as the last best hope of humankind.

In some respects, the rhetoric of neoconservatives deviates noticeably from the accustomed tropes of developmentalism. To begin with, they drop the claim to value-free science of classical development theory in favor of an appeal to "moral truths" and "universal values." Further, the explicit anti-modernism of many elements of their cultural criticism and

---

[36] President Bush used the civilized/barbarian contrast in his Address to a Joint Session of Congress and the American People of September 20, 2001; available at www.whitehouse.gov/news/releases/2001/. But he soon dropped this nineteenth-century rhetoric – which is obviously unsuited to winning friends and influencing people in the postcolonial world – for the contrast between good and evil.

[37] The quoted phrase and the ideas are taken from remarks by President Bush at the 2002 Graduation Exercise of the United States Military Academy; available at www.whitehouse.gov/news/releases/2002/.

social conservatism, as well as their invocation of American civil religion to ground and interpret basic political values are unusual in that discursive domain. And the rhetorical valorization of "traditional values" prevents them from simply replacing the hoary civilized/barbarian dichotomy by the now usual modern/traditional dichotomy. Thus they often deploy the seemingly non-developmental rhetoric of good versus evil, which has the added advantage of playing directly to the large constituency of evangelical Christians. Nevertheless, developmentalism is still at work providing ideological cover. American values are represented as an especially happy realization of universal values that find various expressions in various cultures. Without some recognizable forms of freedom, democracy, and human rights, no people can attain a civilized mode of existence. And this, it is argued, is precisely the predicament of the Islamic world. In consequence of the historical failure of Westernizing elites to create an Islamic modernity combining economic development and political democracy with Muslim identity, and in response to the ever-increasing pressures of globalization in every sphere of life, resentment of Western superiority has grown, as has the temptation to Islamist radicalism.[38] The result is a "clash of civilizations," which, though it is typically articulated in religious terms, is at bottom a matter of failed modernization – hence the importance of spreading, by imposition if necessary, American/Western values and institutions throughout the Islamic world.

These disparate elements were explicitly assembled into a more or less coherent developmental account, which Bush unveiled at the twentieth anniversary of the founding, under President Reagan, of the National Endowment for Democracy.[39] The basic components may be briefly summarized as follows:

(1) While "the progress of liberty" is "the direction of history," it is "not determined by some dialectic of history" but requires the active engagement and political courage of free people. In particular, the moral and military commitment of the US to defending freedom across the globe has been central to its worldwide advance.

[38] Bernard Lewis, *The Crisis of Islam: Holy War and Unholy Terror* (New York: Modern Library, 2003). For alternative views, see J. Cohen and D. Chasman (eds.), *Islam and the Challenge to Democracy* (Princeton University Press, 2004).

[39] United States Chamber of Commerce, Washington, DC, November 2003. Available at www.whitehouse.gov/news/releases/2003/11/print/20031106-2. html. In what follows, the passages in quotation marks are taken from this speech.

(2) Though technological, economic, and social developments are crucial ingredients of modernization, they are not prerequisites that
have to be satisfied *before* a people can become free and democratic.
Quite the contrary: "the prosperity, and social vitality, and technological progress of a people are directly determined by the extent of
their liberty," for freedom unleashes creativity and private enterprise, and that is the key to advances in these other domains. Again:
"it is the practice of democracy that makes a nation ready for
democracy," democracy itself is "the path of progress ... and
every nation can start on this path." In short, liberal democracy is
not the end-point but the starting point and driving force of development – the classical structure of deferral has been inverted.

(3) In some parts of the world, particularly in the Middle East – which
is "of great strategic importance" and "must be a focus of American
policy for decades to come" – there is a "freedom deficit" that
prevents people from entering upon this path and thus "undermines
human development." These "relics of a passing era" – military and
theocratic dictatorships – represent the major challenge of our time
and "the resolve we show will shape the next stage of the world
democratic movement."

(4) As long as "the Middle East remains a place where freedom does
not flourish," it will produce an endless supply of "violence for
export," increasingly armed with weapons of mass destruction.
This is something we cannot accept, and so "the United States has
adopted a new policy, a forward policy of freedom in the Middle
East." As demonstrated in Iraq – "a watershed event in the global
democratic revolution" – a key to this forward strategy is the use of
American power to start oppressed peoples on the path of liberty
and democracy – or, as Charles Krauthammer has put it, to "help
trigger democratic revolutions by militarily deposing their
oppressors."[40]

(5) In doing so, the US is not simply imposing its own values on other
cultures. We recognize that "modernization is not the same as
Westernization," and that democratic governments reflect their
surrounding cultures. But there are also "essential principles

---

[40] "The Hypocrisy Continues," *Chicago Tribune*, March 21, 2005, p. 19. On this
view, then, democracy can be imposed by means of force and violence, and
without consulting the target demos.

common to every successful society," and these are based in the end on universal values, especially liberty. For liberty is not only the "design of nature" and "the direction of history," it is "the right and capacity of all mankind," the "plan of Heaven for humanity," and "the best hope for progress here on earth." This interlinking of nature, history, morality, Providence, and progress may seem extravagant, but it is not unfamiliar: it hearkens back to early modern liberal theory.

Notwithstanding the palpable tensions in this neoconservative ideology of benevolent global hegemony and universal values implemented by unilateral military power, there are presumably defense and foreign policy elites who genuinely subscribe to it. We should not underestimate the self-righteousness of American exceptionalism and the power of national myths. But as with previous high-minded ideologies of empire, critics have been quick to point out the more earthly interests this one serves. Thus, some have noted the predicament in which the American right found itself after the breakup of the Soviet Union. The seemingly inexhaustible supply of fear of "the enemy" it had made available for purposes of political mobilization, social control, and military-industrial expansion dried up almost overnight. In these difficult circumstances, 9/11 was a political bonanza, thoroughly exploited by the Republican right under the intellectual leadership of the neoconservatives. The never-ending "War on Terror," against an omnipresent yet evanescent enemy, reinvigorated "the paranoid style of American politics," which paid immediate dividends in partisan politics, "homeland security," and military spending.[41] Other critics, on both the left and the right, have noted a neoconservative tendency to conflate the vital interests of the United States with the national security interests of Israel as defined by the leadership of the Likud Party and promoted by the Israel Lobby in the US.[42] Moreover, this view of Israel's security interests is widely shared by Christian fundamentalists in the USA, who for their own scriptural reasons – the ingathering of the Jews, the Second

---

[41] This general characterization of American politics is, of course, taken from Richard Hofstadter, *The Paranoid Style in American Politics and Other Essays* (Cambridge, MA: Harvard University Press, 1996).

[42] See, for instance, Francis Fukuyama, *America at the Crossroads* (New Haven: Yale University Press, 2006); and Michael Massing, "The Storm over the Israel Lobby," *New York Review of Books*, June 8, 2006, pp. 64–73.

Coming of Christ, etc. – strongly support Likud/AIPAC (American Israel Public Affairs Committee) policies. And still other critics have emphasized the US geopolitical interest in Middle East oil.[43] This last type of consideration might help explain why someone like Cheney would close ranks with neoconservatives, which was crucial to their recent ascendancy.[44] In any case, it is the interest that much of the rest of the world believes to be behind America's recent actions.

V Toward a critical theory of global development

Our journey from modernization theory to recent policy statements has taken us from the precincts of European developmentalism into the province of American exceptionalism. Echoing Hartz's account of the liberal tradition in America, this has meant another crusade abroad, the neoconservative rationale for which often runs as follows. At the close of World War II, the United States and its allies had defeated one of the two major alternatives to liberal democracy, European fascism. It required another half-century, again under American leadership, to defeat the second, Soviet communism. That was accomplished less through decades of containing communism and managing postcolonial modernization than through the shock therapy administered by the more confrontational policies of the Reagan administration. But just as the final triumph of liberal democracy and the "end of history" were being proclaimed, a new form of fascism, "Islamofascism," reared its

---

[43] See, for instance, Harvey, *The New Imperialism*. This view receives some support from the recent (June, 2008) issuance of no-bid service contracts to five major Western oil companies, who will have the right of first refusal on future contracts to develop some of Iraq's largest oil fields.

[44] In a speech given at the Institute of Petroleum in 1999, shortly before he became Vice-President, Cheney explained: "By some estimates, there will be an average of two percent annual growth in global oil demand over the years ahead, along with conservatively a three percent natural decline in production from existing reserves. That means by 2010 we will need on the order of an additional fifty million barrels a day. So where is the oil going to come from? ... While many regions of the world offer great oil opportunities, the Middle East, with two thirds of the world's oil and the lowest cost, is still where the prize ultimately lies ... Oil is unique, in that it is so strategic in nature. We are not talking about soapflakes or leisurewear here. Energy is truly fundamental to the world's economy. The [first] Gulf War was a reflection of that reality." Available at www. energybulletin.net/559.html.

head and threatened the free world.[45] This has made it necessary to launch a third global struggle – after World War II and the Cold War – a "War on Terror." And the principal means to fight this war are not long-term development projects aimed at ameliorating the conditions that breed and nourish terrorism, but "democratic revolutions" – not patient *Bildungsprozesse*, so to speak, but sudden conversions. For classical modernization theorists were mistaken about the empirical preconditions of democratic self-governance: democratic revolutions "triggered" by external military force can create their own supporting conditions – or so many neoconservatives aver.

Despite the evident differences between this brand of neoconservatism and the progressivism of modernization theory and practice, much has remained constant. From Vietnam to Iraq, liberal universalism has been rendered not only compatible with but even supportive of forceful interventions into postcolonial societies by appeal to some version or other of the modern/premodern dichotomy. From the perspectives of those societies, it might indeed appear that the more things change, the more they remain the same. From the start of the modern era, the pursuit of Western interests in the non-Western world has repeatedly been represented as being for "their" advancement and improvement. In this respect, Mill's characterization of nineteenth-century Britain as a "benevolent despot" is not so different from the neoconservative understanding of the USA today as a "benevolent hegemon."

Thus, one can easily understand why many postcolonial thinkers have rejected the fundamental assumptions of development thinking altogether and called for a "decolonization of the mind," in which we un-learn to think of history as a unitary process opening onto a uniform future.[46] I doubt that our minds can or should be purged of development thinking altogether. As I explained in chapter 5, there are deep-seated features of the world we live in – inescapable "facts" of cultural and societal modernity – that make it impracticable for us simply to dismiss ideas of development. Whichever side one takes in the current debates surrounding globalization, for instance, it is obvious that such discourse lives from the fruits of the historicist enlightenment in the *Geisteswissenschaften* of the late nineteenth and early twentieth

---

[45] Paul Berman, *Terror and Liberalism* (New York: W. W. Norton, 2003).
[46] Majid Rahnema (ed.), *The Post-Development Reader* (London: Zed Books, 1997).

centuries. It is precisely our historically, sociologically, and anthropologically schooled views of the diversity of beliefs and practices that, for
instance, enable *and* constrain the contemporary discussion of "multiple modernities." If we add to this the continuing effects of the earlier
Enlightenment – including the ongoing advances in our scientific understanding of the world and in our technical ability to manipulate it, as
well as the effects these have on traditional systems of belief and on the
normative and evaluative elements of culture intimately interwoven
with them – we can understand why entire *kinds* of reasons have lost
and continue to lose their discursive weight. To such "Hegelian" facts of
cultural modernity, we can add the "Marxian" facts of societal modernity, the global conditions in which all societies willy-nilly find themselves and which confront them with an array of basic challenges they
have to meet if they want to survive and thrive. Cultural and societal
"facts" of these sorts constrain the range of viable "alternative" modernities, especially when we take into account the myriad internal relations and causal connections between them.

From this perspective, it is not surprising that "modernization,"
"development," and related notions are still routinely invoked for
purposes of analysis, assessment, policy, and planning in official and
unofficial public spheres. This is not *only* a matter of the colonization of
our minds, but also of very basic features of the world we live in and of
the ways we think about it. And even if it were possible to dismiss such
notions, not everyone in postcolonial societies would find that desirable, for most people value at least some elements of modernization. For
them, the issue is not whether to modernize or not, but how to do so and
within what constraints. And if that is so, we have no practicable
alternative but to revisit and rethink the idea of development. I shall
conclude with a few "rules for the direction of the mind" when occupied
with that task.

(1) To begin with, the reflexivity of modern cultures has meant that
modernization has been accompanied from the start by critiques of
modernization. Romanticism and Marxism, Nietzsche and Weber,
Gandhi and Fanon are as integral to the discourse of modernity as the
dominant ideologies they opposed. Precisely the claimed universality of
that discourse leaves it *semantically and pragmatically open* to dissent
and criticism from subordinated and excluded others. For this reason,
modernity need not – indeed cannot – be left behind for some putative
postmodernity; but it can be continually transformed from within. In

the present connection, it is significant that the late twentieth century saw the rise of a global discourse of modernity in which postcolonial thinkers have played an increasingly important, critical and transformative role.

(2) If the facts of cultural and societal modernity are as I have suggested, there is little chance of radically different modernities arising and surviving in the world we live in. On the other hand, there is not only the possibility but also the reality of *multiple* modernities. Convergence at abstract, formal, or structural levels is quite consistent with, and indeed necessarily accompanied by, diversity at more concrete levels. Consider the following examples: the abstract norm of equality has been interpreted and implemented in any number of ways, from formal equality to substantive equality, from equality of opportunity to equality of outcome, and in various ways in each respect; freedom of speech is compatible with the proscription of hate speech in many European countries but not in the United States; and freedom of religion is compatible there with established churches but not here; free-market economies look quite different in Sweden, the United States, and Japan; and representative government can mean everything from constitutional monarchy and parliamentary government to the US federal system and Latin American corporatism. The conceptual point is this: *by their very nature*, the universal cannot be actual without the particular, nor the formal without the substantive, the abstract without the concrete, structure without content.[47] Thus the idea that all societies are converging on the American model is based on a fundamental misunderstanding of universality as uniformity. The "dialectic" of the general and the particular would lead us to expect, rather, that different cultures, different circumstances, and different histories – including different histories of domination by, and resistance to, European imperialism – normally give rise to quite different modern cultures and societies, that is, to multiple modernities. Given the extent, intensity, and variety of cultural encounters in the modern period, one would expect to find what one in fact finds: not unilinearity and uniformity but plurality and hybridity – the coalescence of diverse patterns and forms

---

[47] This was, of course, a point already clear to Hegel. Charles Taylor has brought it to bear upon the discussion of multiple modernities in, among other essays, "Two Theories of Modernity," in D. P. Gaonkar (ed.), *Alternative Modernities* (Durham, NC: Duke University Press, 2001), pp. 172–196.

arising from heterogeneous origins. Moreover, how much convergence to expect at the societal level, is partly a practical question of, for instance, what kinds of economic arrangements are fit to function effectively in global markets, or what kinds of legal institutions are suited to establishing an effective rule of law in national and transnational contexts. So the issue confronting postcolonial societies is not whether to modernize at all but how best to do so. Of course, as long as wealth and power are distributed as unequally as they are, the range of answers available to the poorest and the weakest will be vastly more constricted than any "inner logic" of modernization processes itself dictates.

(3) Grand theories and grand narratives of development or modernization always outrun the available empirical evidence. They are macrohistorical interpretive schemes that, as Weber recognized, can never be value-free all the way down. However value-neutral the surface grammar of such theories may appear, they are framed from interpretive and evaluative standpoints that are essentially contestable. Hence the claim to scientific objectivity raised by the varieties of development theory we have examined – excepting the moralistic versions of neoconservatism – has to be seen as ideological. It functions to foreclose or foreshorten moral, ethical, and political debate concerning questions of justice and the common good: "we'd like to do more for those in need, but the iron laws of global markets simply preclude it." And it underwrites a technocratic-bureaucratic form of development practice, implemented by experts, that eliminates or marginalizes democratic input by those being developed. Of course, this does not mean that empirical data and the correlations, connections, preconditions, and consequences they indicate are irrelevant. They place very real constraints on which types of theory and narrative make analytical and interpretive sense, and on which types of policy and planning are practicable and promising. From this methodological standpoint, the current neoconservative strategy of militarily triggering "democratic revolutions" around the world appears as a hypermoralism that treats empirical evidence as largely irrelevant. However, between the scientistic suppression of normative discourse and the moralistic disregard for empirical inquiry there is a broad spectrum of options. In some respects, Kant's understanding of grand metanarrative – universal history from a cosmopolitan point of view – as the object neither of theoretical knowledge nor of practical reason, but of "reflective judgment," was closer to

the mark. On his view, while such metanarratives must take account of, and be compatible with, known empirical data and causal connections, they always go beyond what is known in aspiring to a unity of history. And that can best be done from a point of view oriented to practice: grand metanarratives give us an idea of the kinds of more humane future for which we may hope, but only if we are prepared to engage ourselves in bringing them about.

(4) Since we have no God's-eye view of the past or future, and macrohistorical accounts are always interpretive schemes projected from value-related points of view, it is not surprising that the chief exemplars of this genre of theorizing should retrospectively appear to be so obviously ethnocentric. It is not surprising because most of the major participants in the discourse of global modernity have until recently come broadly from the same cultural setting. This has given their disputes an in-house character, so that notwithstanding the very basic disagreements among Kant, Hegel, Marx, and Mill, for instance, they could all agree that European history marked out the one true path of modernization. The theoretical glorification of Britain's culture, society, economics, and politics in the late nineteenth century and of America's in the late twentieth was not, then, a matter only of inflated self-regard but also of the ethnocentrism endemic to a culture talking only to itself. The antidote to this is not merely gathering more data but further opening the discourse of modernity to non-Western voices.[48] To some extent, in our major cultural institutions this process is already underway; and the increased presence of postcolonial voices in scholarly and popular discourse has begun to have its decentering effects. But in the institutionalized venues of global wealth and power, such voices are still muffled, and that cannot be changed without restructuring the asymmetrical relations that have shaped modernization processes from the start.[49] Until that happens, mainstream development theory and practice are likely to remain deeply ethnocentric.

(5) Nevertheless, the theory and practice of development cannot simply be abandoned in favor of some postdevelopmental thinking of difference. Not only do the facts of cultural and societal modernity

---

[48] Seyla Benhabib, *The Claims of Culture: Equality and Diversity in the Global Era* (Princeton University Press, 2002).

[49] As the growing clout of China, India, Brazil, and some other members of the WTO indicates, this process is already underway. But it remains, for instance, that the US still has an effective veto power in the IMF.

weigh theoretically against that, but the pressing need for organized collective action on behalf of the poorest and most vulnerable societies also make it practically objectionable. Instead, we have to fashion a critical theory of global development that acknowledges its inherent risks and continuously works to contain and counter them. To start with, such an approach would have to reject natural-historical accounts of social evolution that conceal from view the massive and pervasive use of force and violence in the capitalist modernization of the West and imperialist modernization of the non-West. This is not simply a matter of the inherent ambivalence of modernization processes, which Weber among others convincingly portrayed, but of the "surplus" suffering and devastation inflicted by the specifically capitalist dynamics of European–American-led global development. Exploitation, expropriation, dispossession, slavery, colonialism, and imperialism were not just accidental byproducts of a developmental process driven by the exigencies of capital accumulation: they were among its central mechanisms. It is, then, remarkable that mainstream accounts of development have largely agreed in ignoring or downplaying that part of the historical record. Force and violence, power and domination have usually played no significant role in these master narratives, so that they might better serve as dominant ideologies, veiling the interests and strategies actually in play. But the repeated resort to overt force and the evident fact that European–American-led modernization has established deeply unjust and clearly unsustainable modes of economic growth have torn that veil aside. A critical theory of global development must keep in view the violence, destructiveness, and injustice of historical modernization processes and keep alive the memory of the immense suffering and irreparable loss thereby visited upon multitudes in every part of the world.

(6) If European–American development is viewed within the world system it created and dominated from the start of the modern era, the classical picture of self-contained national units with stronger or weaker internal impulses to growth and maturation has to give way to that of an interactive global nexus marked by significant differences in wealth and power. Until these vast differentials are leveled down, there can only ever be "uneven" development: many weak, impoverished, postcolonial societies will never "catch up," and thus the "underdevelopment" constructed by colonialism will become their inescapable fate. That this not be allowed to happen is a demand not only of distributive justice but

of reparative or restorative justice as well.[50] Those nations that have been historically implicated in the expropriation of native lands, the extermination of native populations, the slave trade, colonial exploitation, and imperial domination have a moral-political obligation to remedy the wrongs of their own past injustice, to redress the continuing harms that resulted from it. Critical development theory thus regards remembering and repairing the deep injuries of imperialism as an obligation in justice and not as a matter of benevolent paternalism. If paternalism is to be avoided in practice, the agencies, regulations, reforms, policies, programs, and the like instituted for that purpose have to be collectively organized in such a way that those whose historical underdevelopment is being addressed have an equal say in their design and implementation. The democratization of retroactive justice has to be part and parcel of the democratization of global governance generally.[51]

(7) Since the 1970s, a new, even more intractable problem with "actually existing development" has loomed ever larger on the horizon: the "limits to growth."[52] The mainstream conceptions of development we have examined take it for granted that development means becoming more like "us," particularly in economic respects. That is, under-developed economies have to be brought up to Western levels of production and consumption; and the obstacles to this are primarily cultural and political. Nature is left out of the picture. But bringing the effects of human activities on the natural environment – there represented only as "negative externalities" – centrally into the picture shows this conception of development to be incompatible with basic prerequisites of human – and, of course, many other – forms of life on this planet.

---

[50] The idea of reparations for colonialism was already advanced by Frantz Fanon in *The Wretched of the Earth* (New York: Grove Press, 1963), pp. 102–103.

[51] "Global Governance" need not – perhaps, could not – take the form of a global government. Many contemporary theorists of global democracy emphasize its "dispersed" and "multilayered" character. See, for instance, James N. Rosenau, *Study of World Politics*, vol. II: *Globalization and Governance* (New York: Routledge, 2006); and J. Habermas, "A Political Constitution for the Pluralist World Society," in *Between Naturalism and Religion*, tr. C. Cronin (Cambridge: Polity Press, 2008), pp. 312–352. For a brief overview, see D. Archibugi, "Cosmopolitan Democracy and Its Critics," *European Journal of International Relations* 10 (2004): 437–473.

[52] Bob Sutcliffe offers a brief overview of this discussion in "Development after Ecology," in J. Timmons Roberts and Amy Hite (eds.), *From Modernization to Globalization* (Oxford: Blackwell, 2003), pp. 328–340.

Our way of life is unglobalizable; "leveling-up" all national economies to the production and consumption patterns of the most developed societies would make the planet uninhabitable. In particular, the levels of resource depletion and environmental degradation they entail are physically unsustainable. Thus development has to be reconceptualized not merely as a problem for underdeveloped societies but as a global problem: how to achieve sustainable development on a planetary scale. One thing is immediately clear: this cannot be done with neoliberal, free-market nostrums; sustainable development has an ineluctably political core. Moreover, the tensions between environmental demands and the demands of equity raise a host of new and difficult issues for any critical theory of global development. How can we achieve a more equitable access to natural resources at present without shortchanging future generations? How can we provide for the well-being of future generations without shortchanging those presently living in conditions of extreme deprivation? How might we conceptualize, let alone achieve, development that is both humane and sustainable? It takes no higher mathematics to realize that this would require a massive redistribution of the use of resources and production of pollution. But rich nations are not likely to relinquish their privileged positions voluntarily. Thus, this relatively straightforward course of reflection opens onto the prospect of intense and protracted global struggles.

From whichever angle one approaches the critical theory of development, it becomes clear that the central issue is the distribution of wealth and power. And looking back at the development of national economies in the modern period, that is what one would expect. It required long and bloody struggles to gain even the limited measure of redistribution finally achieved by state regulation of economies, mass-democratic politics, and social-welfare policies and programs. It seems that we are now at the start of another – this time global – struggle to reign in the systemic force of money and power, which may well require a global rule of law, democratic forms of global governance, and a global politics of distributive and reparative justice. Of course, the structures of the nation-state cannot simply be replicated at the global level. And so it will require institutional imagination, experimentation, and proliferation to discover which forms of law, democracy, and politics work best in a transnational context to domesticate capitalist modernization for a second time. If that should prove to be impracticable, then there seems to be no way of avoiding a continuation of the "state of nature" in international politics that Kant bemoaned in "Perpetual Peace" – though not necessarily in the form of a "war of all against all." For instance, one might imagine, as do many (Carl) Schmittians, that the rise of cultural-geographical constellations of wealth and power outside of Europe and America will, in the absence of transnational structures of peace and justice, lead to a continuation of international power politics in the altered forms dictated by a militarily, politically, and economically multipolar world. Macro-sociological theories of historical change are, as we have seen, notoriously weak in predicting the future. But one may at least hope that the neo-Kantian cosmopolitan scenario has as good a chance of being realized as the neo-Hobbesian one.[53]

[53] Jürgen Habermas, "Does the Constitutionalization of International Law Still Have a Chance?" in *The Divided West*, tr. C. Cronin (Cambridge: Polity Press, 2006), pp. 115–193.

Conclusion: the presence of the past

Men make their own history, but they do not make it as they please, they do not make it under circumstances chosen by themselves, but under circumstances directly found, given and transmitted from the past. The tradition of all the dead generations weighs like a nightmare upon the brain of the living.

Karl Marx[1]

The modernization of the West was tied to globalization from the start, and racial formations were integral to that process: racial classifications had constitutive significance for the slave trade, the dispossession and removal of indigenous populations, colonial labor regimes, institutionalized segregation and discrimination, ethnoracial forms of nationalism, restrictive immigration policies, and other central structures of the modern world order. Those structures were not merely – "superstructurally" – justified by racist ideologies, they embodied them: racist schemes of interpretation and evaluation were essential to the intelligibility and normativity of the organized practices that produced and reproduced the order. As the spread of racial domination accompanied the rise of liberalism – with its emphasis on freedom and equality – and the emergence of enlightenment humanism – with its emphasis on universal reason – there were issues of legitimacy at every step. I have defended the view that the infusion of liberal and enlightenment thought with developmental thinking proved to be the most effective means of addressing them. Other cultures, peoples, and societies became bypassed stages of Western development, and thus in need of tutelage – in the form of benevolent despotisms, civilizing missions, and the like – before they could catch up to the West. I have also contended that despite the successes of civil rights movements and decolonization struggles after World War II, new forms of racism and imperialism,

---

[1] "The Eighteenth Brumaire of Louis Bonaparte," in R. C. Tucker (ed.), *The Marx–Engels Reader* (New York: W. W. Norton, 1972), pp. 594–617, at 595.

which are superficially compatible with the formally recognized freedom and equality of individuals and societies, have become integral to the contemporary world order. Neoracist thinking continues to classify human beings into familiar ethnoracial groups and to characterize them in terms of familiar cultural and behavioral stereotypes, which are still used to explain inherited inequalities of life chances and to disguise the pursuit of self-interest. There are, of course, also significant alterations in these familiar patterns – for instance in regard to "rapidly developing" Asian societies – but the overall contours display remarkable continuity with those of classical racism and imperialism.

I have presented only fragments of a critical history of the present in these regards, and provided only scattered indications of a critical theory of development informed by a different practical interest. The focus on *ideologies* of race, empire, and development has unavoidably given a more idealist and voluntarist cast to my characterization of the relevant historical processes than my own view of the ineluctable intrication of agency and structure, lifeworld and system warrants. But I have repeatedly emphasized that racial and imperial ideologies entered into the very structures of national and international orders in the modern period, and that those structures have to be changed along with our thinking about them. The idea of global governance aimed at politically reflexive regulation and reform of global economic structures represents one possible form of the interplay between collective agency and social structure. It addresses the Darwinian character of the struggle for survival that has been endemic to the modern state system by proposing a "postnational constellation" in which sovereignty is multi-layered and widely diffused.

Moving in that direction will require radically altering the conception of human development that has been integral to European–American self-understanding and to our understanding of relations to darker "others" across the globe. And that in turn will require that we become more fully aware of the barbarism at the heart of our own civilizing process. In the wake of the horrors associated with World War II, Europeans seem to have learned some of these lessons, as their movement toward the postnational constellation of the European Union suggests. But the United States, spared the wartime devastation of its homeland and emerging as the only remaining great power, has, it seems, yet to learn most of them, as the Vietnam and Iraq invasions indicate. Together with our anomalous policies on trade, development, energy, environment, "preemption," unilateralism, and a host of other things, they suggest that national false consciousness and self-righteousness have scarcely abated. This is unlikely to change, I have argued, until the American public seriously comes to terms with its own illiberal and unenlightened past. Like Locke, America's founding fathers decried the enslavement of Englishmen while countenancing that of Africans. And while America's imperialism was largely continental rather than intercontinental before the closing decade of the nineteenth century, it became the dominant neoimperialist power of the post-World War II period and has continued the authoritarian streak of liberal internationalism into the present. The long postwar period now appears to be approaching its close, and if that is to be less cataclysmic than the ending of the prewar period, raising a more critical historical consciousness in America's political culture is of great importance, for the legacy of centuries of racism and imperialism is everywhere at work.

As the burgeoning discussion of "transitional justice" amply documents, when past injustice is persistently ignored or misrepresented, that is often experienced by its victims and their descendants as a form of public disrespect, to which they frequently react with widespread resentment.[2] If it is an injustice whose aftereffects still reverberate in present inequities, ignoring the historical roots of the latter, while blaming them on those who suffer under them, is usually experienced not only as a refusal to acknowledge past wrongs and redress continuing harms, but also as a form of public humiliation. The transitional justice discussion also makes clear that, in the face of such refusal, forging the democratic solidarity and collective agency needed to address such accumulated inequities is highly unlikely. In my view, this holds for global transitional justice as well; achieving the degree of global solidarity required to deal effectively with global problems depends on coming to terms with pasts that are still present.

Given that traditional theories of development regularly served as ideological rationalizations of the dispossession, enslavement, and colonization of ethnoracially identified "others," and that contemporary versions are often made to serve the purposes of neoimperialism, it is no wonder that talk of development and underdevelopment meets with

---

[2] See the literature cited in chapter 4, and David Bell (ed.), *Memory, Trauma, and World Politics* (Basingstoke: Palgrave, 2006).

such widespread skepticism today. Trumpeting the superiority of liberal democracy has come to sound like a warning signal for liberal interventions in pursuit of geopolitical interests – all the more so in the neoconservative version that singles out democratization, even when militarily imposed, as the "trigger" for all other modernization processes, and thus can no longer appeal to the structure of deferral built into mainstream modernization theories to excuse the installation and support of authoritarian client regimes.

A critical theory of development has to remain aware of the horrors historically perpetrated in the name of human development and to struggle consciously against the ambiguities and dangers inherent in developmental modes of thought. At the same time, it cannot deny the evident advance of human learning in numerous domains and the enhancement of our capacity to cope with a variety of problems. For both internal and external reasons, there can be no "going home again," no return to authentic pasts. The discussion in Part Two affirmed that we are now all moderns in an important sense, and that the globalization of commerce and communication has given rise to a global discourse of modernity which is increasingly polycentric and multivocal. The question now for societies all over the world is not whether or not to modernize, but which forms of modernity to develop, in light of structural constraints and pressures emanating from the global system. If we hope to mitigate the destructiveness of historical forms of capitalist development, the regulation and steering of the economy arduously achieved by the nation-state will have to be somehow reconstituted on a global scale. And this brings us back to questions of global governance.

If the latter is to be cooperative in any meaningful sense, coming to terms with humankind's racist and imperialist past is unavoidable, for that past "weighs like a nightmare on the brains of the living." We cannot have a future that is qualitatively different from it so long as we refuse to deal with it. Thus attention to the "politics of memory" also pertains to a critical theory of development.[3] As explained in chapter 4, this refers to a form of political-cultural activity that involves public debate about representations of the past. Given the great diversity of

---

[3] Max Pensky, "Critical Theory and the Politics of Memory," unpublished. I am grateful to Pensky for making this and other chapters of his work-in-progress on memory politics available to me.

historical, cultural, and political positions of global participants, this will evidently have the form of a conflict of interpretations, that is, of competing public representations, narratives, and images of the past. And as I argued there, recourse to the standards of historiographical objectivity is necessary, if we are after more than politically useful fictions: though this will not eliminate the conflict of interpretation, it can reduce it to the dimensions of "reasonable disagreement." We can hope that this transpires peacefully, within public spheres constituted by norms and principles on which we can achieve at least an "overlapping consensus" among diversely positioned societies, peoples, and cultures.

Beyond this, a critical theory of development has to take into account the costs as well as the benefits, the risks as well as the rewards of modernization processes, in which good and bad are inextricably entwined and the choice between goods that cannot be harmonized is unavoidable. Unlike classical development theory and practice, critical theory abjures force and violence as a means of imposing modernization on societies, for its normative framework – whether expressed in Kantian, Rawlsian, Habermasian, or other terms – rests on the equal respect for all persons, everywhere and at all times. Translated into legal-political concepts, this makes basic human rights and personal and political autonomy, or non-domination, standards by which to judge developmental programs and policies. And because the extent of equality of opportunity and political equality depends upon the degree of socioeconomic equality, democratic global governance will have to address distributive issues too, in order to sustain the conditions of its own possibility by supporting the development of capabilities required for civil and political participation.[4]

About the immensely complicated – theoretically as well as empirically – and ever-expanding discussion of global governance, I have had little to say here. I have several times noted the growing trend toward conceptions of global governance without a global government or world state. This reflects empirical tendencies toward a decentralization of decision-making authority and other governmental powers, and a disaggregation of the functions of sovereignty. The formation of transnational regimes and negotiating systems that regulate domains historically

---

[4] See Kevin Olson, *Reflexive Democracy: Political Equality and the Welfare State* (Cambridge, MA: MIT Press, 2006) for a good account, in a Habermasian framework, of this reflexive relation.

under the authority of the nation-state, the proliferation of non-state global actors – agencies, organizations, networks, multinational corporations, INGOs, and the like – who participate in decision-making and policy-setting processes, and the "nesting" of political communities from the local to the global level have led many political theorists to conceive of global governance as "dispersed" and "multileveled." I am generally sympathetic to these more decentered approaches, but I want here to emphasize two respects in which the *global* character of global governance is crucial: human rights and global justice.

Since the adoption of the Universal Declaration on Human Rights in 1948, there has been a continuous broadening and deepening of "human rights culture" across the globe and a proliferation of human rights institutions – such as international courts – and organizations – such as Amnesty International and Human Rights Watch – dedicated to monitoring and protesting egregious human rights violations everywhere. Beyond eliciting spontaneous reactions of horror and indignation at such violations, this culture and these institutions and organizations have shaped an expanding, mass-mediated, and digitally connected global public sphere concerned with the extension and protection of basic human rights. Transnational advocacy networks are thus able to pursue a "politics of human rights" that frames and publicizes rights issues, mobilizes public opinion around them, forces them onto national and international agendas, and brings public pressure to bear on states and transnational organizations. That has proved to be an important source of transnational solidarity across sociocultural boundaries.[5] At the same time, the growth of global solidarity has been inhibited by the tendency of many developed societies to emphasize civil and political rights over the economic and social rights stressed by many developing societies. As the rights discussion has expanded from a Western to a global discourse and become increasingly decentered in the process, the conflict of interpretation arising from this disagreement regularly blocks overlapping consensus and reasonable agreement. Some major human rights agencies, such as Amnesty

---

[5] Jeffrey Flynn, "Human Rights, Transnational Solidarity, and Duties to the Global Poor," forthcoming in *Constellations*, is an interesting analysis of some of the issues involved. For a good overview of the historical and theoretical background to this discussion, see Hauke Brunkhorst, *Solidarity: From Civic Friendship to a Global Legal Community*, tr. J. Flynn (Cambridge, MA: MIT Press, 2005).

International and Human Rights Watch, have recognized this and now include subsistence rights on their agendas.

In the view adopted here, this is not only a practical-political exigency; it is a moral-political obligation. The demands of global justice cover not only the actions of individual and collective actors but also the basic structures responsible for the distribution of rights, opportunities, and goods (including membership, as in matters of citizenship and immigration).[6] By this measure, existing transnational institutions and arrangements are fundamentally unjust and immoral. As in the case of racial injustice examined in Part One, we are dealing here with historically accumulated and systemically reproduced inequalities of wealth and power, and thus with issues of reparative as well as distributive justice. Centuries of expropriation, extermination, enslavement, and empire, which were part and parcel of the rise of capitalism in the West, left its beneficiaries with vastly more power than its victims to set the ground rules of the postcolonial global order. The laws and conventions, treaties and organizations, procedures and institutions that constitute this order tend to systematically advantage the already advantaged and disadvantage the already disadvantaged. Among the global multitudes who live and die in abject poverty are the tens of thousands who die each day from easily preventable causes – so that anyone who lives to an advanced age in one of the wealthier societies will have coexisted with hundreds of millions of preventable deaths from the consequences of poverty during his or her lifetime, significantly more than the number of deaths by violence in the "bloody twentieth century."[7] If the latter was a good reason to outlaw wars of aggression and write human rights into international law, then mass death by extreme poverty is an equally good reason to redesign international institutions to ensure a fairer distribution of resources, opportunities, and goods. It is also an argument for placing rights to subsistence – to meeting such basic needs as those for adequate nourishment, clothing,

---

[6] Thomas Pogge and Darrel Moellendorf (eds.), *Global Justice* (St. Paul, MN: Paragon, 2008). Pogge draws on Rawls's theory of justice but, unlike Rawls, applies its distributive principles to the global level. See his "An Egalitarian Law of Peoples," reprinted in *Global Justice*, pp. 461–493. Cristina Lafont does something similar with Habermas's theory of justice in "Alternative Visions of a New Global Order: What Should Cosmopolitans Hope For?" *Ethics and Global Politics* 1 (2008): 1–20.

[7] See Pogge's "Preface" to *Global Justice* for some relevant statistics and sources.

and shelter, for safe drinking water, basic sanitation, and preventative health care – on the human rights agenda; for unless such needs are met, civil and political liberties cannot be effectively exercised. And like other rights, subsistence rights entail correlative duties, including the duty of individual and collective agents to restructure the global system in such a way as to end their gross violation.[8]

Global poverty is not the only problem beyond the capacity of any single nation to resolve and thus requiring some form of global governance. Some of the many others are preventing war and other forms of international violence; halting the proliferation of weapons of mass destruction; combating global terrorism; dealing with the pollution of the environment, the exhaustion of non-renewable resources, and global warming; controlling the spread of infectious diseases; responding to ethnic cleansing and failed states; and regulating the mass migrations caused by famine, drought, civil violence, political oppression, persistent unemployment, and extreme poverty. Many theorists argue that for global governance to deal with such problems in ways that have global legitimacy, it will have to incorporate forms of democratic transparency, accountability, representation, and participation.[9] And these forms will have to accommodate deep cultural differences and allow for a conflict of interpretations of basic norms and principles whose validity is generally accepted. I shall conclude with the Kantian question, whether we may reasonably hope to achieve such a just, democratic, pluralistic world society.[10]

Some progressive theorists have argued that this is too little to hope for, that it amounts to de-fusing the fusion of utopian hopes and historical consciousness that emerged in the eighteenth century. Seeking to retain at the global level the gains achieved by nation-states in respect to individual rights, democratic participation, and social welfare is a fundamentally defensive reaction to the ravages of globalization.[11] The utopian element

---

[8] Henry Shue, *Basic Rights: Subsistence, Affluence, and U.S. Foreign Policy* (Princeton University Press, 1980).

[9] For instance, David Held, *Global Covenant* (Cambridge: Polity Press, 2004); and Jürgen Habermas, *The Divided West*, tr. C. Cronin (Cambridge: Polity Press, 2006).

[10] See chapter 5, section III.

[11] See, for instance, W. E. Scheuerman, "Global Governance without Global Government? Habermas on Postnational Democracy," *Political Theory* 36 (2008): 133–151.

in progressive politics is thereby severely contracted, even if, like Habermas, one envisions restructuring political institutions to ensure more democratic control not only of the economy but also of the state, thus reigning in the systemic force of power, as well as that of money, with the communicative force of autonomous public spheres.[12] Privileging historical continuity in this way, the argument goes, amounts to giving up hope for a radically different future (Bloch), something wholly other (Horkheimer), or the irruption of the new into history (Benjamin). But while the contingency of history makes utopian hopes – and, of course, dystopian fears – *possible* in principle, we are concerned here with what it is *reasonable* to hope for and work towards, in light of what we know about past history and present circumstances – for though "men make their own history, they do not make it as they please ... but under circumstances directly found, given and transmitted from the past."

On the other, "realist," side, a variety of critics have argued that cosmopolitan hopes of the sort sketched above are a species of wishful thinking that ignores the realities of conflict built into the nation-state system, the clash of civilizations at the global level, and the ongoing reconfiguration of the world into continental power blocks. Cosmopolitan theorists usually respond by elaborating upon the acceleration of global interdependency discussed in Part Two. But the issue should not be framed in terms of the empirical evidence for competing *predictions*. Development theory is a theory of practice.[13] Like other theories of practices – for instance, of education, child rearing, business, city planning, health and well-being – it is constructed, as Kant said of universal history, *in praktischer Absicht*, from a practical point of view, with a practical intention. Such theories marshal empirical and theoretical knowledge in the interest of realizing valued outcomes, the feasibility of which is judged in light not only of empirical and theoretical

---

[12] J. Habermas, "The New Obscurity: The Crisis of the Welfare State and the Exhaustion of Utopian Energies," in Habermas, *The New Conservatism*, tr. S. Weber Nicholsen (Cambridge, MA: MIT Press, 1989), pp. 48–70.

[13] See Hans-Georg Gadamer, *Reason in the Age of Science*, tr. F. Lawrence (Cambridge, MA: MIT Press, 1981), for some interesting reflections on theories of this type. Stephen Toulmin has also had interesting things to say about the distinct logic of such theories in a number of his works. I am grateful to Simone Chambers for her comment on an earlier presentation of my argument, which made me aware of the need to clarify this logic.

considerations, but also of the ability and willingness of relevant agents to bring them about.[14]

Ultimately, the practical point of view informing the developmental approach I have adopted here is, like Kant's, a moral point of view; and the valued outcome, global justice, is, like his "perpetual peace," a moral-political end. Though they belong to the same cosmopolitan family, the "global justice" conception underscores the democratic, egalitarian, and multicultural aspects of the global rule of law in ways that Kant's did not. It retains the purpose he ascribed to it of containing and diminishing the violence and oppression that has been so prevalent in human affairs; and it adds those of ameliorating unnecessary suffering and expanding people's capabilities to lead the kinds of lives they value. Given such twentieth-century horrors as total war, the first use of atomic weapons, the threat of mutually assured destruction, bureaucratically administered genocide, and totalitarian oppression, and given such twenty-first-century challenges as environmental collapse, resource exhaustion, the spread of weapons of mass destruction, global terrorism, and extreme global poverty, the particular conception of global justice projected here is obviously a response to perceived exigencies: it is a historically situated projection of historical hopes. I have claimed for it neither predictive certainty nor high probability from the vantage point of a disinterested observer. I have proposed, rather, that it is an attainable goal – a future condition that is consistent with our knowledge of historical patterns and present tendencies, and that it is reasonable to set as a goal of progressive politics. More particularly, it is a future that continues lines of historical developmental sketched here – the directional accumulation of learning processes in many cognitive domains, from pure and applied science to historical, social, and cultural studies; the directional expansion of our problem-solving capabilities in a multiplicity of dimensions, from technique, architecture, and engineering to organization, administration, and planning; the directional development of practical reasoning correlative with this massive shift in our stock of "good reasons" for doing one thing rather than another, and in this way rather than that; the expansion of individual freedom in connection with the growth of reflexivity and critique, which

[14] And such engagement is subject to the old adage: "if at first you don't succeed, try, try again." Who could have predicted, or would have bet, a few years ago that an African American would be elected President of the United States in 2008?

Kant and Hegel took to be the hallmark of modern culture; and the development of social, economic, and political institutions that embody that freedom, which the liberal tradition saw as the great accomplishment of modern society. Adapting the egalitarian thrust of social democratic thought and the pluralist thrust of multicultural thought, I have added that development theory and practice must also incorporate the *substantive* freedoms – in Sen's terms, the capabilities – that will make the personal and political freedoms formally achieved by liberalism concrete realities. And this means opening diverse paths to multiple modernities rather than following the same path to a single modernity. Again, the question is whether this is too much to hope for, whether it is in the end a "realistic," "feasible," or "practicable" hope.

There is no doubt that the historical record warrants the melancholy that Walter Benjamin experienced in contemplating it; nor is there any denying the disappointment of hopes for progress by the events of the twentieth century. But though these must remain integral to our "postmodern" sensibility, a politics premised solely on melancholy or disappointment – or on some other form of historical pessimism, that is, on the abandonment of hope for a significantly better future – would not be a progressive politics. This is not to deny that these are *possible* responses to universal history, in conjunction perhaps with one or another of the alternative readings that Kant considered possible: history as a story of decline, as a farce composed around the endless cycle of human folly, or as a random play of chance events, signifying nothing.[15] Kant rejected these other possible readings on moral grounds. Accepting any of them, he argued, makes non-sense of striving for the improvement of the human condition, which is our moral duty. In particular, moral-political engagement for the global rule of law sketched in "Perpetual Peace" requires a reading of history that makes attaining it possible. In the view presented here, this means a reading that is not merely compatible with the facts of history, as we know them, but is a plausible interpretation of those facts, and one that makes the hope for improvement a "reasonable" hope for an achievable end.[16]

---

[15] "The Contest of Faculties," in H. Reiss (ed.), *Kant: Political Writings*, 2nd edn (Cambridge University Press, 1991), pp. 176–190, at 178–180; and "Idea for a Universal History with a Cosmopolitan Purpose," in *ibid.*, pp. 41–53, at 48.

[16] Though Kant himself sometimes refers to "reasonable" hope for a "practicable" future, he more often requires only that the goal be a "possible" one. This follows

Kant was not entirely consistent as to whether this could be had without religious faith, that is, on purely natural-historical grounds. He sometimes took the tack that the plausibility of the progressive reading and the reasonability of progressive hopes depended in the end on viewing nature – in the broad sense including human history – as having a providential design, such that what morality commands is in fact attainable.[17] The approach I have presented here does not appeal to religious faith, and so the case for the plausibility of a developmental reading had to be made on broadly naturalistic grounds, that is, in light of the comparative plausibility of competing interpretations of historical change and contemporary globalization. And the interpretation I have sketched – and which I am supposing could be further elaborated so as to enhance its plausibility – was intended to provide reasons to believe that the gradual realization of greater global justice is an attainable goal, one that it makes practical-political, as well as moral-political, sense to pursue. This form of reasoning is not peculiar to the matter at hand but belongs to the practical logic of any political undertaking: the goal pursued must be judged politically achievable for the undertaking to make sense. How strong or weak our confidence in the chances of success must be before our engagement is reasonable obviously admits of no precise answer.

A question we raised at the start of this study may well be posed anew at its conclusion: given the widespread depredation in which developmental thinking has historically been implicated, why continue with it at all? I have tried to show that the idea of human development is not exhausted by the misuse to which it has been put; that there is much more than a kernel of truth in the view that human history evinces considerable advances in learning, problem solving, practical reasoning, functional differentiation, economic production, the rule of law,

from his conception of moral commands as unconditional – or, rather, as subject only to the condition that what be commanded be possible, that "ought" implies "can." As I am working with a detranscendentalized conception of morality derived from discourse ethics, which entails that conditions and consequences be taken into account, I adopt the stronger requirements that an interpretation be plausible, a hope reasonable, and a goal achievable.

17 See, for instance, "On the Common Saying: 'This may be True in Theory, but It Does Not Apply in Practice,'" in *Kant: Political Writings*, pp. 61–92, at 90. In the twentieth century, a number of religious thinkers argued that belief in historical redemption without faith in God was thoroughly discredited by events. For an influential statement of this view, see Reinhold Niebuhr, *Faith and History* (New York: Charles Scribner's Sons, 1951).

political organization, and other respects; that as a result developmental thinking is irrepressible, and it has proven dangerous to leave this field to those who misuse it; and that practically oriented reflection on historical change is a fruitful way to think about contemporary challenges and possible responses to them. I have also tried to show that we can and should construct a critical theory of development, at a higher level of reflexivity, which takes into account and tries to avoid historical distortions and misuses of developmental thinking. In particular, critical development theory has to remain cognizant of the ambiguities built into rationalization processes, to which critics of enlightenment views of progress from Hegel through Weber to Horkheimer and Adorno alerted us, especially the ascendancy of subject-centered, instrumental-strategic conceptions of reason – or rational choice – that has led to the objectification and instrumentalization not only of nature but of other subjects, and even of ourselves. As Habermas and others have argued, this has to be superseded by an intersubjective notion of communicative reason, which is always embodied and embedded in society, culture, and history. In this view, Western rationalization has been truncated and distorted by its subjectivist and instrumentalist fixation, and thus we still have much to learn about human development. The idea of sustainable development raises this issue in regard to our relation to nature; and the idea of global dialogue with non-Western cultures raises it in regard to our relation to others.

The critical conception of development I have sketched here points away from dichotomy and domination and toward diversity and dialogue. Disaggregating the various domains, processes, strands, and logics of development, makes different adaptations and combinations not merely possible but probable, and thus replaces the idea of a single path to a single modernity with that of a multiplicity of hybrid forms of modernization.[18] Each society will have to work out its own form, with its own accounting of costs and benefits, but under the not inconsiderable constraints of the global system – which, of course, it can try with others to alter – and the growing normative constraints of the emerging world order – which it can try with others to shape. One thing is clear: we are all in this together. Constructing a just and sustainable world order will require further development of *every* society, including

---

[18] Charles Taylor has stressed this line of thought in his writings and in conversation.

already "developed" societies. The question of whether, or the extent to which, such an order can be achieved is obviously an open one. The uncertainty is exacerbated not only by realist skepticism concerning the possibility of ever getting beyond conflicts of interest and balances of power, but also by postcolonial objections against the imposition of normative conceptions developed in the West upon other societies. This is a notoriously fraught issue; but given that all nations have recognized the UN Charter and that most have ratified at least part of the International Bill of Rights (comprising the Universal Declaration of 1948 and the two International Covenants of 1966), as well as a number of other conventions, we have what may be regarded as the beginnings of a global "constitutional project."[19] That is, disagreements concerning, say, the relative weight of civil and political rights to social, economic, and cultural rights, or concerning whether certain rights conceptions are overly individualistic, may be understood as debates within an emerging global constitutional tradition concerning the proper interpretation and implementation of norms that all parties take to be valid in one sense or another. From this perspective, interpretations can be legitimately *imposed* only by internationally recognized bodies and agencies (e.g. international courts) in the areas of their jurisdiction. Various forms of "soft power" compatible with international norms belong to the bag of political tools that may be used to advance the cause of global justice in other areas. But the kind of forced modernization that culminated in imperialism in (what was to become) the "Third World," totalitarian communism in the "Second World," and fascism in parts of the "First World," is incompatible with the critical conception of development defended here. This leaves the problem, among many others, that some societies will continue to reject some preconditions and elements of that very conception. In this connection, we will have to learn to accept smaller steps that open the way to further steps, and hope that the push and pull of economic, social, and political globalization, as well as of the globalization of information, communication, and culture, together with the rapid expansion of global civil society and the proliferation of global public spheres, will eventually lead to those further steps.

---

[19] J. Habermas, "A Political Constitution for the Pluralist World Society?" in Habermas, *Between Naturalism and Religion*, tr. C. Cronin (Cambridge: Polity Press, 2008), pp. 312–352.

Index

Abrams, Elliott 213, 215
Adenauer, Konrad 99
Adorno, Theodor 14, 106, 152
affirmative action 30, 98–107, 213
Agassiz, Louis 73
Alliance for Progress 194
Almond, Gabriel 201, 203, 205, 206
American Historical Association 108
Amin, Samir 198
Amnesty International 235
ancient Greece 134, 138
Anglo-Saxonism 71, 72, 73, 80,
    81, 109
anthropology
    cultural anthropology 82, 83
    emergence in Germany 48
    Kant 44, 45–47, 68
    Kantian sources 47, 49
    physical anthropology 70, 82
anti-Islamism 9, 216, 217, 220
anti-Semitism 8, 96, 102
Arendt, Hannah 3, 7, 8, 96
Aristotle 5, 42
Armenian genocide 100
Augustine, Saint 134, 136, 150
"Auschwitz lie" 104–105
Austria, memory of Nazi period 106

Balibar, Etienne 4, 5
Baran, Paul 197
Barkan, Elazar 83
Benedict, Ruth 83
Benhabib, Seyla 186, 225
Benjamin, Walter 61, 102, 131, 153,
    238, 240
Bentham, Jeremy 168
Berger, Peter 212
Bernstein, Richard 27
Beveridge, Albert 79–80
Bhabha, Homi 16

Bitburg incident (1985) 101
blaming the victim 87–88, 203
Bloch, Marc 238
Blumenbach, Johann Friedrich 48,
    70, 82
Boas, Franz 82–84
Bohman, James 117, 163
Bolton, John 213, 215
Bourne, Randolph 82
Bowers, Claude 108
Boxill, Bernard 39
Bretton Woods system 196, 208
bureaucratization 148, 159
Bush, George H. 215
Bush, George W. 80, 212, 214, 216,
    217–219
Butler, Judith 38, 116

capitalism
    democratic control 163, 212, 227,
        234–235, 237
    global development and 17, 23,
        148–149, 195–200, 207–212
Chakrabarty, Dipesh 183, 188
Cheney, Dick 215, 220
Chicago School 83
China 79, 81
Christianity
    imperialism 24
    Kant 56–57, 67
    philosophy of history 134–135,
        153–154
    slavery and 42
civil rights movements 2, 13, 24, 29–30,
    90, 108, 110
civilizing discourse 24, 26–27, 81,
    109, 178, 187, 192–194,
    216, 231–232
clash of civilizations 217, 238
climate 50

Clinton, Bill 215
Cold War 110, 195–196
Colombia 79
colonialism. *See* imperialism
Commager, Henry Steel 110
Condorcet, Marquis de 77, 153
contextualism 37–41
cosmopolitanism
  hope for 165, 238–245
  Kant 53–55, 56, 66, 68, 154, 165,
    224–225
  modernity and 154, 238
  neo-Kantianism 229
craniology 73
critical theory
  cultural racism and 12
  elements 14
  Frankfurt School 14
  global development 16, 220–229,
    231–243
  Habermas 13, 133
  methodology 38
Crummell, Alexander 114
Cuba 79, 81
culture
  cultural anthropology 82, 83
  cultural modernity 155–158
  cultural racism 10–13, 86–93, 118
    blaming the victim 87–88, 203
    Mill's ethnoculture 82, 175–176
  Hegel on cultural development 138
  human rights culture 235–236
  Kant 54, 68, 239
    convergence 186
  learning 142
  legal cultures 159
  multiculturalism 158, 159–160,
    213, 240
  politics 126–127
  reflexivity of modern culture
    222–223, 239

Darby, Derrick 118
Darwin, Charles
  See also social Darwinism
  evolution 141
  gender 75
  genetics 75–76
  learning process 157
  natural selection 5

race theory 75
  survival of the fittest 76
  teleology and 53
De Greiff, Pablo 105, 126
decolonization 2, 30, 182
Decter, Midge 212
democracy
  control of capital 163, 212, 227,
    234–235, 237
  and development 202–203
  Habermas 14, 185, 238
  modernist assumptions of 190
  rule of law 163
Denton, Nancy 124
dependency
  development and 195–200
  neo-Marxism 194
Derrida, Jacques 47, 182
destinarianism 72–73, 79–80
development
  See also history; Third World
  concept 18–19
  critical theory 16, 220–229,
    231–243
  dependency and 195–200
  end of history 132, 165, 210
  ideology 3, 178, 180, 183, 198, 217,
    219, 224, 232
  liberalism and empire 64, 166
    Kant 169–171, 179
    Locke 166–167
    Marxist critique 177–178
    Mill 168, 171–177, 178,
      179, 186
    postcolonialism 180–185
  limits to growth 227–228
  metanarratives 131–133, 137–142,
    187, 224–225
  modern discourse
    cultural modernity 155–158
    global capitalism 17
    reasonable disagreement 160–165,
      187, 234
    reflexivity 155–158, 222–223,
      239, 242
    societal modernity 158–160
  modernization. *See* modernization
  neoconservatives 212–220
  neoimperialism 2–4, 180–185,
    212–220

development (cont.)
  neoliberalism and globalization 16,
      17, 149, 153, 185, 194,
      199–200, 207–212
  philosophies 134–142
    dialectics of progress 59, 62,
        142–149
    Hegel. *See* Hegel, G. W. F
    hope 153
    Kant. *See* Kant, Immanuel
    lessons 155–165
    Marx. *See* Marx, Karl
    morality and modernity 150–154
    post-Kant 137–142
    pre-Kant 134–136
    progressive 131
    universal history 43, 44, 55,
        136–137, 224–225, 238
  political displacement 186–191
  postcolonial concept 180–185
  previous discourse 26–27
  race and colonialism 1–2
  sustainable development 242
Dewey, John 82
distributive justice 226
Dixon, Thomas 108
Douglass, Frederick 114
Du Bois, W. E. B. 24, 25, 41, 83, 109,
    110, 114
Dunning, William 109, 110
Durkheim, Émile 131, 145, 146,
    151, 201
Dworkin, Ronald 39

East India Company 167, 168, 177
empire. *See* imperialism
end of history 132, 165, 210
Enlightenment
  ambivalence of ideas 18
  continuing effects 222
  growth of knowledge 143–144
  Kant as representative 43, 54
  progress 242
  Scotland 139, 168
  universalist metanarrative 38, 158
environment
  limits to growth 227–228
  sustainable development 242
Erhard, Ludwig 99
ethnology 73

eugenics 24, 74, 84
Eurocentrism 14–15, 50–51, 56,
    182–185, 187
evolution
  Darwin 75–76, 141
  modern synthesis 84
  social Darwinism and race 76, 84
  teleology and 53

Fair Deal 123
Fanon, Frantz 222
Federal Housing Administration 123
Feith, Douglas 213
Ferguson, Adam 77
Flynn, Jeffrey 235
Foucault, Michel 13, 38, 181
Frank, Andre Gunder 198
Franklin, John Hope 109
Frazier, E. Franklin 86
Frederickson, George 119
French empire 3
French Revolution 62, 143, 146
Friedlander, Saul 105
Friedman, Milton 207
Fukuyama, Francis 132, 210
functionalism 141–142, 201

G-7 4, 211
Gadamer, Hans-Georg 186
Galileo Galilei 157
Gandhi, Mahatma 222
Gaonkar, Dilip 116
gender
  Darwin 75
  Kant 52
  marginalization 23
  Rawls 28–29, 32
  social Darwinism 74, 76
genealogies 13, 38, 181
genetics 5, 75–76, 82, 84, 93–95, 109
Germany
  Bitburg incident (1985) 101
  dealing with Nazi past 96–97,
      98–107
  East German past 106–107
  emergence of anthropology 48
  historians' debate 99–105
  immigration violence 107
  Jewish reparations 97
  partition of Samoa 79

ghettos 120–126
Gilman, Nils 201
Ginzburg, Carlo 105
Glazer, Nathan 212
global justice 186, 189, 191,
    236–241
globalization
    capitalism and 17, 23, 148–149,
        195–200, 207–212
    critical theory 16, 220–229,
        231–243
    democracy and 163, 212,
        227, 234–235, 237
    global governance 163, 234,
        236, 243
    market economies 158
    Marx on 17, 139–140
    modernization and 230–231
    multiculturalism 158, 159–160
    neoliberalism 16, 17, 149, 153, 185,
        194, 199–200, 207–212
Gobineau, Arthur de 73
Goldhagen, Daniel 102
Gooding-Williams, Robert 12, 25,
    117, 126
Gossett, Thomas 80
Grant, Ulysses 80
Griffith, D. W. 108
Guam 79
Gulf War (1990) 215

Habermas, Jürgen
    on background assumptions 40
    communicative action 151–153, 242
    on critical theory 133
    cultural learning 142
    democracy 185, 238
    ethics 14, 151–153
    German historians' debate 100,
        101–103, 105
    global constitutional project 243
    modernization 147–149
    Rawls and 35
    social change theory 131, 137
Haider, Jörg 106
Hartz, Louis 193–194, 220
Hawaii 79
Hayek, Friedrich von 207
Hegel, G. W. F
    critique of enlightenment 242

cultural modernity 222, 239
    Marx and 131
    morality 150–151
    philosophy of history 137–138, 145
    reason in history 53, 186
    reflexivity 155, 239
    "slaughter bench of history" 65
Heidegger, Martin 131 **180**
Herder, Johann Gottfried von 61
Herskovits, Melville 83
Hilferding, Rudolf 197
Hillgruber, Andreas 99
Himmelfarb, Gertrude 212
History
    See also development
    and Austrian Nazism 106
    and East German Nazism 106–107
    end of history 132, 165, 210
    German historians' debate
        99–105
    German memory of Nazism 96–97,
        98–107
    Marx on history making 90, 230
    objectivity 104–105
    pessimism from 240
    selectivity 96, 102
    unfairness to victims of history 105
    United States
        memory of racial injustice 96–98,
            107–117
        politics of public memory 111–117
        racist historiography 108–111
Hitler, Adolf 99, 100
Hobbes, Thomas 135, 229
Hobson, John Atkinson 197
Holocaust 2, 24, 96, 99–100, 102,
    104–105
Home Owners Loan Corporation
    123–124
Hong Kong 199
Honneth, Axel 14, 37
Horkheimer, Max 14, 152, 238
Horton, James Oliver 112, 114
human development. *See* development
Human Development Index 197
Human Freedom Index 197
human rights
    conventions 243
    culture 235–236
    debate 187

human rights (cont.)
Kant 188
modernist assumption 190
social v individual 243
Human Rights Watch 235

immigration
East and West Germany 107
European discourse 11
racism and 9–10
social Darwinism and 74
imperialism
development and 1, 177–180,
186–191, 214–220
liberalism and 166–177
Kant 169–171, 179
Locke 166–167
Marxist critique 177–178, 180, 188
Mill 168, 171–177, 178, 179, 186
meaning 2–3
modernization and 23–24,
200–207
neoimperialism 2–4, 180–185,
212–220
postcolonialism 180–185
race and 1, 78–81, 230
United States. *See* United States
India 168, 173, 175, 177–178
institutionalized racism 88–92
International Monetary Fund (IMF) 4,
194, 196, 209, 211
IQ testing 74, 84, 94
Iraq 4, 214, 215, 216, 220, 231
Islamism 9, 216, 217, 220
Israel 99, 219

Jackson, Henry "Scoop" 213
Jefferson, Thomas 71
Johnson, Lyndon 86, 204

Kagan, Robert 213
Kallen, Horace 82
Kames, Lord 48
Kant, Immanuel
anthropological sources 47, 49
cosmopolitanism 53–55, 56, 66, 68,
153, 154, 165, 224–225
culture 54, 68
convergence 186
modernity 239

Enlightenment representative 43
Eurocentrism 50–51, 56
frame of reference 15
gender 52
Habermasian recasting 14
impure ethics 44–47, 68
nature 229
inequalities 67
radical evil 58
teleology 53–54, 57–58, 61, 65–68,
178, 188
theodicy naturalized 58–64
perpetual peace 19
philosophy of history 51, 53–58
critique 64–68
French Revolution 62
hope 55, 136–137, 153, 190,
240–241
imperialism 169–171, 179
influence 77
metanarrative 187, 224–225
morality 150, 153, 189
nature's purpose 61
point of reference 134, 135–137
practical reason 140
progress 61, 62, 64–68
Tahitians 61
tensions 26, 70, 188
theodicy naturalized 58–64
universalism 43, 44, 55, 136–137,
224–225, 238
practical anthropology 44, 45–47, 68
practical orientation 133
race theory 14–15, 48–53, 70, 81
English-speaking scholarship 43–44
geographical differences 50–51
monogenesis 48
original race germs (*Keime*) 5, 48
teleology 51–53
Rawls and 30, 31
reflective judgments 187
religions 56–57, 150
Christianity 56–57, 67
theodicy naturalized 58–64
republicanism 67, 150
slavery and 43, 62–64, 70
unsocial sociability 144–145
Keime 5, 48
Kennedy, John F. 206
Keynesianism 197, 207, 211

Kinder, Donald 117, 118
King, Desmond 122–123
King, Martin Luther 29, 206
Kipling, Rudyard 81
Kirkpatrick, Jeanne 213
knowledge, growth of 143–144
Kohl, Helmut 99, 101
Krauthammer, Charles 213, 218
Kristol, Irving 212
Kristol, William 213
Kroeber, Alfred 83
Ku Klux Klan 110

Lafont, Cristina 236
Lamarck, Jean-Baptiste 75, 76, 84
Lasswell, Harold 206
Latschar, John 113
law
   legal cultures 159
   legitimation 158–159
   modernization of 158–159
   natural law 135
   rule of law 163, 190, 202
Le Conte, Joseph 77–78
learning, cultural 142
Lenin, Vladimir 197
Libby, Lewis 213, 215
liberalism
   autonomy 176
   complicity with slavery 37
   critical theory and 38
   imperialism and development 64, 166
      dependency 195–200
      Kant 169–171, 179
      Locke 166–167
      Marxist critique 177–178
      Mill 168, 171–177, 178, 179, 186
      postcolonial critique 180–185
   Marx on 198
   nonideal theory 27, 28–36
Lipset, Seymour Martin 205
Locke, John 25–26, 135, 166–167, 232
Louden, Robert 50
Lowie, Robert 83
Luhmann, Niklas 141
Luxembourg, Rosa 197

McGovern, George 213
McKinley, William 79
Mandeville, Bernard 59

Marshall Plan 196
Marx, Karl
   capitalist globalization 17, 139
   commodification of life relations 148
   conquest 23
   historical materialism 131
   history making 90, 230
   on imperialism 177–178, 180
   on liberalism 198
   modernization 146, 147
   morality 150
   philosophy of history 139–140, 145
   political economy 139–140
   race relations 23
   utopia 153
Marxism 11, 222
Massey, Douglas 124
Mead, George Herbert 151
Mead, Margaret 83
memory, public
   Austrian Nazism 106
   East Germany 106–107
   German historians' debate 99–105
   German Nazi past 96–97, 98–107
   politics of memory 111–117,
      233–234
   selectivity 102
   unfairness to victims of history 105
   US racial injustice 96–98, 107–117
      politics of public memory 111–117
      racist historiography 108–111
Mendel, Gregor 75, 82
metanarratives 131–133, 137–142,
   187, 224–225
methodology 28–41
Mexico/US war (1848) 72, 80
Mill, James 167–168, 175
Mill, John Stuart
   custom 172
   development and empire 168,
      171–177, 178, 179, 186
   ethnoculture 82, 175–176
   good despotism 180, 221
   liberty 172–173
   race 82, 175–176
   utilitarianism 172, 176
Mills, Charles 29, 31
Mises, Ludwig von 207
MIT Center for International Studies
   201, 204–205

modernity
  conquest and 23–24
  global modernity 15
  multiple modernities 222, 223–224, 240
  reflexivity of modern culture
    222–223, 239
  universal discourse 222
modernization
  concept 197
  domination and 200–207
  globalization and 230–231
  hybrid forms 242
  Third World 195
Mommson, Hans 100
monogenesis 48
Monroe Doctrine (1823) 3
Monthly Review 197
Morison, Samuel Eliot 110
Mormons 176
Morton, Samuel George 73
Moynihan, Daniel Patrick 86, 212
multiculturalism 158, 159–160,
    213, 240
Muravchik, Joshua 213
Myrdal, Gunnar 85–86

Nagel, Thomas 39
Nandy, Ashis 182
National Association of Real Estate
    Brokers 122
National Endowment for
    Democracy 217
nationalism, racism and 7–10, 79
natural history 134, 135
natural law 135
Nazism 74, 84, 96–97, 98–107, 110
neoconservatives 195, 212–220
neoimperialism 2–4, 180–185,
    212–220
neo-Kantianism 229
neoliberalism
  anti-welfarism 194
  development and 145
  globalization 16, 17, 149, 153, 185,
    194, 199–200, 207–212
neo-Marxism 197–200
neoracism 4–13, 93–95
Netherlands, empire 3
New Deal 122, 123, 196, 207, 208
newly industrializing countries 199, 209

Nietzsche, Friedrich 13, 131, 143,
    147, 222
Nolte, Ernst 99
Nott, Josiah 73
Novak, Michael 212
Novick, Peter 109, 110

Obama, Barack 11, 117
objectivity 163, 224
Ogletree, Charles 97
oil 220
Okin, Susan Moller 28
O'Sullivan, John 72

Panama 79
Park, Robert 83, 86
Parsons, Talcott 131, 141, 151, 197,
    200, 201–202, 205
Patterson, Orlando 87
Pensky, Max 233
Perle, Richard 213, 214, 215
Philippines 79, 81
Philipps, Ulrich 109
Podhoretz, Norman 212
political economy, Marx
    139–140
political modernity 183
political philosophy
  marginalization of gender 23
  marginalization of racism 23–28
  methodology 28–41
  neglect of slavery 42
polygenesis 48, 73
Portugal, empire 3
positivism 27–28
postcolonialism
  critique of development 180–185,
    221
  modernization and 195–197,
    202, 210
post-Fordism 98
postmodernism 183–185, 240
power
  postcolonialism 180–185
  race and 7, 13
  soft power 243
Prebisch, Paul 197
progress
  dialectics of progress 59, 62,
    142–149

Enlightenment discourse 242
growth of knowledge 143–144
Kant 61, 62, 64–68
Puerto Rico 79, 81
Pye, Lucian 201, 203, 205, 206

race theory
    See also racism
    18th-century 6, 48–53
    19th-century 1, 5, 8, 70–82
    20th-century 82–85
    culture theory of race 86–93, 118
        blaming the victim 87–88, 203
        Mill 82, 175–176
    Darwin 75
    genetics and 5, 84, 93–95
    historiography 5, 71–73, 108–113
    Kant. *See* Kant, Immanuel
    Nazis 74, 84
    non-biological elements 6, 11–12,
        83–87
    post-Kantian development 70–74
    power and 7, 17, 72–82, 92–93
    science and 5–6, 7, 8, 10–11,
        27, 70, 93–95
        19th-century United States
            73–74, 82
        decline 82–85
        neoracism 4–7, 82–85, 91–92
    social construction 6–7, 11
    social Darwinism 69–70, 74–78,
        82–85
racism
    colonialism and 1–2, 230
    "common-sense" racism 6, 12
    critique of 2, 40–41, 83–93
    development and 1, 48–53,
        62–64
    ideology of 25–27, 77–81, 87–89
    immigration and 9–10
    institutionalized racism 87, 88–92
    marginalization in political
        philosophy 23–28
    nationalism and 7–10, 79
    neoimperialism 2–4
    neoracism 4–13, 93–95
    Rawls and 29–33
    reparations 126–127
    science and 5–11, 82–85, 93–95
    survival 17

Rawls, John
    basic structures 8>
    critical theory and 38>
    gender 28–29, 32
    Habermas and 35
    ideal and nonideal theor
    neo-Kantianism 30, 32
    racism and 29–33
    terminology 23, 155
    theory of justice 28
Reagan, Ronald 97, 101, 208,
    217, 220
reflexivity 155–158, 222–223,
    239, 242
religions, Kant 56–57, 150
reparations 126–127, 226–227
Reparations Coordinating Committee 126
restorative justice 17, 126, 227
Roman Empire 132
romanticism 8, 71, 222
Roosevelt, Franklin 123
Ross, Dorothy 71
Rostow, Walt 201, 202, 204, 205
Rousseau, Jean-Jacques 30, 59,
    135, 143
Royal African Company 25, 166
rule of law 163, 190, 202
Rumsfeld, Donald 215

Saddam Hussein 215
Said, Edward 181
Samoa 79
Sanders, Lynn 117, 118
Schmitt, Carl 229
Schönhuber, Franz 106
Schumpeter, Joseph 152, 202
science
    See also race theory, science and
    17th-century revolution 5
    18th-century natural history 6
    comparative anatomy 70
    craniology 73
    objectivity 224
    positivism and 27–28
    race and 5–6, 7, 8, 10–11, 27, 70
        decline 82–85
        neoracism 93–95
        United States 73–74, 82
Scotland, Enlightenment 139, 168
Scott, James 207

...ne for Africa 2
...Amartya 184, 240
...elby, Tommie 33, 39
Shils, Edward 201
Singapore 199
slavery
   Christianity and 42
   Kant and 43, 62–64, 70
   liberalism and 37
   Locke 25, 166–167
   philosophical neglect 42
   US 78, 86, 107, 109–110
Smith, Adam 59, 77
social Darwinism
   Darwin and 77
   decline 82–85
   dominant theory 74–82
   gender 74, 76
   race and biological evolution 1, 75–82
   survival of the fittest 76
   US dominance 69–70
   US imperialism 78–82
   US race theory 74–78
Social Science Research Council 201
social sciences 10–11, 192, 200
societal modernity 158–160
sociology
   legitimation of law 158–159
   race relations 83, 84–86
soft power 243
South Korea 199
Soviet Union
   Bolshevism 100
   breakup 210, 214
   Cold War 195–196
Spanish American War (1898) 69, 79, 80
Spanish empire 3
Spencer, Herbert 69, 75–76, 77, 78
Stalinism 106
Stanford-Binet intelligence test 84
stereotypes 88, 94
Strauss, Leo 214
Strong, Josiah 81
structural adjustment programs 211
structural functionalism 201
structuralism 141
Stürmer, Michael 99
Sugar Islands 63

Sumner, William Graham 75, 77, 78
sustainable development 242
Sweezy, Paul 197
Switzerland, SVP 9
systems theory 145, 153, 199–200

Taft, William Howard 81
Taiwan 199
Taylor, Charles 159, 191, 223, 242
teleology 51–53
Teutons 71, 73
Thatcher, Margaret 208
Third World
   dependency 195–200
   modernization 195
   modernization and domination 200–207
   neoimperialism and neoconservatives 212–220
   neoliberalism and globalization 207–212
   sociocultural retardation 92
Thomas, W. I. 83
Thompson, Judith Jarvis 39
Tocqueville, Alexis de 192
transitional justice 232
transnational regimes 234, 236
Truman, Harry 123, 194
Tuck, Richard 27
Turgot, Jacques 59, 143
Turkey, Armenian genocide 100
Turner, Frederick Jackson 79

underclass 10, 13, 87, 125, 126–127
UNDP 197
United Kingdom
   empire 3, 168, 173, 175, 177–178, 221
   Thatcherism 208
United Nations
   Charter 2, 243
   Economic Commission for Latin America 197
United States
   affirmative action 30, 98–107
   African Americans
      disenfranchisement 117
      ghettos 120–126
      institutionalized racism 88–92

labor market segregation 125–126
Plessy v *Ferguson* 77
politics 117–127
reparations 126–127
segregation 7, 17, 24, 111–112, 122–124
social Darwinism 76, 77–78
sociology 84–86
stereotypes 88
underclass 125
Agency for International Development 194, 196
Asian Americans 116
Carolina Constitution 166–167
civil rights legislation 97
civil rights movements 2, 13, 24, 29–30, 90, 108, 110
Civil War
  Gettysburg commemoration 111, 114
  lost-cause view 104
  memory 111–114
culture of poverty discourse 10
exceptionalism 70, 71–73, 192–194, 219
Fair Deal 123
Great Society programs 97, 213
historiography
  history teaching 113–114
  master narrative 113
  racist history 108–111
immigration
  Chinese exclusion acts 81
  non-European increase 98
  politics of memory and 114–117
  racism and 8, 24
imperialism
  19th-century expansion 3–4, 72, 79, 109
  destinarianism 72–73, 79–80
  modernization and domination 203–207
  social Darwinism 78–82
  Texas annexation 72
Israel Lobby 219
memory of racial injustice
  failure 96–98, 107–117
  politics 117–127
  politics of public memory 111–117
  racist historiography 108–111

messianism 193–194
Mexican War (1848) 72, 80
native Americans 50
  expulsion 72
  extermination 78, 80
  social Darwinism 76
  Wounded Knee massacre 77
neoconservatives 87–88, 97, 125, 212–220
neoimperialism 192–195
neoliberalism and globalization 207–212
New Deal 122, 123, 196, 207, 208
preemptive national security strategy 214
racism
  blaming the victim 87–88
  culture 86–93
  historiography 108–111
  neoracism 93–95
  politics 117–127
  science 73–74, 82
  social Darwinism 69–70, 74–78
Reconstruction 7, 78, 97, 107–111
slavery 232
  abolition debate 72
  public memory 104, 107–117
social reform 82–85
Spanish American War (1898) 69, 79, 80
underclass discourse 10, 13, 87, 125
war on terror 215–216, 219, 221
Universal Declaration of Human Rights (1948) 2, 235, 243
universalism
  Enlightenment metanarrative 38, 158
  Kant 43, 44, 55, 136–137, 224–225, 238
  modernity discourse 222
  neoimperialism 181
  slavery and 42
utilitarianism 168, 172, 176
utopias 153, 154, 237

Vietnam War 206, 216, 231
Voltaire 48

Wake Island 79
Waldheim, Kurt 106

Wallerstein, Immanuel 199
Walzer, Michael 40
Ward, Lester 83
Washington, Booker T. 114
Washington Consensus 209
Watergate 206
Weber, Max 131, 142, 143, 145, 147,
    148, 163, 222, 224, 226
West, Cornel 69
Wilson, William Julius 124

Wilson, Woodrow 78, 80, 109, 110,
    111, 215
Wolfowitz, Paul 213, 214, 215
Wood, Allen 49
World Bank 4, 194, 196,
    209, 211
world systems theory 199–200
WTO 211

Zimmerman, Jonathan 113